About the Author

Luke Waldron was born in the village of Ballyroe in Knock, County Mayo. He studied Philosophy and Theology and has a degree in Social Science. Education that gives priority to motivating people to think for themselves is one of his great passions. He studied educational methods that helped promote awareness among the marginalised of their dignity and rights. One of those aids was the production and use of video documentaries. In his day he was a keen Gaelic football and soccer player; he took to jogging and cycling in later life. One of his dreams is to see his native county win the All Ireland.

To my wife and companion, Carmen, who initially
encouraged me to write and supported me all
through the process.

'The man who writes about his own life and times is the only man who writes about all people and all times.'
– George Bernard Shaw

'When I feed the poor, they call me a saint. When I ask why the poor have no food, they call me a communist.'
– Dom Hélder Câmara

A Dawn Unforeseen

Journey from the West of Ireland to the Barrios of Peru

Luke Waldron

The Liffey Press

Published by
The Liffey Press Ltd
Raheny Shopping Centre, Second Floor
Raheny, Dublin 5, Ireland
www.theliffeypress.com

A catalogue record of this book is
available from the British Library.

ISBN 978-1-908308-43-6

Printed in Spain by GraphyCems

CONTENTS

ACKNOWLEDGEMENTS

My special thanks to David Rice and Kathleen Thorne and their Hedge-School of Writing, which Carmen and I attended and where I first tested the waters. It was David too who, after reading my manuscript, put me in touch with Fiona Clark: thank you Fiona for your dedication to the task of editing.

I sent a draft copy to a small group of resigned Columbans and am deeply grateful for their genuine interest, useful suggestions and unreserved support. My special thanks to Joe and Teresa O'Grady-Peyton.

Some Columban friends enthusiastically gave of their time to read my memoir: I greatly appreciate their positive comments and warm encouragement.

Many a day I have sat in a quiet corner of our local Hotel Hilamar in Kinnegad. There I most often plied my new-found trade of writing: my sincere gratitude to Robert Bagnall and the staff for always making me feel at home.

I must thank our children and their partners (Kathy and Dale, Willie and Grainne, Tony and Linda): they were always eager to learn of my progress and encourage me on my way. I often had to call on their computer know-how and even their artistic touch.

Lastly, I want to thank David Givens at The Liffey Press for his patience and guidance as we prepared the book for publishing. Likewise, I am indebted to Sinead McKenna for her expertise on design of the cover and her willingness to take on board suggestions from me and my family.

1.

DECISION TIME

I CAN STILL VIVIDLY recall the moment. It had been a long but fulfilling morning visiting schools in the *barrios* or shanty-towns. As I walked along the narrow, dusty streets, which sprawled out on top of the centuries old city rubbish dump, I was in a pensive mood.

The midday, end-of-summer sun beat down relentlessly in Lima that day. The streets were deserted except for children playing in huddles at the doorsteps of precariously built houses. Dogs, crouched in the shade, barely opened an eye as I shuffled by. All the hustle and bustle at the street market had eased and sellers were taking down their stalls. Everything was the same and still, except inside me.

I was in my early thirties and had built up a good relationship with the people. Despite the slowness of the work, and the near impossibility to quantify it, I knew I was part of an important process. Many aspects of my life were meaningful and satisfying.

The nearly nine years that had passed since my arrival in Peru had been literally life-changing. So much learning from experience and soul-searching too. But, of late, I had begun, very gradually at first, to experience a sensation of being trapped.

Working with the marginalised people in the *barrios* or shantytowns was something I wanted to continue doing. It was at the centre of who I had become, a long-term commitment. But two matters, which more and more seemed to threaten the continuation of my commitment, had come to occupy my innermost thoughts. They stemmed from my condition as a Catholic priest.

One of those 'limitations' was the blanket imposition of celibacy on all priests. Over the years since my arrival in Peru I had become more conscious that the struggle of the people in the *barrios* for social inclusion was going to be a very long one. As I came to grips with this reality I felt the need for a female partner, for a companion with whom I could share my commitment and my whole life.

The other 'limitation' that had begun to weigh on me had to do with the clerical institution itself. Like many of my priest companions, I had tried to be close to the people, but one always felt set apart, a member of an elite and powerful institution.

Trudging along towards the parish house, I quietly admitted to myself that I would like to get married. I gave myself the permission and freedom to do so in the future. What surprised me then, and still does, was how lacking in interior struggle this was. The actual carrying through on that decision would not be without its pains. However, that morning I felt a distinct relief at having been able to make a momentous personal decision.

Several decades later I am motivated to share the story of my searching for answers, and commitment with the struggle of the poor. It covers half a century of closely following the onward march and counter-march of society and the Church: nearly three of those decades were of direct personal involvement, at a time of extraordinary change in society, and of heated debate and often bitter division within the Church, not just in Peru but across Latin America, and in far-flung 'mission countries'.

Why tell the story now? Because I am convinced that the issues it highlights are highly relevant for Catholics today, relevant indeed for people of all faiths and none, relevant for all who dream of a better world. Whether we are members of the shrinking number who go to church regularly, or belong to the increasing number of the disaffected, an understanding of recent Church history is vital if we are to comprehend, and face, the burning issues of the moment. For the heated debate, and often bitter division, which I relate, have only increased in the fifty years since the Second Vatican Council first started. That mammoth assembly sat for three years and opened a period of great hope. But that window has long since been shut. The agreed proposals – to bring some democracy into the Church's governance, and update its approach to cultures and the modern world – have been shelved by the Vatican elite.

In a world where accountability, transparency, and access to information are acknowledged by most democratic governments worthy of the name, the Church has retreated more and more into its own world of autocracy, control and secrecy.

I consciously try to be fair and respectful towards the missionary organisation to which I belonged, and to which I am still bound by enduring friendships – the Society of St. Columban. It fostered a breed of men who were brotherly, committed and unassuming. When given roles of authority they tended to go by the book.

It is my hope that some of this account will be of interest to many of the vast army of supporters of missionary efforts in the 'home countries'. And that they will not be shocked to learn, that in going to do what we saw as God's work, we took on some subordinate obligations for which we were neither prepared nor suited.

Some felt they could continue their mission under the yoke of celibacy and clericalism and remained. Some of us felt we could not and should not and left the priesthood. Our deepest values have not changed.

Though this memoir will concentrate on the missionary organisation of which I was a member, the deep division between traditionalists and reformers, recalled in these pages, was in no way unique to it. That painful struggle was, and is, common to missionary and local clergy organisations, right across Latin America and beyond.

TWELVE YEARS BEFORE I took the decision to leave the clerical institution, when going through my third year in the seminary, I was having serious doubts about whether I should continue. I did not feel comfortable talking about this to any of the priests in the seminary. The first people I spoke to were my parents. I was home on holidays in our small farm in the West of Ireland.

After breakfast one morning I let my mother know that things were not all well.

'Mom, it's about the seminary,' I said, mustering all the courage I could.

'That's alright, Luke. Tell me what's troubling you.'

'Well, this last year, I haven't been happy at all. And I am thinking of leaving the priesthood.'

'That would be very drastic. What exactly is bothering you? I thought you were very happy there.'

'Well, now I feel I don't want to be a celibate for ever. You know, not ever being able to get married.'

'I understand son, but always remember that you have a wonderful vocation, helping all those poor people.'

'Mom, that is easier to say than to do. Imagine, going all those years without sex, without a female companion.'

'Let me tell you, Luke: sex is not that special.'

'How can you say that, Mom?'

'It's nothing to shout about, believe me. But, anyway your mind will be on your work with the poor people.'

'Well, I am young. You were too, when you met Dad. You remember that, don't you?'

'Oh, yes Luke. All I am saying is that it's worth giving it a try. You can do so much good, you know.'

'But, one has to be happy and I haven't been. When I go back to the seminary, I'll see how I feel, and then I'll take a decision. Thanks for the chat, Mom.'

'God bless you, Luke. Give me a hug. You'll be alright.'

Walking out of the kitchen, I was glad for that heart-to-heart chat. Dad was down in the cow-house milking the last of the three cows. When he had finished, he got up, stepped onto the path behind the cows, and placed the bucket on the stool. Though I hadn't milked a cow for some time, it was all so familiar: the cows chewing on the hay, the smell of the warm milk and the odours from the place, all blended in the wintery morning air.

'Dad, I was just talking to Mom about how I have been unhappy in the seminary lately.'

'Tell me, Luke.'

'Well, it's about that whole thing of not being able to get married and have a family. I don't think I can go through with it.'

'I'm very sorry you're not happy up there at the seminary. I thought you were.'

'Well, I was at the beginning, but now, what it all means, has been sinking in.'

'I hear you. Look, all we ever wanted was that you would be happy at whatever you chose to do. Think it over, and remember always, that whatever you decide, we will be behind you.'

'Thanks, Dad. I'll go back there, more at ease now.'

As I told him of my inner struggle, he had been preparing to smoke his pipe. My nervousness must have been obvious, but he appeared relaxed. Our conversation had stayed with him down the years. Recently, my youngest sister Mary told me how he had related the whole episode to her, years later.

Back in the seminary, I decided to persevere. My mother must surely have influenced my decision. But I never felt fettered by her advice nor carried it as a weight around my neck. Rather, when the time to cross the bridge did come, I could walk free and look back with gratitude to my Father and Mother; they were not just parents but friends too.

I was grateful also to the Columbans. They had given me a training that was standard in seminaries at the time. In spite of its limitations, I believe it contributed to the acquisition of some positive habits for life. Their charism of showing welcome and friendship to the visitor was special. With them I had ventured out on an unknown road at a time of enormous change. Along that way I had learned to value the culture of the poor, join their struggle for full citizenship, and make friends for life. Last, but not least, I had met my soul-mate and life companion.

I WAS VERY AWARE THAT acting on the decision to get married, which I had taken walking back to the presbytery that morning, would carry with it automatic exclusion from the clerical institution.

Although I had not fully worked things out for myself, I had begun to question the justification for the division of the Church into those who had status and power, and the vast majority who listened and obeyed. Certainly, nothing Jesus had said in the gospels, as far as one could see, pointed towards that kind of organisation. It seemed obvious that the clerical structures had much more to do with historical influences, going as far back as the adoption of Christianity as the official religion of the Roman Empire.

My immediate concerns were about how best to communicate my decision to the people, and the small group of priests, mostly younger than me, who were my closest friends. For them it would be a real shock. For it was 1970 and the big exodus had not yet begun.

Leaving behind security, status and privilege – well into mid-life in most cases – to face into the real world without any career counselling or re-training seems now to have been a hugely daunting task. And it was. It always amazes me that it did not paralyse so many of us.

In coming to my decision to leave the clerical institution, I knew that the years I had spent working with the poor in Lima had not only taught me lessons for a lifetime, but nurtured and formed a commitment that I wanted to continue. The whole experience made it easier to see the way forward and gave me the motivation to go there. That was then, but nearly nine years earlier I had arrived in Peru a very different person.

2.

CULTURE SHOCK AND QUESTIONING IN THE BARRIOS

THE MISSIONARY SOCIETY of St. Columban had sent a few priests to Lima in 1952. By the early 1960s the number had grown to just under thirty, made up of members of the Society and priest volunteers from dioceses in Ireland and England. Pope John XXIII had appealed to the 'home mission' countries to send priests, nuns and brothers from religious organisations and dioceses to Latin America. In the late 1950s and through the 1960s there was a huge influx of foreign missionaries, men and women, into the continent.

When the time came to set out on my missionary journey, my father and I took a taxi to Ballyhaunis. Mother could never get herself to say good-bye at the train or bus station. The train journey to the port of Cobh, in County Cork, was the loneliest I have ever taken. I was tempted to get off more than once.

At the port, I met my classmate Pat. Both of us had been assigned to the same country, Peru. We had no say in the making of that decision. My classmate's presence had a calming effect on me. Though he didn't play any sports, and wasn't a great talker, he always appeared to be more grown-up than the rest of us. The fact that he smoked a pipe added a certain gravity to his demeanour. I was glad of his company as we boarded the waiting ship.

It hadn't escaped me that it was from this same port of Cobh that my parents had made the difficult sea journey several decades earlier. But above all, Cobh was etched in the Irish psyche as the place from which millions of its citizens left, as they fled the horrors of the Famine in the 1840s. That avoidable tragedy had started a phenomenon of emigration that was to continue for many decades to follow. The vast majority of Irish emigrants went to the United States but a good number went to countries like Argentina and Canada.

On our way across the Atlantic by boat, we encountered a severe storm. We had foolishly dared to go up to the top deck and witness nature's turmoil. It was pitch-black as we held on to the railing and watched the towering waves, with their white caps, come rushing at us. I was getting my first big lesson on the awesome power of nature. Pat, as usual, was outwardly unperturbed.

We docked for a week or so in New York and I visited my aunts, uncle and cousins in Philadelphia. I stayed in Aunt Babe's and her daughter Mary's home. My cousin Mary would be the chief motivator of the clan. All were on my father's side: Aunt May, Uncle Pat, Uncle Denis, Uncle Tom (then deceased) and their extended families. A number of get-togethers were organised where I was given a royal welcome and presented with a cheque for 'your work on the missions'.

Meeting my cousin Eddie, his wife Kate and their five children had been an especially emotional encounter. He had been orphaned at an early age, when his mother, Dad's sister, had died suddenly in Philadelphia, and shortly afterwards his father had passed away there also. The five children were taken into care by the uncles and aunts. Eddie had come to Ballyroe with my parents and was raised in our house. He was the big brother, maybe fifteen years older than me. In his twenties he had returned to Philadelphia.

My immigrant extended family held priests, especially missionaries, in high regard. Now they had one of their own heading for the missions, and they showered him with appreciation and support.

The second boat journey brought us through the Panama Canal and on to Peru. We were about to disembark in the port of Callao, the gateway to Lima. It was September 1962.

Before coming to Peru, some Columbans had been on mission work in China. With the coming to power of Mao and the communist party, some had been imprisoned and later all were expelled. While the communist regime was in no mood for dialogue with the Catholic Church or its missionaries, it is also true

that the latter were very poorly prepared to discover and assimi-
late the values of the rich Chinese culture.

When Pope John XXIII made his call for missionaries to go to
Latin America, the Church had special interests there. The vast
majority of the population was nominally Catholic, but priests
and members of religious organisations were scarce. Rome and
the local hierarchies were fearful of what they perceived as an
imminent danger – the advance of communism. They were also
worried about the inroads Protestant sects were making. This
added urgency to the appeal of the Pope and helps to explain in
part the impressive response.

The winds of change were blowing in the continent. The successful Cuban revolution of 1959 was an inspirational event for
the marginalised masses and left-wing parties. In many countries, the centuries-old structures that held the peasants captive
in the most miserable of conditions were beginning to crumble.
Social mobilisation in the countryside, and mass migration to
the cities, would soon become the order of the day in Peru.

As I look back now, I am struck by our lack of preparation for
the venture we were about to undertake. Equally stunning is our
lack of any awareness that this was the case. We were 'blissfully
ignorant' of just about everything – the social, cultural, economic and political realities that we were about to face. The seven
years of preparation in the seminary, by omission of these topics,
had convinced us of one thing. All mission work was basically
the same, no matter where one was sent. That was the practical
belief and attitude that had sustained our colleagues in Asia and
it would do the same for us now.

Our job was to get people to church, administer the sacraments and, when we had a certain command of the language,
teach the catechism. Indeed, even the language was not strictly
necessary, for Mass and the sacraments were still in Latin and
were effective of themselves. This was what missionaries did
wherever they went. It was, we believed, a well-travelled road,
with clear signposts to follow.

As we stepped off the boat, the small group of Columbans,
waiting by the quayside, stood out in their white soutanes or

cassocks. It was a comforting sight and one which we expected. Showing welcome and hospitality to one and all was a trait that had been instilled in us. It was our special charisma. After a warm reception, we drove away from the busy commercial and fishing port, with all its activity, smells and sounds.

We were in a Volkswagen beetle, rocking and rolling over the rounded stones of the dried-out river bed, raising a cloud of dust. We made our way, between the rows of bamboo huts, towards the newly built parish church and house. Both were imposing buildings. They stood out and I felt they signalled a successful missionary endeavour was in progress. We had come to a halt at the presbytery and our driver, who was also my new boss, ushered us in.

Miguel was tall, broad-shouldered and had a commanding presence. A native of County Cork, he had already been in the country for a full decade and was now the Columban Superior in Peru. In an entertaining way, over the following days, he regaled us with stories about work in the new mission. He even took it on himself to give us a sense of the importance of the city of Lima. During the almost 300 years of Spanish colonisation (1532-1821), Peru had been made a Vice Regency for a time and Lima was the administrative centre for most of Spanish-ruled South America. The seasoned missionary encouraged us to take some time to look around the capital city.

As I walked its streets, the signs of its colonial past were very evident in the style of public buildings and monuments. They were also visible in the lavish mansions and homes of the rich. The ruling class was mainly made up of *criollos* or the descendants of the Spanish through inter-marriage. They still lived within the city. Later they were to move out to exclusive suburbs.

But what impressed me most was the ubiquitous presence of the recently arrived migrants. The rich and the poor were sharing the same public spaces, much to the irritation of the former Miguel had told me. They felt their city was being taken over by rustic peasants and they were totally out-numbered by them.

Whole streets in the city centre were occupied by street-sellers, all pedalling their wares, trying to make a living. One could get anything from a shoeshine to a document typed, right there on the sidewalk.

Public transport came in all shapes and sizes. The most ubiquitous were the *micros* or mini-buses. Transport was cheap, chaotic to my unaccustomed eyes, but effective. The waiting time was minimal. As each vehicle arrived at the street corner, the driver's assistant, who was hanging from the door, jumped off and made sure everyone got on. He was there if a push was needed and there was always room for one more! '*Al fondo hay sitio,*' 'There's room at the back,' was the familiar cry.

Another aspect of life in Lima that soon came up in conversations with Columban colleagues was the widespread use the middle and upper classes made of the migrants' cheap labour. Many people from Columban-run parishes, especially women, worked as servants in the homes of the better off. Despite the latter's negative attitude towards the migrants, they could not manage without them. The bigger mansions could have four or more people doing jobs like cooking, cleaning, gardening and security. The maid servants, who got their keep and little else, were lodged most often in a little room on the flat roof.

The flat roofs were everywhere. Rain was not a problem. 'It never rains here, well maybe a couple of times a year,' I was told. We were in the tropics but Lima had a freak climate. So did most of the coast of Peru – it was a desert.

Except for the rivers that came down from the mountains, there was no water. Nothing would grow without irrigation. So the precious liquid was channelled, in small canals, allowing the river valleys to become productive.

The high Andes Mountains blocked the rain clouds of the *selva*, or rainforest, from crossing over to the coast. On the other side, the cold Humboldt Current, which ran along the Peruvian coast, did not allow evaporation. Instead, it caused condensation, with low clouds and mist in winter, and fog on summer mornings. Humidity was always very high but temperatures were mild with no extremes – an average of about thirteen Celsius in winter and twenty five in summer.

It was easy to see that this kind of weather had some obvious advantages, like people being able to get by with the most rudimentary kind of shelter and move about at all hours, every day of the year. But it did have one especially serious down-side for the millions of newly arrived.

They were short of stature, had larger lungs and hearts than people born at sea-level. Accustomed to living at heights of up to 4,000 metres, where the air is rare, they had to breathe in more of it. The top soccer teams from the coast dreaded having to play their rivals in Cusco and nearly always lost.

But in Lima the high humidity often caused these up-rooted people serious breathing problems. They missed the dry clean air of the *sierra* and suffered a lot from tuberculosis.

As I was getting my bearings, in the historic and rapidly changing capital city, it was also important to learn about how the Columban work had developed. I would, after all, be expected to build on it.

From Miguel I learned that the Society had been given charge of a big area north of Lima's river Rimac. The vast majority of the city's population lived on the south side. At the beginning the new 'parish' was sparsely populated, some 14,000 people. Just north of the river was the *Barrio Obrero* or Workers' Village. It was made up of four groups of housing estates. They were built by the government of a populist military dictator, on the back of a strong growth in exports.

The rest of the area was made up of *haciendas* or landed estates. This form of land and labour exploitation had been established from the early days of the Spanish colony. Just as had happened all over Latin America and in Ireland too, land was seized and granted to colonial agents and friends. Some estates were huge. One of the largest, depending on the demand on the foreign market, produced cotton or sugar cane. It stretched all the way from the coast, right across the Andes and took in a swipe of the jungle region also.

The *haciendas* in the new 'parish' were smaller than in other parts, but the system was the same. Cotton was the main crop and extra migrant workers came from the highlands at harvest time.

From the beginning, in 1951, the few Columbans in Lima went to live among the poor people they were going to serve. This was a big step at the time. They were the first group of missionaries to do this in Lima. Other organisations had parishes in upper class areas, and taught English and catechism to the children of the rich.

The first church that had been built was in the *Barrio Obrero*, and at the insistence of the Columbans the parish was named after Blessed Martin de Porres, a black friar to whom there was great devotion in Lima and, coincidently, in Ireland too. The problem was, he was not yet officially declared a saint. Rome was holding out and Columbans believed that the efforts of the local Cardinal were crucial in getting permission to use the name.

In the *haciendas*, Mass was said for the owners and their families. The same was done for the workers who lived in the most miserable conditions: rows of one-roomed shacks. Friendly relations developed with the owners, who contributed financially to the mission, and sometimes donated a truck or a car for Miguel and Mal to get around.

From the early 1950s on, Columbans had made contacts with the other religious organisations in the city. Some schools run by nuns began to send groups of catechists, once a week, to teach Christian doctrine in the new parishes. Women from the upper classes came to help out with social services, supplying medicines and food.

The rich still felt safe to come to the poor and give social and religious help. On the surface, Peruvian society had clear social hierarchies and there was apparent order and peace. Lima, and the cities of the coast, appeared stable. The vast majority of the poor were still far away in the provinces, out of sight and out of reach.

Whatever appearance of stability had been around was rudely shattered one morning at the end of the 1950s. The Columbans had woken up to find that some 10,000 families had 'invaded' the dried-out bed of the river Rimac. The make-shift huts stretched away, in endless rows, towards the airport.

By this time, Miguel was on friendly terms with the mayor of Lima, one of the biggest *hacienda* owners in the area. He had also cultivated a personal relationship with the President of Peru, and with his wife, who was known for her charitable work. In this, Peru was not dissimilar to Ireland. In both countries there was close collaboration between Church and State. It was understandable that Miguel would use his close contacts at the highest levels to try to get help for the newly arrived parishioners.

He went to his powerful friends in *Palacio de Gobierno*, the Government Palace. Help arrived speedily in the form of sheets of matted bamboo, blankets and food. There was technical help to plan the layout of the future *barrio*: areas were set aside for future churches and schools.

Support of catechists from the rich side of the city continued to grow. Soon the Columbans helped set up a credit union. People were poor but in those years of the 1950s work was still available and they were able to save: over time they could pay for the basic services of water, light and sewerage. Through their contacts once again, those pioneers of the Columban mission got a mobile bank to come to the area.

In the space of a few years, the original parish had been split into four. Each had a social service centre that distributed food from Caritas, the Church's international organisation for delivering aid to the poor countries. Usually there was also a doctor, a dentist and a social worker available.

As a brand new arrival, I was impressed by what I was seeing and hearing. It was easy to believe that I was in the presence of a successful missionary endeavour. What was being done seemed logical, effective and efficient. People appeared to have trust in the Church and were coming to receive the sacraments.

Yet, without knowing it, we were at the end of an era. For some years, social unrest had been growing in the *sierra*, that huge area in the highlands, still home to the majority of Peruvians. People there had to eke out a bare subsistence on tiny plots of land or work as serfs on *haciendas*. Villages were isolated, nestled in gorges of the rugged mountains, at altitudes of anything up to 4,000 metres. Roads of poor quality only served the bigger towns. Transport was difficult and suffered from the risk of constant landslides in the rainy months. In those areas, the State's presence was weak and vital services, such as health and education, were poor or non-existent.

The breaching of this physical isolation got a big impulse when the transistor radio became accessible to the millions of poor. Social researchers say this phenomenon was an important element in awakening the dream of a better future, and of fuelling the mass migration to Lima and the cities of the coast. Life surely would be better there.

For some weeks after my arrival in Peru, I had received short sketches on the reality, history and development of the Columban mission, mainly from Miguel. I felt confident of being able to follow in the path already laid down by Columbans. But first it was necessary to go to a language school for three months. It was run by another missionary outfit, the Society of St James the Apostle, founded by Cardinal Cushing of Boston in the United States.

From Monday to Friday we worked at mastering the basics of Spanish. On weekends we went to help out with Masses and baptisms in the parishes.

It was exciting to get to live with that mixed bunch of students. They came from the US and Ireland and numbered about twenty, as far as I can recollect. Those of us who were recently ordained were in the minority. The older men were responding to the call from Rome, but were also, I sensed, searching for more meaning in their lives. I got the impression that a certain boredom with the work at home had set in.

Refreshingly, our days in that school were not all taken up with learning Spanish. What stands out for me, from those three months, is the effort the Director of the school made to give us a quick introduction to some of the cultural and social realities of Peru. He got some speakers in, and they weren't status quo people. The message we were given was that we were going to have to face a complex situation, in both society and Church. And we were clearly told that we did not have all the answers. In addition to feelings of inadequacy around the language, now our self-sufficiency was rocked.

On weekends out of language school, we visited each of the four existing parishes. The churches and parish houses, all newly built, mainly with money from the home regions, were the only finished, solid structures in the whole area.

Masses were well attended. Preparing a five minute sermon in Spanish, and mustering the courage to speak to some people in the *despacho* or parish office, were the big challenges. People were welcoming and most understanding of our stuttering efforts.

As we were about to finish at the language school, the Society leadership in Ireland made a surprising intervention in the running of the mission in Peru. Miguel, our best known Columban in the country, was replaced by someone who had worked in China prior to coming to Lima. There he had suffered imprisonment and expulsion.

Owen was, in so many ways, the opposite of Miguel. Whereas Miguel was always well-dressed and looked the part, our new Superior, tall and stooped, never paid attention to appearance. He was in his fifties, I think, a simple man, most at home in his wellingtons and old work clothes. Digging, ploughing and sowing, in the acre or so of land around the centre house, our headquarters, was what he enjoyed most.

He was a retiring kind, and one got the impression that he never really wanted the job. But I also got the distinct feeling that once he had been given it, because of his clerical acceptance of 'blind obedience', he was determined to see it through. The experience of imprisonment in China seemed only to have strengthened his basic beliefs and hardened his resolve. There would be no room for questioning, reflection or compromise. His predecessor, on the other hand, had seemed to revel in the job and was capable of some flexibility.

Soon after finishing at the language school, I was asked by my new boss to meet him early one morning at the centre house. After breakfast, we sat on a bench on the veranda. It was a summer morning in January and we were observing the potato drills he had recently prepared. The pigeons, just feet away, were busy fighting over the bread crusts he had brought from the kitchen.

As we sat there, talking mostly about the variety of potatoes in Peru, it being the home of the potato, Owen started to prepare his own cigarette. I was fascinated, as I had not witnessed the process close up, except in the cowboy movies. As he licked the wrapping paper and sealed the cigarette he casually said:

'I've decided to send you to the Holy Cross parish. You should be alright there.'

Then he stood up, blew a puff of smoke into the warm morning air and put his hand on my shoulder:

'Now Luke, I want to give you some advice. You may hear ideas going around about this and that. Just remember that all the thinking has been done for us. You don't have to rack your brain. Just put your head down and plough ahead.'

He smiled reassuringly as we parted.

You couldn't help having a soft spot for this unassuming big fellow. As well, here was a man who had suffered for the 'cause'. The short visit was soon over and I left with his advice lingering in my mind. But I was also aware that it was not what I had heard at the language school – that we didn't have all the answers.

In spite of the conflicting messages in my head, there was some reason for me to feel happy. I was going to join two Columban colleagues who were just a few years my senior. We had been together in the seminary. Michael, who hailed from County Galway, was three years older than me – he was the energetic and out-going parish priest. Gerry, from Cork, was just a year my senior – he was observant, intellectually inquisitive and had a keen sense of humour. Joe was older, an Irish volunteer priest who had worked in England. He was quiet and more set in his ways. But we were all clerics who would be expected to follow the beaten path.

Nobody knew how many people lived in the parish. The guess was 30,000 to 40,000. It was still growing and would soon reach the motorway that ran alongside the airport. One of the first things we decided to do was to try to get to know the people, and their situation, by visiting them in their homes. I also saw it as a great opportunity to begin to practise my Spanish.

The 'house-visitation' became a sobering, first-hand experience of how the poor lived and what their worries and hopes were. It became clear, very quickly, that they had very different priorities to us priests. Their priorities had to do with very down-to-earth matters.

They still hadn't got the basic services, like water, light and sewerage. Their leaders were putting pressure on the Municipality but the wheels of bureaucracy turned slowly. Meanwhile, they had to purchase water by the barrel and make do. With no State social welfare, it was a question of people having to work at anything, work or go hungry. Street markets and street sellers abounded. The exodus from the highlands was only starting. Impressive as it seemed at the time, it was to pale in comparison with the massive numbers that were to flock to Lima in the decades ahead. There were still some jobs available, in the textile line particularly. The parish was a hive of activity, with people working on their homes and transporting materials in their all-purpose tricycles.

Education for their children was hugely important to the parents. They spared no effort in making sure there were sufficient classrooms when school started in April. They kept continuous pressure on the Department of Education to build. When they saw that the building would not be started or finished on time, they organised community collections, and community work, to provide provisional classrooms.

Every family was desperately trying to save to buy a load of bricks. Lima is prone to earthquakes. It is on the San Andreas fault which runs along the coast from southern Chile all the way to Alaska. This, of course, significantly adds to the cost of building. All structures have to be reinforced with steel and concrete columns.

Life for our parishioners was a constant struggle, but I was not picking up a sense of despair. Hardship and deprivation were everywhere to be seen, but somehow hopes and dreams shone through. It seemed that, even then, they could glimpse their town as it would be. They were, literally, building their future.

But where there is grinding poverty there is disease. One night shortly after my arrival to the parish, I was called out on a 'sick call'. The teenager was crouched on a make-shift bed in a room made of bamboo sheets and cardboard. A candle shed its dim light on the drawn, ashen face of the boy. Though his body was consumed by tuberculosis, and he was unable to talk, he was still conscious. As I tried to say a few words of comfort to him, and perform the last rite of the Church, his fixed stare questioned me deeply. It would stay with me over the years. I was sure he was saying,

'Padre, look at these conditions, look at what they have done to me.'

As Catholics, we had always been led to believe that poverty was somehow acceptable, part of human existence, the destiny of the poor. Priests, and lay people alike, were encouraged to show compassion and try to alleviate the sufferings of the poor. This was carried out in the traditional way, by doing works of mercy: giving food, clothes or medicines. Our parish, like the others the Columbans worked in, had a social worker, who oversaw the distribution of food to those most in need.

But now Michael, Gerry and I had begun to ask ourselves questions about the limitations, and negative effects, of this aid. Many more questions and much more searching followed in quick succession. Unknowingly, we had embarked on an ongoing process of reflection and action, the results of which we couldn't have envisaged. The other priest in the parish, Joe, was not interested in joining our reflections. He was at ease continuing on the traditional path and we respected his option. For as long as we were together we had a good relationship.

Questioning accepted thinking and practice was not something that I had done openly up to then. All through secondary school and the seminary, my strategy had been to keep quiet, and certainly not run the risk of asking any awkward questions. One didn't have to be a genius to figure out that it was the safest way to go. In the prevailing system, the teacher transmitted information, the students listened, took some notes and memorised.

But for the odd exception, teachers did not see their role as being about motivating or stimulating us to think. Whether the information given was relevant, up-to-date or otherwise was none of the students' business.

So, in those twelve years, the many 'off-limits' questions that came to my mind were, by force of habit, quickly shut down. It was a survival strategy for those times.

In my new parish of Holy Cross, the situation had totally changed. I was with two friends, Michael and Gerry, and all three of us were faced with the same reality – *barrios* teeming with thousands of impoverished families, all in a hurry. We began to ask questions about the traditional pastoral approach. I was timidly finding the courage to do some thinking of my own.

The sheer numbers of poor in the parish, and the scale of the poverty staring at us every day, was an inescapable fact. Set against that harsh reality, the parish social services, good and all as they were, amounted to no more than the proverbial drop in the ocean. There was no arguing with that.

Little did we know that what seemed liked an ordinary enough observation would start us off on a personal, and intertwined, journey that would lead to many more questions and a deeper search for solutions.

I imagine myself at the reek of turf, outside our house in Ballyroe, filling a bucket to bring in for the fire. As long as I keep picking the sods from a safe spot there is no problem. But if I pick one from the bottom, one that is sustaining many others, a part of the reek will come tumbling down. So, too, I visualise the consequences of those first diffident steps, tampering with an important block of my beliefs.

What the three of us were really doing was focussing on something that was taboo, by highlighting the limitations of the traditional 'works of mercy'. Obviously, the poor were grateful for the charity received. They were outwardly friendly towards us and towards the Church in general. But the question was, aside from the outward expressions, on a deeper level, what sort of effect was the receiving of handouts having on them? Personally, I had become aware of how, when I encountered women leaving the parish clinic with their little bag of food, they kept their heads down. *'Hola Padre'* they said as they went on their way – they made no eye contact.

Our conversations and reading began to focus on fundamental notions like the dignity, self-respect and rights of the poor.

Getting to know and appreciate the culture of the people was hugely important in motivating us to continue the process of searching. Early on, we had underestimated their qualities and potentialities. Because our people were poor and uneducated, it was easy to look on them as a lesser people. As priests we saw them as people who needed above all to be taught the Christian doctrine, they were souls to be saved.

Gradually, we began to realise that it was our privilege to be working among a people, who were inheritors of an immensely rich culture. When 'discovered', it had surpassed in several aspects the achievements of the western world of the time.

The capital of the Inca Empire, Cusco, when taken over by the Spaniards in 1534, had running water, sewerage, street lighting and gold and silver smiths, something many European cities did not have at that time. The ability of the Incas to build and cultivate terraces on the rugged slopes of the Andes and irrigate them, often by bringing water against the gradient, is a marvel of ingenuity and engineering.

Their empire stretched north-south, from Colombia to Chile, and from the coast to the jungle. They had built some 14,000 miles of roads on the most difficult of terrain. Some 500 years ago, they had experimental agricultural stations dotted across the *sierra*.

It was a vertical society, with a caste system, but it was also a caring one for its time. Deposits were built at strategic points to store food in preparation for natural disasters, famine or war.

The Inca people were very religious. Their spirituality, like that found in the Celtic culture in Ireland and other European countries, and indeed in other cultures around the world, was firmly rooted in nature. They had a deep reverence for the universe, the earth and its Creator. They believed in more than one god. The three principal gods were:

Wiracocha, the Supreme god, was the one who had revived the earth after the flood.

Pachamama, the Earth goddess, was venerated especially by those who worked the land. That special connection with the earth, centuries later, came with the emigrants from the *sierra* to the *barrios* surrounding Lima. At *fiestas* out in the open air, I often watched a ritual that had been handed down through the centuries. As a group of friends shared *chicha*, a homemade fermented drink, or a bottle of beer, they passed a glass from one to the other. As they did so, some ritually spilt a few drops on the ground as a respectful acknowledgement of Mother Earth.

Inti, the Sun god, was venerated each year at the celebrations of the winter solstice. It was an act of homage by the Inca, for he was considered a direct descendant of the Sun god. At the end of winter, when the sun was farthest from the earth, the Inca pleaded for it to return, warm the earth and ensure good crops. When the Spaniards banned these celebrations they went underground. They were considered to be contrary to the Catholic faith.

In 1944, the *Inti Raymi*, Festival of the Sun, was revived. It was reconstructed from descriptions found in chronicles from the time of the Spanish conquest. Today it is celebrated on 24 June and draws hundreds of thousands of people not only from Peru and Latin America but from around the world.

As we were getting to know the culture of our parishioners, recently arrived from remote villages in the Andes Mountains, the three of us were immersed in a process that involved personal growth. We were also in search of a new type of pastoral approach – one that respected and built on the cultural and community values of the poor. We had more questions than answers. Fortunately, help from an unexpected source was available.

I believe it was Miguel, during his time as Director, who had introduced the Columbans to the Alvarez Calderon brothers. They belonged to an old aristocratic family that had *hacienda* and business interests. Their parents' initial plans for them were probably very different from the path the young men had chosen. We heard how they had travelled to Europe to choose suitable universities for their future studies and careers in the family businesses. Contrary to family expectations, they ended up picking a progressive seminary to study for the priesthood, and had returned with new ideas about evangelisation, especially about how to bring the gospel to the poor.

If we *gringo* priests had to make every effort to get to know the cultural values and mentality of our parishioners, in hindsight I realise that the Alvarez Calderon brothers must have had to go through a similar process too.

They were to have a powerful influence on my awakening, on that of some of my Columban colleagues, and indeed on clergy in Lima and other parts of the country. Both were in good standing in the archdiocese, despite their radical pastoral approach. The then archbishop of Lima, Juan Landazuri Rickets, had been superior of a Franciscan monastery, before being put in the big job. He was no radical, neither by persuasion nor inclination. However, he seemed to realise that the wheels of change were already in motion in society, and the Second Vatican Council had started – the Church could not stand still.

Carlos Alvarez Calderon, the older of the two brothers, was the national chaplain for the Young Catholic Workers' lay movement, and Jorge worked in one of the shantytowns, and was chaplain to a lay, adult workers' movement. On meeting them I was greatly impressed by their knowledge of Peruvian society and by their radical thinking on pastoral work. Equally impressive was their enthusiasm to share their insights and thinking with us.

They had begun to organise mornings of reflection for priests working with the poor. We discussed the cultural aspect of our work, lay formation and our own personal growth. These meetings were the perfect complement to our own reflections in the parish.

For the first time, I was daring to think for myself and beginning to shed some of the shackles that held my mind captive. At first, it was not the most comfortable of feelings. As clerics we had been moulded in the tradition of obedience to the superior.

Yet here I was, involved in what would be seen as some kind of conspiracy. We were kicking the traces, and asserting our right to question accepted pastoral thinking and implement alternatives. My boss, I was aware, would not be at all amused with my present company. Exactly how displeased he was would soon be revealed. But I was not on my own, and there was safety in numbers, or so I preferred to think.

In the parish, we were beginning to implement a pastoral plan that had the building of community, based on small groups, as the core. Once we had made our own the basic idea of the innate dignity of the poor, and had learned to value their rich culture, the next steps in our own growth process were more straightforward.

We had moved on from the traditional, passive acceptance of poverty as something that could be explained by destiny or 'God's will'. Instead, it was a structural problem of society. The poor had rights that were being denied, and that problem was a matter of injustice. They were an oppressed people and had the right to organise and make their demands felt by the State and its institutions.

Though we reformers didn't talk much about it among ourselves, we all knew we were heading for trouble. It was clearly evident that carrying through on our new vision and convictions would not only bring us into conflict with the traditional Church authorities. It would, sooner or later, bring our presence and work in the *barrios* to the attention of those in the different government institutions. Our message was 'subversive' for those in power. They were still intent on patching up the old order.

We knew it was the beginning of a long road. Achieving some measure of success in getting basic services installed was going to be a crucial step in the struggle for the people in the *barrios*. But their growing awareness of the glaringly unequal distribution of the country's wealth would also be a defining step. Though underdeveloped, huge wealth was being accumulated by the upper classes. They paid ridiculously low taxes and the tax system itself was woefully inefficient.

Education took centre stage in all our work. We took advantage of all occasions to motivate people to reflect, starting with examples from their lives, and the reality in which they lived. We were discovering that our role as educators had a lot to do with being alert to ask the right question, at the right time. It was about provoking people to reflect and begin to think for themselves. Mass, sacraments, blessings, funerals and fiestas of patron saints were all occasions that were used to help raise personal and collective awareness. But it was in our work with small groups that a deeper process of growth, reflection and action took place.

In line with the documents coming from the Second Vatican Council, the Christian message was no longer centred on sin, guilt, punishment, rules and regulations. The emphasis was on the living Christ and His core message of love and the dignity of all people, especially the marginalised poor.

The Council had also turned on its head the prevailing concept of salvation. We were now told that it was already present, and at work in history through the action of Jesus. It was present in all cultures and all religions. As missionaries, we weren't bringing salvation anywhere.

Gone was the basis for believing that we were somehow superior, and that our mission was to convert the heathen from their wicked ways. Rather, we were to look for, and see, the presence of salvation, already at work, in the multiple manifestations of the people's culture and lives.

The Council had also insisted that the Church's mission was to immerse itself in the world, in daily life. As salvation was already present and at work in the world, there was no longer any place for the traditional 'distinction of levels', which implied a dual vision of history. On the one hand, there was temporal history, which we called 'the world', where evil and sin abounded and where people had to live and work. Then there was the totally different level, that of sacred history, where salvation was worked out. The two were like two parallel lines, never touching.

With that kind of understanding of Church and faith, religious practice easily became an individualistic type of experience, which had little or nothing to do with the realities of this world. It was more about religious practices and devotions, and gaining merit for the next life. One could be a daily Mass-goer and feel no need to have any involvement in neighbourhood problems, beyond perhaps doing some acts of charity.

The new teaching said that there was but one history, at the same time temporal and sacred. For the Church, and for Christians, it was a matter of being witnesses to the message of Jesus in the world. The Church did not need to be politically powerful to fulfil its mission. Rather, history showed that when it had more temporal power it strayed further from its true mission. Neither did Christians need to form 'Christian' political parties to gain hegemony in society. Instead, they should accept the diversity of political options.

As we reflected on, and assimilated, these radically new ideas, they began to influence our approach to pastoral work. We became very conscious of our own position of power. As white *gringos* we knew we were perceived as powerful by the poor.

In our parish, as in others, discussions about how to give testimony to a simpler lifestyle, and a less 'powerful' approach in pastoral work, were taking place. They were topics that cut very deep, questioning as they did the accepted Columban and traditional Church approach at that time. Calling into question the highly sensitive issue of the size and scale of churches and parish houses, already built, proved to be one of the most divisive matters. Our personal lifestyle was another area that heated up the debate. For example, we questioned whether playing golf, an upper class hobby in Lima, was acceptable.

Positions were beginning to polarise. Those of us on the side of change began to meet among ourselves. Lack of trust on both sides had crept in and was poisoning the atmosphere. After closing the parish office at night, we started to go to a newly formed parish to meet up with other reformers.

The new parish in Reynoso, on the other side of the river Rimac, belonged to the diocese of Callao. Though not actually far from the other Columban parishes, because of its location it seemed to be a bit isolated. Two young Irish priests had begun to work there.

Johnny, from County Armagh, had joined the Columban Society after finishing his training in the national diocesan seminary in Maynooth. This jovial man, with his thick-lensed glasses, always looked the intellectual. After ordination, he went back to

Maynooth and received a doctorate in theology there. In his own unpretentious way, he fitted into our group easily. Inspired by the Alvarez Calderon brothers, Carlos and Jorge, he had embraced the challenge of working with the poor from the new perspective. Always ready for a discussion, no topic was out of bounds for him.

P.J. was Johnny's companion in the parish. From County Limerick, he had also studied in Maynooth. Intense and practical, he was grappling with the new ideas and intent on putting them into practice.

We used to meet in the small presbytery. Some of the rooms were not yet plastered, none were painted. That was their choice. There was no electric light. We gathered around the rough wooden table, in the centre of which sat a kerosene lamp.

In the winter evenings the heat it gave off was welcome when we arrived. A few of the priests smoked cheap cigarettes that gave off a distinct odour. At the beginning of the meeting, we all sat close around the table. But as the night wore on, the heat from the lamp and the thick smoke gradually forced us to draw back. We ended up sitting by the walls, and barely able to see one another. But the atmosphere and discussions were captivating, and the sessions continued into the small hours.

Sometimes, we found ourselves discussing the momentous events of the Protestant Reformation and the Catholic Counter-Reformation. We saw a connection with our own time. The Church had taken a defensive position back then. Now, Pope John XXXIII had convoked the Second Vatican Council to 'open the windows and let in fresh air'. There was a historic and exciting opportunity at hand.

The Council of Trent (1545- 1563), the Church's response to the call for change, implemented some institutional reforms. It eliminated gross forms of corruption, such as no more selling of indulgences, accumulation of landed estates and great wealth, or open political meddling, among others.

But it had strengthened the role of the Pope as an absolute ruler. Any collective form of governance was closed off. The gap between the clergy and the laity had widened – the training in the newly formed seminaries had seen to that. The new Roman

Catechism, and many rituals and devotions added in the following years, would serve as a basis to indoctrinate, and domesticate, the laity.

Late into the night, we chatted and reflected on how the Church had failed to take advantage of a great opportunity for serious reform. We were at one as regards what was needed: a return to the spirit and simplicity of the message of Jesus, priority to be given to witnessing to that message and putting in place truly democratic structures in the Church. It was a tall order. But we were hoping against hope that the Second Vatican Council could deliver.

'It seems to me that there is hope for real change this time around. John XXIII is very strong on it,' comes a voice from the corner.

'Right enough, the momentum appears to be there, especially among bishops from Latin America and the developing world,' says another.

'But, we can't kid ourselves. The hierarchy and the Roman Curia won't allow their power to be weakened without an all-out fight,' another chips in.

'Surely, there can be no going back now,' I venture.

'It's a hard one to call, lads. There is a huge buzz around the Council and there are great expectations everywhere. Some progressive bishops have brought along their theological experts, like Hans Kung and Gustavo Gutierrez. But there is an awful lot of politics going on. Let's not forget how the Curia had taken control of the preparatory commissions, and their proposals were thrown out at the very first session. They haven't gone away though,' Johnny reminds us.

'I agree, and Paul VI, is not John XXIII. Montini was a Vatican bureaucrat, Head of the State Department for thirty-two years. He was one of the close advisers of Pius XII. So, I can't see him backing the kind of changes that are needed,' warns another.

'All I'll say is that we're in a modern world now, under the spotlight of the media. They won't be able to hide or cover up as before. If they screw it up this time, things will never be the same again,' a voice from a corner of the room, predicts gravely.

3.

A LONG WAY FROM BALLYROE

AS I LEARNED in later years from colleagues who had left the clerical priesthood, making the decision to leave, especially in the early 1970s, had meant for many a long and painful struggle. The clerical culture had been inculcated in us all, but it seemed to have taken root more deeply in some. As I revisit my own cross-roads moment, I am struck by how I had taken no counsel and had relied on my inner feelings, values and instinct.

I am drawn to reflecting on my own roots, those values of home and community on which what we learn afterwards must rest, that hidden place where inner strength comes from. I find myself going back in my mind to that little farm in Knock, County Mayo, in the West of Ireland.

It is late August and my father and I are harvesting. It is near the end of my school holidays. My other siblings will be on hand later to help stand the sheaves upright, making them into 'stooks' (about ten sheaves put standing up close together) that will protect them against bad weather. But now we are alone and I can hear that comforting, measured sound the scythe makes as it cuts a swath in the golden oats. A fresh, earthy smell surrounds us. The newly-mown corn rustles as I gather it into sheaves and tie each one, by giving a couple of twists to a small fistful of straw. I am stretched but content.

At last my father gently lays down the scythe and we both make our way towards the ditch. This is a regular ritual and I look forward to the break. We go to the can of oatmeal-flavoured drink my Mother has prepared. It is great for quenching the thirst on a sunny harvest day. Dad reaches for his jacket and rummages for the pipe and other accoutrements to prepare his smoke. Out comes that precious little block of tobacco. It was my mother who always knew when his supply had run out or was dangerously low. He would get edgy, and one of us children was dispatched to the shop in the neighbouring village to get a fresh supply.

From another pocket he retrieves the well-worn pen knife, and holds the tobacco between the thumb and forefinger of his left hand. As he cuts, the bits fall into the cupped palm below. Putting away the knife he begins to tease the tobacco pieces, rubbing them against the palm with the fingers of his right hand, before loading the pipe, anticipation written across his face.

Today is so calm, not a breeze. He needs no lid for the pipe and has no difficulty lighting up. The first puff of smoke rises slowly and just hangs in the air. I am comforted by the familiar aroma of his favourite brand. Butterflies flutter lazily around, seemingly intent on showing off their multi-coloured wings. Even the usually busy honey-bees appear to be less in a hurry than usual. We rest and survey our work. Peace is rooted there. I breathe it in and feel secure.

It was in these moments that I got to know my father and he passed on to me his lessons for life.

'Be proud of your roots, and never be ashamed of where you came from,' he would say. He spoke to me about the importance of work, not at all in an intellectual way.

'Don't ever be afraid to take on any job,' was his advice. The school of life had taught him it was work that gave value to things.

Born at the turn of the last century, he was one of twelve children brought up on a little farm in the village of Cloonbook, in the next parish, six or seven miles away. These were the years leading up to the 1916 Rising, which spelled the beginning of the end for English control of what is now the Republic of Ireland. But this was also a time of massive emigration from Ireland, mainly to the United States. Seven of my father's siblings, including him, went to New York and settled in Philadelphia.

Leaning against the ditch, my father recalled, with an ironic sense of humour, some of the many jobs he had to turn his hand to. Recalling working on the Holland Tunnel he said, 'It was so hot one day that a mule just keeled over and the ganger told us that it was time to go home for the day.'

He told me that one of his jobs had been driving a cab on night shifts. Sometimes a few men got in and told him to keep the engine running, or drive around the block, while they went into a building.

'No questions were asked and I always got a tip,' he would add. These were the years of Prohibition, when the sale of alcohol beverages was banned and the illegal trade was rampant.

He worked as a waiter in a café where an older brother had been made manager. It was there that he first met my mother, even though they were both from either side of the town of Ballyhaunis, a few miles from Knock in Ireland. She was an only child. Her parents had travelled to the US a number of times and her father worked in construction with a cousin who had set up his own company there. During one of those trips my mother was born. When she was just a few months old, her parents returned with her to their home on the farm in Crossard, near Ballyhaunis.

Like my father's, her home was also republican. My memories of her singing to us by the open turf fire are vivid, ballads like 'The Woodlands of Loughlinn' or 'Down by the Glenside'.

The years when the 'Black 'n Tans' roamed the countryside had created a lasting impression on her and, through her vivid recounting, on us too. She made sure we knew of their origin and their actions, how they were recruited from prisons in England to terrorise the people into submission, and how, as they drove around the countryside, they would randomly shoot farm animals.

One story is still etched in my memory. It was about a young, red-haired lad from her village who was cutting turf in the bog. They captured him, tied his feet to the back of the army truck and dragged him screaming all the way to the square in Ballyhaunis. He was still alive when they got there and they shot him.

Despite living through this dramatic period, as a young girl she had travelled to England just after the 'Troubles' were over, to train as a nurse. Her parents knew a local woman who was matron in a hospital over there. That experience must explain how she could later separate political loyalties from place of work. I think this was something that my father could never quite work out. He once told me that he had vowed never to set foot voluntarily on English soil.

The ancestral home of my father's clan was in the village of Ballyroe in Knock, where we were born and reared. It was from there that his father, our granddad, had moved to Cloonbook, leaving behind his brother Tom to run the farm. 'Tom Billy' the locals called him.

A few years after my parents had married, they received a letter at their home in Philadelphia. It said:

'Come as fast as boat will bring you. This place needs looking after, and bring a safety razor with you. Uncle Tom.'

Shortly before that, my father had passed the exam to join the police force. He would never get to be part of the force and I suspect he always regretted that. At that time he would have willingly stayed on in Philadelphia. My mother, on the other hand, was happy to return home. She told us that the idea of raising a family in the big city never appealed to her. So they packed and took the boat across the Atlantic.

The farm in Ballyroe had some thirty acres; about half was suitable for tillage. This was typical of all the farms in the village. These were the first generation of Irish people to own their farms after more than 700 years of English domination.

Now, after gaining independence, they were a proud people indeed. There were no complaints back then about having to pay the 'rates' or land tax. Rather, it reinforced the awareness that this land was theirs at last.

My parents were close. Dad would survive his soul-companion by just a few years and in that time he had a few strokes. He told me how, on one Good Friday, he was alone when he felt another coming on. For such an eventuality, he kept one of those small, flat bottles of whiskey in the inside pocket of his jacket.

'I took a few slugs of Paddy's and prayed with the rosary beads in the other hand. I knew the Man Above would understand,' he told me with a mischievous smile.

Both of my parents were traditional Catholics but my father always seemed to have held on to a certain independence of mind. My decision to leave the clerical state in 1971 had not appeared to bother him. All through the twentieth century, the power and prestige of the Catholic Church in Ireland had only grown. For another decade it would remain a formidable and feared institution.

Like most Irish mothers of her day, my mother was very proud to have a son a priest, and would never have allowed herself to even contemplate the possibility that he might one day leave and become, overnight, a failure and a shame on the family name, become what was commonly called a 'spoiled priest'.

One could hardly overstate the status and power of the Catholic Church in the Ireland of those years. It was felt at all levels, local and national. We have been called a priest-ridden society and not without cause. Their power reached far beyond the silent pews in church, to education, health and the political sphere. One of the most blatant cases of clerical interference in politics came when the hierarchy toppled probably the finest Minister of Health the new Republic has seen.

Noel Browne was a medical doctor by profession. His family, and he himself, had been stricken by that dreaded, almost unmentionable disease – tuberculosis. In a few years, due to his influence, new hospitals, clinics and sanatoria were built all over Ireland. Treatment and medicine were made available, free of charge. Some 2,000 extra beds had been provided in a little over two years for TB patients. He had rid the country of that centuries old curse – all that, at the end of the 1940s and the beginning of the 1950s, when we were a very poor country.

Then he planned to introduce the Mother and Child Scheme, whereby there would be free family doctor, consultant, and hospital care for every mother and her children up to sixteen years of age.

The Minister was not making a solo run in 1950. In fact, his scheme was based on a Health Act, which permitted the introduction of the Mother and Child Health Scheme, and had become law three years earlier. He had also got Cabinet approval.

But opposition would come from wealthy doctors, represented by the Irish Medical Association, and above all from the Catholic hierarchy. He had crossed swords with the latter already. The run-down, out-of-date health service was in the control of religious orders of nuns and brothers and the bishops would fight to ensure that it remained that way.

In his book, *Against the Tide*, Noel Browne tells how he was summoned to meet the then Archbishop of Dublin, John Charles McQuaid. At Cabinet, he was told that the existing protocol demanded that he go to meet the Archbishop, not the other way around. They also told him that he could not bring his Departmental Secretary. He was to have no witness.

When he arrived, to his complete surprise, he was met not by one bishop, but by three! They read a letter from the hierarchy to the government. It stated bluntly that the State, by implementing the Mother and Child Scheme, would be taking on powers which,'If adopted in law, they would constitute a ready-made instrument for future totalitarian aggression.'

Not long afterwards, the government gave in to the hierarchy's demand. All parties in the coalition, including his own, abandoned him. Noel Browne had to resign.

After reading his autobiography, I wrote to him and we communicated by letter when I was in Peru. Back in Ireland I visited him and his wife Phyllis in Connemara, with my friends Des and Sean, both of whom I had first met in Peru. As we drove up to the neatly-kept thatched cottage, we saw a tall, slender figure in muffled coat and cap at the reek of turf. It was indeed the great man himself! We were welcomed into their cottage by his wife Phyllis and over a glass of whiskey first, and later tea and scones, we chatted freely for a couple of hours.

Driving away one couldn't help but be refreshed and uplifted. At the evening time of his life, this frail man and his faithful partner lived tuned-in to the events in Ireland and beyond. They were content in simplicity, surrounded by none of the trappings available to a government minister.

In my youth there was another deep-rooted but less conspicuous force than that of the Catholic Church at work in the rural villages: the community spirit of the people. It was strong and vibrant, even though it had recently come through the severest of tests.

I was growing up barely two decades after the Treaty of 1922, which had created the Irish Free State. The compromises in the Treaty fell short of complete independence, and left the six northern counties under English control. It was unacceptable to many republicans and led to nearly a year of bloody civil war in the twenty-six counties. The wounds left by that internal conflict, involving pro- and anti-treaty forces, affected not only neighbours but divided many families also.

Our history classes stopped at the heroic 1916 Rising. The tragic events that followed were too raw and divisive to be touched upon in class. Loyalties, in the new democracy, were centred on the two main political parties, of pro- and anti-treaty tendencies.

Looking back now, I am amazed how well people in the village, and surrounding areas, were able to deal with those deep emotional wounds. The smouldering hurt was never talked about, as far as I can remember. Not in our presence anyway. People let time serve as the great healer.

Around our area, small farmers were economically all in the same boat. This was the basis for a community solidarity that I saw in action many a time. I remember especially when a neighbour died suddenly leaving behind his wife and young children. Immediately, the *meitheal*, that unwritten law of community help and support, swung into action. Neighbours joined together to cut and save the widow's turf and crops. We saw the same community spirit at work on several occasions each year.

'Threshing time' was one of much excitement for us children. The horse-drawn machine, and its cortege, started at one end of the village and continued its work from one neighbour to the next. Getting access to the corn, in the stack-yard, was often an exercise in team-work, which captivated our attention.

The wheels of the machine often got bogged down in the mud. The horses would have enough to do to get themselves free, never mind pull. After the scramble for stones and timber, voices were raised and language used which it would not have been wise to let the parish priest in on. After much pulling and puffing, the horses and machine were finally stationed at the precise spot between the stacks of corn.

The operation itself, when all hands were on deck, was a sight to behold. There were men on stacks throwing the sheaves to those on the machine, in what looked like perfect coordination. They in turn cut the straw rope with one deft stroke of the knife and fed the loose corn into the thresher. As it swallowed, it made a bellowing noise that rose and fell, echoing around the village.

The mangled straw came out at the back and was forked immediately to the four men making the big stack. Unshapely at first, it gradually took on that familiar thatched-cottage look. It, too, would later be thatched against the winter rains. The precious grain flowed out at one side. It was carefully monitored and bagged. For us children, it was a most impressive display of organisation and cooperation.

We had our distractions, too, when we chased after mice, and the odd rat, as they scampered from the scene. But the workers concentrated on the job at hand – except on one day. There was that hilarious occasion when a frightened mouse raced up the leg of Tommy Mac's trousers. Unfortunately for him, it took refuge where it was least welcome. Bouncing on the stack of barley and roaring to no avail, he struggled to loosen his belt. It was the only time that I remember the owner stopping the machine, so that all could recover some composure.

In the afternoon, when the work was all done, the whole group made their way to our kitchen. My mother would have been busy all the while preparing a hearty meal.

Another yearly opportunity to see the community in action was at the killing of the pig. The animal would have been duly fattened for months before. It was always the same neighbour who did the needful, the actual 'sticking'. Again, we were allowed to miss school. From early morning there was activity in the yard as my father and three or four neighbours prepared the scene. We watched on and our excitement grew by the minute.

A wooden platform was built for the main event, and a couple of barrels, full of water, were laid on stones that circled a turf fire. The screeching and wailing of the pig easily revealed where the operation was taking place. Once the pig's blood was gathered in a bucket, without delay boiling water was poured over the carcass. Then it was easy to scrape away all the hair. Next it was strung up on a ladder, disembowelled and cut in pieces. Growing up on the farm, we children were present many times at the birth of the animals. However, pigs and fowl were the only ones whose planned demise we witnessed. We watched on and winced, with a mixture of wide-eyed shock, sadness and acceptance. Our elders, by allowing us to be present, were handing on life's lessons and skills.

Next day the bigger chunks would be salted and put away in empty tea chests. Later they would be removed and left hanging from the kitchen ceiling. From there they would be used to make those delicious dinners of bacon and cabbage that I can still smell and taste. But on the day itself there was still work to be done, late into the night.

We children helped mother to make the black pudding. The big pot was on the fire, well into the small hours. Next morning, my older sisters and I went around to the neighbours' houses bringing the choice bits of pork and, of course, the black pudding. They would return the favour when their pig-killing-day came around.

There were occasions when the community spirit was called on to respond to an emergency. One of our fields bordered on a lake. It was boggy land and many times was the scene of neighbourhood solidarity. Inevitably, once or twice a year, one of the cattle would over-stretch for a bit of grass that lay enticingly on the far side of a swampy drain. Once the animal got the front feet stuck it was more than likely that all its efforts to get free would only make the situation worse.

When the alarm was raised all available hands were mobilised. There was no rushing in blindly to the rescue. The situation was assessed from all angles. Solutions were proposed and discussed and only after agreement did the operation proceed. Sometimes the animal might have been in the drain for hours and would be very weak. But I never remember one dying. It would be rescued and nurtured back to health. The community spirit would have come through once again.

There was another more hidden and uncomfortable aspect of life in Ireland in my youth. As youngsters in Ballyroe, as in all the other villages of the parish, we were warned about drink by our parents and the Church. We were told that it was a lethal destroyer of lives. It only brought ruin and misery on whole families. So, in Church we all took the 'pledge'.

Father Mathews had founded the Total Abstinence Society in Ireland in 1838. In our time, it was called the Pioneer Association and the majority of young people made the solemn promise not to take a drink until they were at least twenty-one. Even though we grew up some hundred years after the founding of the movement, the Church still felt that people could not be relied on to handle drink. Something drastic was needed.

Ireland, after the endless years of colonisation, of rebellions and defeats, had very serious problems of alcoholism. It was, at the time of the founding of the abstinence movement, the poorest country in Europe. At its peak, it is estimated that at least half the adult population of the time joined the organisation. Besides the charismatic leadership of the priest, the movement's strong community aspect seems to have given it a special appeal in the countryside.

Growing up, I had not witnessed the more destructive effects of alcoholism. The relationship with alcohol in general did not appear to be an easy one. Use of alcohol seemed to be carefully controlled, and was certainly not anything like the way families on the continent of Europe enjoyed their glass of wine with a meal. In most families – mine being no exception – there was always some port wine and the drop of whiskey for the visitor. But there were occasions when caution was thrown to the wind.

My mother's parents, who had been living with us, both died within a short time of one another. Their wakes are part of my childhood memories. Granddad was laid out in his coffin in their room. Granny and a few other women were on vigil there. Most of the other neighbouring women were in the kitchen with my mother. After a few glasses of wine, tea and cake were served on and off during the night.

The men were out in the small yard, at the back of the house. It was summertime and the door was open. People came, bringing chairs and benches, and sat around in groups. The busiest place was where the keg of beer was located, just to one side of the back door. Comings and goings were frequent, as Dad poured the pints.

Some neighbours had come with a few bottles of poteen, the treasured home-made brew, distilled from barley or potatoes. It was not part of the licensed trade! The bottle and small glass were passed around, and chatter and laughter filled the yard until day broke. Then the parting ritual began: the 'quick one for the road', the expressions of sympathy, and the slow, unsteady procession, in twos and threes, made its way down the 'boreen' or lane.

As youngsters we would witness an ingenious way of getting a pint, in a tricky situation. Some men used to start doing the Stations of the Cross after last Mass on Sunday. These ran in a semi-circle outside the church building. With impressive devotion, these male parishioners showed no undue haste until they reached the Seventh Station. Then suddenly they would disappear behind the bushes. They were on their way to Harry's thatched pub for a few pints.

My father's opportunities to indulge came with the fair days. I accompanied him a number of times. My only brother, Liam, was four years younger, so the privilege was mine. The days I most enjoyed were the pig fairs. The cattle fairs were more troublesome. In the dark of the early morning, we had to walk the animals the four miles to Ballyhaunis, and back again, if we didn't sell. They continually strayed off the main road and it was my job to anticipate this possibility, as much as I could, running ahead to the next danger spot.

For a while we had two sows and there were two litters to sell in the year. After having cared for the piglets (we called them bonhams) for several months it was time for them to be sold.

A fair day was always an early morning start. I would wake up to that heart-warming, sizzling sound of frying in the kitchen.

My mother made sure we had a real breakfast for the long day ahead. Excitement filled the early morning air. It would be possible to pay off the grocery bill, which had grown and stretched our credit to the limit. Fair days were very welcome ones for the shopkeepers too.

On occasion, we might have as many as twelve bonhams to sell, and the horse and cart would be required. Often a couple of the litter were kept and fattened. One was to provide us with bacon and the other was sold.

The trusted kerosene lantern broke the darkness as we made our way across the yard to the stable. Dad hung it on the outside wall of the pig-house. Inside we worked by the light of a candle. Firstly, mother pig had to be enticed, with some food, to leave the brood. She was put into another pig-sty, as trying to handle her offspring in front of her was a risk Dad, to his cost, had learned not to take.

We were both in the stable one day, and for some reason he had picked up one of the bonhams. The anxious mother stared fixedly in his direction for a brief moment, before lunging forward at surprising speed. He desperately tried to open the door but it was too late. She had pinned him against the door and grabbed him by the rear end. He roared with pain. She only let go when she was good and ready. Mission accomplished, she did an about turn, back to her care. My mother had to use her best nursing skills to treat the injured part.

'For once you're lucky to be so skinny. That sow couldn't get a right grip on you,' she said with a laugh.

I had fun chasing and catching the bonhams. Once I had caught one, Dad took over. Screeching and wriggling, each one was carried to the waiting transport. The cart had a nice bed of straw which immediately aroused their curiosity. The front rail had been removed and fitted between the side rails; it would provide a small space up front and a seat for us. Once our precious cargo was loaded, there was no time to waste, and we started off down the narrow, winding lane to the main road. It was important to get to town early and be able to pick a good spot to do business.

The fair was held on the main street on the small square in the centre of the town. We usually picked a place about mid-way down the street. The donkey and cart were reversed towards the sidewalk. It was the ideal viewing position for prospective buyers. People were arriving and setting up shop; in about an hour the place looked crowded. As soon as the day dawned, the pubs opened. My father left me in charge, joined a neighbour or acquaintance, and headed for a pub. On his return it was my turn to have a treat, a cup of coffee and a sandwich. They tasted extra special on a fair morning.

Business started, with buyers and sellers alike getting a feel for the lie of the land. They walked about freely looking at what was on offer, and sometimes stopping to chat with a neighbour or friend. It was a fascinating ritual for a ten-year-old to observe. The owner would not let an opportunity slip by. The man observing his bonhams would pretend not to be really interested, but Dad would always initiate a conversation.

'How are you doing there, boss? Are you looking for many today?'

'Ah, just looking around,' he would mutter as he ambled away.

'Ok, boss. Come around again. I'll do right by you.'

Often as not, it would be someone he knew who stopped by. Dad and he would chat for a while. For the first hour people came and went.

'Are we ever going to sell today?' I would ask.

'It's very early yet, son, they'll be back.' Dad would say.

Some of these same people returned later and did a deal. I could never read the early signs of an interested buyer. The first sale was exciting. Before that my father, like the other sellers, had sized up the situation. The number of jobbers present was a good sign, as was the general buzz and atmosphere. A jobber was someone who bought large numbers, which he later sold on.

Dad seemed to have a good idea of his asking price. The difference between that and the eventual price agreed was never much. But, I gathered that it was very important, especially for one's own self-esteem, not to make a bad sale. To ensure this, a process of negotiation was required to get to the finishing line.

When either of the two parties suggested, 'We'll split the difference', it was a sign that business was serious. The said difference would be little, but it was important to go through the process. The buyer would start to walk away. My father would quickly respond:

'Come back John. I won't do wrong by you, just look at that pair at the front.'

After duly observing them once again, there would be more haggling and slapping of hands, but I could see that the deal was as good as done.

'Alright then but you will give me a good luck-penny,' the buyer would say. This usually meant that the two of them would go to the pub, the money would be handed over, and Dad would stand him a drink. Another hand-slap and they sealed the agreement. Before they left, the pair of bonhams were duly marked, to the new owner's satisfaction. Most people bought two but it could be just one or, on the rare occasion, three. The same procedure followed until all were sold. By that time Dad was merry, having had numerous visits to the pub. As the day had progressed, these visits seemed to last longer.

With all our business done by early afternoon, I could share with my old man the satisfying feeling of a job well done. Dad asked one of the people beside us to keep an eye on the donkey. Patiently, it had stood there all day, harnessed to the cart and munching on a bag of hay. It would throw an anxious eye in our direction, as if to say, 'don't drag it out now, you two'. We went to the fish and chip shop for a special treat.

Before hitting the road, there was one more important matter to be attended to. We called at Jordan's grocery. After some rummaging in his pockets, Dad produced the list of purchases to be made. It would include some special goodies, like jelly and custard and ingredients for sweet cakes. Mother would use them so that the whole family could feel they shared in the sale. This was the day that the slate was cleaned, and all the accumulated debt paid. I took the reins and Dad hummed and drowsed contentedly, as we trotted our way home.

≈ ≈ ≈

THE LIFE I KNEW so well, the one that imprinted so many cherished memories, was drastically changed far sooner than I would have wished for. At the end of primary school, Master Ryan, our teacher at Knock National School, had prepared a few of us to sit for the County Council examination, so I got a scholarship to study secondary school as a boarder. In those years, few small farmers' sons ever got that opportunity, not around our area anyway. My parents were very excited, and the decision, regarding which school to go to, was easy.

Even though it was located in neighbouring County Galway, they chose St. Jarlath's College. It was a minor seminary, run by priests, and that had to be good. I don't think most of us boys gave it much thought, but my mother surely had hoped that I might opt for the priesthood at the end of the five years. There would be no easy way to have a gentle leave-taking. I was the eldest child and was leaving the nest, much too early for my liking. That was the simple truth of it.

It was early September 1950 when my father and I took the bus from Ballyhaunis for Tuam. We were joined by a friend of Dad's from the next village, with whom he used to team up each spring for the ploughing, a two-horse job. Both men were on the same mission, bringing their sons to the boarding school.

The college lay in the shadow of the cathedral. On one side was the Presentation Convent School for girls, with whom we would have no contact for the duration. We presented ourselves, and were welcomed by a priest, who led us to a first year dormitory and assigned us our beds.

After putting our bags under the bed, we walked along the time-worn corridors and went outside. We were all making an effort not to show our nerves and the silence at times was awkward.

It was a warm, sunny afternoon. We two boys joined a group who were kicking a football on the Gaelic pitch beside the college. Our parents looked on. I was aware of their presence, and could only imagine the mixed feelings they were having. The first year students had come a day early. We had the place to ourselves, and kicking the football was an easy way for us to get to know each other.

An incident occurred that would help lighten the atmosphere. One of the lads, who had obvious footballing ability, had paused to light a cigarette. This in itself was an impressive statement back then. Of course, once in the system, this habit would merit drastic treatment. He had barely time to complete the operation, and put the box of matches back in his jacket pocket, when the ball was kicked in his direction. Instinctively, he raced after it and, as he did so, smoke began to bilge from the pocket. He didn't notice anything and raced on, fanning the fire. We chased him down, slapped him around, much more than required, and put the fire out.

Then, suddenly, Dad and his friend were on their way. There would be no handshake or hug. When I noticed them, they were going up the steps. I began to follow them but realised it was too late. They had reckoned the goodbyes would be too much for us all, I thought. Maybe, too, they felt we needed to start getting used to what lay ahead.

We were not released until just before Christmas. Life for my sisters and brother would go on and I would not be part of it. Like the other boys, as the days and weeks went by, I had to put my nostalgia for home life to the back of my mind, as much as possible.

The one and only means of contact with home we students had was by letter. Mom was a good letter writer, and she would always get Dad to put in a paragraph at the end. Like her generation, and our own too, handwriting was an art.

I made some friends, and Gaelic football became my safety valve and distraction. All the festivities and celebrations that surrounded Mayo's two successive All-Ireland titles in 1950 and 1951 gave me a warm feeling and a sense of pride. And, of course, it helped that the captain was from my mother's home village. But we dared not forget that we were in the territory of our football rivals. There would be no showing off.

Of the twenty plus teachers in the school, only two were lay people. All the others were priests. Sent to work in the school right after their ordination, we students never heard that they had any special training in education or work with teenagers. They were a decent group of people. A few gave extra dedication to getting the best out of us on the sports field and in organising the yearly musical. We got an education that matched that of other schools at that time. Yet, there was one negative aspect that was never faced – physical punishment.

It was the priest in charge of discipline who did the most damage to us physically and emotionally. He used a thick cane, a 'jobber's stick' we called it. For misdemeanours, like talking after lights were out, one could get, depending on his mood, four to six lashes on each hand. If he was in a particularly vile mood, which as rumour had it, coincided with a full moon, he would make sure the stick came down on each wrist for good measure. Blisters and cuts were the result. It was noticeable that when he had a personal dislike for a particular student the punishment could go much further.

After final prayers, one night, he raided the dormitory. There was too much noise for his liking, and he ordered a number of us to line up outside his room. As each of my companions entered the room, he closed the door. Still, the agonised cries echoed along the corridor. Before I entered, one of the better footballers on the team was about to leave. He was bent forward in pain. With speed, the punisher slammed the door shut, trapping the lad. His head and arms were outside but he was caught. The blows rained down on his bottom, as he screamed for mercy.

Trembling, crippling fear took hold of us in these situations. There was embarrassment, deep humiliation and lots of anger as well. After the evening meal, some would discuss how to face up to that man, even physically. The president of the school, also a priest, couldn't but have known what was going on. Still, he never, to our knowledge, intervened. Neither did we do anything except talk. When, many years later, that priest was finally changed and given work in a parish, he was already an alcoholic. Sadly, I reflect on how a man, in urgent need of help and treatment, was left in such a crucial job for so long.

Our parents were more than reluctant to get involved. They would even try to justify the cruel punishment by suggesting, 'You must have been doing something wrong and got into trouble.' To our young minds, it was obvious that it was a lost cause – the Church then could do no wrong.

I survived the boarding school regime without distinction or disgrace. At eighteen years of age, one was expected to be grown up, and ready to take a big decision about what to do for the rest of one's life. Ready or not, we all did.

During my last year in St. Jarlath's, several representatives of missionary organisations visited us. They were looking for recruits. One was a Columban, who knew the two priests of the Society, Kieran and John, from my own parish. The three of them struck me as down-to-earth people, who were devoid of airs and graces.

The Columban magazine, called *The Far East* after the original idea of mission to China, came regularly to our house. It portrayed the efforts of nuns and priests in far-off countries. Going on the missions appealed to me as something worth doing.

Midway through the summer holidays, I told my parents of my decision. For weeks beforehand, I had tried to muster up the courage to do so. Of the many thoughts and emotions that went through my mind, there was a question that bothered me most. As the eldest of the children, and the first to get a secondary education, was it not my responsibility to get a job and be in a position to help out financially?

I felt confident that my decision to study for the priesthood would be welcomed by my parents, but surely, they would ask themselves, why did he have to choose the foreign missions? Perhaps that question did not weigh too heavily on them. Parting of the ways, and the long goodbyes, were part of the Irish psyche of the times.

Ireland of those years had already sent, and would continue to do so for some decades more, thousands of nuns, priests and brothers to the missions. All through those years, it lost tens of thousands of its youth to emigration. Many were never to return.

Though the farewells were so common, I doubt if it made them any easier for those left behind.

My parents did indeed support my decision. However, there was no sharing of the mixed feelings of joy, sadness or fear that they must have had. Very quickly, I noticed that I was being treated differently, and with a special deference, by my mother. My siblings had begun to call me Luke, no longer Lukie. They would tell me it was at mother's request. I got a special place at our humble kitchen table and was served first. It was uncomfortable for us children, but the approach of my entry into the clerical ranks had, in my mother's mind, to be acknowledged in our home.

After breaking the news, the rest of the summer seemed to fly by. My brother Liam and my sisters, Ann, Patsy and Mary, were growing up quickly. Now I was leaving them, and not just physically. I would be set apart.

Thankfully, I didn't fully realise how much our paths were going to diverge. Without having yet put on a Roman collar, I was already different. I think we were all in a kind of daze. A mixture of social values and religious beliefs, forces beyond our control, were taking over.

My parents, putting their bravest faces on the situation, would have thought to themselves, 'Well, at least he will be in Ireland for another seven years'. That was the length of time the training was to take. First year students were not allowed home during that year. We could receive visits. My parents never made it to the seminary until the day I was ordained, six and a half years later. In those times, it was a long way from Ballyroe, or anywhere in Mayo, to Dalgan Park, near Navan in County Meath.

In many aspects, life in the seminary was a most welcome change from that of the secondary school. A genuine spirit of comradeship pervaded the place. It was fostered and practised. Men in their last year mixed freely with students from lower years. We were trusted to report our own misdemeanours. This was so incredibly different and refreshing.

But we had to be moulded to fit the role that we aspired to fulfil one day. The whole purpose of the daily routine was to have us acquire the habits, knowledge and spiritual life required.

From our early morning rising, to our last visit to the chapel, our lives were ruled by bells.

As the months and years went by, the whole notion of who we were training to be was patiently drummed into us. We were trainee clerics, hoping one day to be part of the clerical institution.

As such, we were special people, chosen and set apart to spread the gospel, especially to the pagans or non-believers. Even though, during my student days, I felt uncomfortable with the constant insistence on the idea, that we belonged to a special class of people, I preferred to put those feelings aside. 'It will be different on the missions,' I would muse.

On occasions, the idea of being special and set apart became especially awkward, like when my old boyhood pals in the village felt inhibited from chatting freely as before. But it was something I could do nothing about. Once I had put on the soutane and collar or the black suit, people immediately knew their place.

Right through the seminary years, another powerful idea was constantly put before us, namely that of self-sacrifice. It was not just the fact that we had taken a vow of chastity, and so could not marry or engage in sexual activity. We had to be ready to face up to, and stoically bear, whatever difficulties the spreading of the gospel might impose on us. This included paying the ultimate price.

Even as a young organisation, the Society of St. Columban already had many martyrs, men who had lost their lives on the missions due to disease or imprisonment. Some of those who had survived prison ordeals addressed us from time to time. They appeared to be humble men, not looking for any special attention but, for us, the message was powerful. They were heroes. We should aim to be like them.

Those who have studied the origin and rise of the missionary movement in Ireland in the last century believe it was greatly influenced by the Easter Rising of 1916. The insurgents took on the might of the British military, knowing full well the uprising would not be successful, and that they would lose their lives in the attempt.

One of the most charismatic of the leaders was Padraig Pearse, a poet, lawyer and educator. The insurrection failed and

Pearse, along with the other leaders, was captured. Waiting to be executed, like his comrades, he wrote a poem called 'The Fool' to those who did not share his dream. Lines like the following would prove to be prophetic:

> *And the wise have pitied the fool, who strove to give a life*
> *to a dream,*
> *That was dreamed in the heart and that only the heart can*
> *hold.*
> *O Wise Men, riddle me this: What if the dream come true,*
> *What if the dream come true and the millions unborn*
> *shall dwell*
> *In the house that I shaped in my heart?*

The heroic self-sacrifice of the insurgents, and their leaders, profoundly touched the soul of the Irish nation. It sparked the War of Independence and opened the road to freedom at last. In addition, it was the touchstone for the start of an extraordinary missionary movement.

Just months after the Easter Rising, the Maynooth Mission to China, later called the Society of St. Columban, was founded. Many other missionary organisations of men and women would follow, inspired by a mix of religious fervour and idealistic nationalism. It is estimated that Ireland had around 7,500 missionaries, women and men, working around the world in the mid-1960s. This was an extraordinary number for a small country.

One of the founding group of Columbans wrote of his personal reflection, after hearing the confessions of volunteers, on their way to join the uprising:

'If they can do it, why can't we, who are priests, risk and give our lives for the gospel?'

Some years after the Society was founded, a Columban wrote a rousing hymn that became our anthem. Interestingly, reminiscent of a crusade-like mission, its title is 'Who has a Blade for a Splendid Cause?'

4.

CONFLICT AND CRACK-DOWN

IN THE PARISH of Holy Cross, a number of months passed and there was no visible presence or intervention by the boss. I cannot remember any general meeting being convened to discuss pastoral issues. Then suddenly Owen decided to do a round of the parishes.

He came to inform us that he was establishing what was in effect a curfew. Nobody, he said, was to leave the parish house after work was finished in the *despacho* or parish office, at 9.30 pm. He was aware of the secret meetings we were holding in the parish of Reynoso, and this was his way of dealing with our deviant conduct.

The prohibition would not work. We were totally immersed in what we were trying to do and having tasted the freedom to question, think and implement new ideas in pastoral work, we were not for turning back. So we continued to meet. And Owen decided to watch us more closely. He visited the parish a few times and laid down the law as regards our duty to follow the traditional pastoral lines. It was obvious that his attitude towards us was hardening and that his determination to put a stop to what we were doing was growing.

To get the people to receive the sacraments he organised a mission to be carried out in each parish. It was to be a time of special effort by us priests to motivate people to come to church, a time to stir up religious fervour.

One evening during the mission, Owen was observing proceedings. The church was half empty and he was obviously not a happy man, as he paced back and forth inside the main door. In a desperate move, he approached me and said, 'Luke, come with me.'

I followed my boss out onto the plaza. It was an area the size of a football pitch, full of the now familiar rounded stones. In the centre there were a few large rocks that had been deposited there by the floods of long ago. It was a gathering place for the youth and he was making a bee-line for them.

As we arrived, he muttered something about the Mission, and without pause he put a long arm on the shoulder of one lad, then another. 'Vamos muchachos' – 'let's go lads' – he said, and proceeded to march, with the two boys in tow, towards the church. There were no objections. The operation was sudden and he was an imposing figure. Seriously embarrassed, behind his back I made some kind of apologetic gesture in the direction of the general group, and started back towards the church. A couple of the lads followed me. Once in the building, Owen deposited the vagrant sheep in an empty pew, and we went in search of more.

On my own path of discovery at that time, the thought of dragging people into church was unthinkable. I was very embarrassed. But from Owen's perspective, a little fatherly tug never did a lad any harm, neither in church or at home. He was basically a good man and was only following what had been drilled into him from childhood, school and seminary. He had also seen it work in his years as a priest. And yet, there and then, I knew that he and I were miles apart.

The stark truth was dawning on me – we would never be able to see things in the same light again. It was a sad awareness that welled up inside me, and does to this day, as I remember old Columban friends, many no longer with us. He had been put into a job that he had not wanted and, given that time of momentous change, one that he was not prepared for.

Almost two years had passed since my arrival in Peru. I had become accustomed to asking some uncomfortable questions and living on the edge. No longer did I have that feeling of quiet confidence and security, or indeed a certain smugness, which came from unquestioned beliefs.

I was in the process of growing as a person. True, I was doing pastoral work from a new perspective, and got satisfaction from thinking things through and trying out new ideas. But mainly, I was learning, and felt I was receiving more than I was giving.

There was, however, another side to this process. This approach to life and work inevitably brought with it risks and new challenges. At times I missed the comforting feeling of being protected by the big institution. But there would be no returning. From now on, one had to be true to oneself.

But I was not alone. Though Michael, Gerry and I were very different personalities, we bonded and quickly became a team. People in the parish noticed this and commented favourably. We read many of the same books, attended meetings and took our days off together.

I remember when we took our first drink and broke the 'pledge', that solemn promise we had made back in secondary school not to drink alcohol until we were at least twenty-one. The three of us had kept to our promise but at this stage it was just another one of the taboos that had to be faced. It belonged to the years of our domestication, when we didn't yet know of personal freedom.

Dressed in civvies, as normal when not on official duty, we sat in a bar on Colmena Avenue in Lima, on a dreary winter's evening, and ordered our first *pisco sours*, that typical drink which newcomers to Lima must savour.

We had all changed in Peru and Michael probably more than any of us. In the seminary he had been a sacristan, a job given only to the most enthusiastic observers of the rules in general, and liturgy in particular. Now, true to himself, he was an extrovert and relishing the occasion.

With more volume and urgency to his voice than I would have preferred at that moment, he summoned the *mozo* or waiter across the length of the pub. On the latter's arrival both engaged in animated conversation, the result of which meant we were given a special demonstration on how the famous drink was prepared. Peruvian pisco is, on its own, a strong spirit, but laced with whipped white of egg, lemon juice and a few other ingredients, it 'seems' to lose its bite. That of course carries its own complications. It is a delicious drink that can catch the unfamiliar imbiber 'unaware'.

With our three drinks sitting temptingly in front of us, Gerry was first to raise his glass:

'Salud, cheers ye pair of rascals, your mothers should see ye now!'

'What your mother doesn't know lad won't bother her. Cheers, slainte and salud to ye both,' Michael responded.

Just back, after facilitating a workshop with a mixed group of adults from the parish, he was all excited.

'Lads, it was an amazing experience. I just sat there and listened.'

'What were ye discussing?' I asked.

'The main theme was really a question. What problems are you having rearing your children?'

'Well, you wouldn't know anything about that anyway, so just as well you let them do the talking,' Gerry said, tongue in cheek.

'Being smart again, eh? Seriously, though, it was very moving to hear parents express, in their own words, the problems they faced daily, like not having a suitable corner in the house, or light, so the children could do their homework.'

'When you hear this first-hand from the people, it really brings home the practical difficulties they are faced with, doesn't it? Well done, Michael, let's celebrate a good day's work,' I said, and we raised our glasses.

As we relaxed, some of the lighter moments of missionary life came easily into the conversation. We used to play a seven-a-side soccer game with some of the school teachers in St. Martin de Porres parish. The playground was surrounded on three sides by a three-storey school building. Our sporting efforts always drew an enthusiastic crowd, made up of teachers and students.

'That was some fun at the game last week, Gerry. Tell us about the Dunner's escapade,' I said provokingly.

'Well, ye know that the same man was never slow when it came to a bit of fun. We were winning the game by a couple of goals. The bould Tom was our usual goalkeeper. Without any warning, and to the surprise and merriment of the spectators, he ballooned the ball up into the air and out over the school building. After some students recovered the ball, I could see that he was shaping up to do the same antic a second time. So I ran up to him and began to give out.'

'Ah, Gerry, will you cop on,' he said, 'Sure the people love it!' And they did!

Then Michael had a story he was bursting to tell. He had worked at the Holy Cross parish a little before Gerry and me. Mal, the parish priest, was a quiet, unobtrusive man with a wicked sense of humour. It was Thursday of Holy Week and he had spent quite a bit of time arranging and decorating a special altar, outside the railings of the main altar. It would hold the consecrated hosts from the Mass commemorating the Last Supper.

'Well, Mal was preaching away, when he spotted this big, shaggy dog come up the main isle, take a sharp right turn for the newly made altar, lift his back leg and begin to piddle all over the spotless altar cloth.'

'Come on, Michael, you're exaggerating as usual,' I muttered.

'Not a bit, lad. True as I'm sitting here. Can't ye just let me finish.'

'Go ahead then, but try and keep your voice down. You're putting on a show as usual.'

'Well, as I was saying, when I was rudely interrupted, Mal, undaunted, never stopped preaching. Instead, he pulled his clerical garments above his knees, threw a leg over the altar rails, then another, and shooed the dog down to the door.'

'Are you saying he was still preaching down at the door?'

'Can't you wait and let a fella tell the full story? At the door, our Mal threw an almighty kick on the unfortunate animal's hindquarters. It scampered howling across the plaza, while Mal did an about turn to his place on the altar, preaching all the while and without as much as a smirk on his face.'

After prolonged bouts of laughter: 'How did the people react?' we asked.

'There was some half-smothered sniggering and giggling went on alright, but it was Holy Week and they would have to wait until after the ceremony to really let go. You know, Mal was

54

known in the parish ever after as '*El Padre de la pata segura*' – 'The Padre with the sure foot'.

We had spent a most enjoyable and relaxing evening. The couple of *pisco sours* that each of us drank had certainly contributed to a memorable occasion. But it was not something that I would write home about. After all, we had just broken the 'pledge'.

After my first year in Holy Cross parish, the friendship and team spirit that Michael, Gerry and I shared had deepened. And, at last I was beginning to feel comfortable with my Spanish. Hours of listening, especially in the company of young people, had paid off. There was plenty of laughter at my gaffs but I always felt we were all enjoying the fun. As the months rolled on, I was picking up more popular sayings and having the courage to use them in conversations. This served to create an immediate bond with the listeners. Many proverbs were not only profound but witty too.

One of the most popular was, '*El que no llora, no mama*' – 'He who doesn't cry, doesn't get to suck'. It applied, not just to the obvious situation of the baby letting his mother know he was hungry, but to all situations where people wanted to let their needs and grievances be known. As they grew in awareness of their rights, the poor used it to motivate and inspire themselves to organise and make demands on the authorities.

Midway through that second year, I felt much more at home. I was part of a community, and liked to think it was a more horizontal relationship than the traditional clerical one. A bond had been formed with the youth group I was responsible for and, not to be forgotten, my football companions. I could not have imagined myself ever damaging that relationship. However, I was to learn a hard lesson.

One morning I was in a school classroom talking to the pupils. Some of my footy friends were there. One of them, in spite of my pleading, had continued to mess around. I came up beside him and gave him a slap across the cheek. Immediately, I was ashamed and mortified. This was not who I thought I was. Even though I apologised to the boy after class, I was shaken and looking for an answer. Where had that sudden reaction come from? How had I lost control so completely? It was a humbling and frightening experience. But it did not take much reflection on my part to feel sure that I knew the answer. Wasn't that what I had seen, on a regular basis, in secondary school?

Busy and absorbed as Michael, Gerry and I were in Holy Cross parish, we hadn't fully appreciated how much, and how quickly, the relationship between colleagues, in the whole group, was deteriorating. People were labelled as pro- and anti-reform, and sometimes put into one or other camp all too easily. These mistakes caused understandable annoyance, and it was to stay with some men for years.

Those of us, who were perceived as being on the side of radical change were nicknamed the *discipuli* or disciples – we were followers of the Alvarez Calderon brothers, instead of the traditional Church.

At that time, nearly half the total number of priests working in parishes run by the Columbans in Lima were not members of the Society. They were what we called 'volunteers' from dioceses in Ireland and England; they had been released by their bishops to work for a number of years with us. A few of these men became ardent proponents of the Second Vatican Council's thinking and pastoral reform. Thus, the lines of bitter division were not confined just to us Columbans. Indeed, talking to members of other missionary organisations, then and afterwards, it is clear that the division along theological and pastoral lines affected most, if not all, of them.

There was little practical need to meet with those in the other camp and we didn't – birds of a feather flock together. We had our own days of reflection and less formal get-togethers. Our visits to the centre house were less frequent, and the atmosphere there had noticeably cooled.

In our parish, even though Joe didn't share most of our ideas and pastoral approach, we nevertheless had a good relationship. He was happy to continue to do what he had always done. We went out for a meal together now and again, and played the odd game of cards. The situation in other parishes was more complex, and relations were strained. The Society leaders must have decided that the spreading of the radical pastoral approach was stoppable but that it had to be done quickly.

We knew we were being watched but, naively, we hadn't expected any big intervention coming from the top. So we were more than surprised when it did happen. Owen, a man of few words, appeared in our parish house early one morning and bluntly announced that he was separating us. Michael would momentarily stay on in Holy Cross parish, Gerry and I were to be moved on.

There was no way one could put a 'nice face' on this intervention by Owen. It was ruthless and dictatorial. No attempt whatsoever was made to try to understand what we were trying to do. We were condemned and punished without any kind of due process. The monolithic and autocratic Church to which we belonged had its way of dealing with dissenters. Owen would have received instructions from those at the top of the Columban Society.

One of the *haciendas*, with a small, mostly migrant population of workers, was where Gerry was banished to. That would keep him out of sight and cut his wings. For some reason, the boss seemed to suspect that he was culpable for a lot of the dangerous ideas we were associated with. As for myself, there were other plans. I would go to work in a parish that the Society had taken over a few years earlier which was located on the other side of the river Rimac.

Of course, we were very aware that the purpose of Owen's intervention was to dismantle the team, and deliver a serious blow to the line of pastoral action we espoused. For me, those two years had not only been memorable but also invaluable. From being an outwardly secure, but in fact diffident cleric, I had embarked on a process of growing up. For people out in the world, this is rarely a straightforward process, but at least it is accepted as what one should try to do. To do so within the clerical structure was, to say the least, proving to be most complicated.

I had begun to claim the right and freedom to think, ask questions and search for answers – and was no longer able to trot out pat answers which belonged to another age. I was young and had so much more to learn and try to do. It was easy for me to empathise with the words of the poet, Robert Frost:

> *The woods are lovely, dark and deep.*
> *But I have promises to keep*
> *And miles to go before I sleep*
> *And miles to go before I sleep.*

Though I was very apprehensive about what was coming down the road, at some level I knew that this new challenge was a continuation of my journey. The break-up of our team would somehow, I kept telling myself, have a positive outcome.

In spite of that basic, positive outlook, Owen's desperate attempt to 'stamp out' our pastoral approach was a huge blow for me personally. While the three of us were to continue to meet up occasionally, and attend some of the same seminars, I was now, in effect, on my own.

The unforgettable team effort, that had given me so much, was now abruptly ended. I was frightened and saddened but could not afford to show it. The feeling of 'I've been here before' kept coming to my mind.

The sense of loss and sadness that comes when one is separated, by the force of circumstances, from family or friends and in this case a community, had been a constant in my life since the age of twelve.

As a cleric, I had been trained to distrust personal feelings. They were dangerous, likely occasions of sin, and had to be covered up, not opened up or admitted to. The problem was that I was no longer a fully domesticated cleric. So, in the weeks after we rebels were scattered, I allowed myself to go down memory lane, and recall the separations that had cost me most.

In deciding the break-up of our team, Owen had shown a tough, uncompromising side but he was not acting alone. The top men in the Society were extremely worried about the radical pastoral approach being carried out in Peru. They were determined to make every effort to eradicate it.

Soon Owen was to get support in the form of a Columban who, like himself, had worked in China and been imprisoned there. Ted had been released from prison and was headed for Lima.

My feelings towards Owen and Ted were mixed. I still had a lingering respect for them. But my frustration was growing. On one level I saw them as people who had suffered for what they believed in. But I no longer shared their traditional beliefs about Church and mission. My earlier hopes had waned. I used to encourage myself, saying that a spirit of tolerance would prevail. That we would finally agree to live and let live. That the leadership of the Society would accept that what we were thinking and doing, though seen by many as too radical, was in line with the Second Vatican Council.

For that was where we pro-reformers got our inspiration. The number one priority was to get to know the people and their culture more and more, discover their richness and values and see salvation at work among them. We did not see ourselves as really needing to convert anyone. We were there to give witness to Christian values, and to draw people's attention to the fact that their own daily efforts at promoting unity, understanding and forgiveness were clear signs of Christianity at work among them. Now that the three of us were to be separated, I held on to a faint hope that our pastoral approach would not be seen as a direct threat. Would we be allowed some measure of freedom?

My tentative hopes were unfounded. Ted's release, after a lengthy period in prison, had created a stir within the Society and in the media. He was appointed to the parish of St. Martin de Porres, where Columbans in Lima had first begun their missionary work. Early on, he let it be known that his job was to make sure that the line of pastoral action we were following was eradicated.

This man, who had suffered imprisonment for his faith, was showing us a hard, intolerant side. He would not shrink from imposing the version of Church that he had been given in the seminary – the recommendations of the Second Vatican Council did not form part of his creed. His experience in China seemed to have convinced him, for ever more, of the rightness of his approach. We were not to hear him say anything about what he had learned from the whole experience.

It was sad and sobering to see how a well-read, witty person could leave aside his compassion, understanding and tolerance, and become ruthless in an attempt to impose his beliefs. I had thought that only happened in Church history books.

Though the Columban Society had been set up initially to contribute to the missionary effort in China, I cannot remember one class, in my time in the seminary, which touched on the rich culture of that vast country, nothing about the positives and negatives of the missionary efforts there. The name of Mateo Ricci was not mentioned.

Ricci, an Italian Jesuit priest, and his small group of fellow missionaries, made extraordinary efforts to understand, appreciate and respect the Chinese culture. An erudite man, he not only became proficient at the language, but contributed to the knowledge of the country in mathematics, and cartography especially. In a country which was highly distrustful of foreigners, he gained the trust and appreciation of people at all levels of society, including that of the emperor.

On the basis of profound respect for its people and culture, he accepted the Chinese term Lord of Heaven, as expressing the concept of the God of Christians.

This is what the Second Vatican Council stated nearly four centuries later: salvation was already at work in all cultures and among all peoples. Ricci, a man way ahead of his time, was always looking for the Christian values already at work in the lives of the people.

After his death in Beijing, in 1610, a heated debate broke out among members of all the missionary organisations in the Far East (Jesuits, Dominicans, Franciscans and Augustinians). Some were to say that Ricci had gone too far, and accused him of defiling the purity of religion, by allowing Christians to take part in superstitious ceremonies, among other things. The arguments and the visits to Rome continued for nearly a 150 years until the Pope finally ruled against Ricci's approach to missionary work.

Owen, Ted and the other Columbans had travelled to China, with the crucial matter already decided by Rome. If they attempted to bring any other missionary approach, except the one imbued with European culture, they were out of order. The silence, and omission of any discussion in the seminary, had in itself given a clear message. There were to be no experiments regarding how to spread the gospel.

Strange, and almost incomprehensible, as it seemed to me at the time, now I can see the lack of any shared evaluation of the Chinese experience as fitting into a picture. Missionary work, as dictated by Rome, whether in China or Peru, was considered to be basically the same. So, there we were in the different countries of South and Central America, foreign missionaries and local clergy, arguing and wrangling as the Second Vatican Council turned the traditional approach on its head. We were divided over the very nature of the Church's mission; divided over something as fundamental as recognising and embracing the Christian values and richness of each local culture; divided over promoting awareness among the poor of their rights, and of the oppressive nature of the social, economic and political structures under which they lived.

5.

A HOUSE DIVIDED

THE NEW PARISH to which I was ordered to go was part of a densely populated area which lay between the river Rimac and one of the main industrial arteries, Argentina Avenue. It was divided into two parishes. The first was run by a French priest. It started at the *Coliseo Cerrado*, National Basketball Arena, under a bridge over the river Rimac, and harboured one of the worst slums in the city, called Carcamo.

The next parish, named The Virgin Mediatrix, was to be my new home. It covered three different barrios or neighbourhoods. Two of them, El Planeta and Mirones Alto, were built alongside the old rubbish dump for Lima. The other, Villa Maria, popularly known as 'El Montón' (The Heap), was entirely built on it. In this latter *barrio*, the church and parish house were located.

The change from across the river was dramatic. Here there were no wide streets and open spaces, no rounded stones and sand of the dried-out river bed. Instead, metres of rubbish lay underfoot and a pervading burning smell filled the air.

The lower parts of the rubbish dump had been levelled out and built upon, but an enormous mountain, several football fields in area and several storeys high, still stood there. A cloud of smoke hovered over the summit, which smouldered continually.

A fine, grey dust, several inches deep, covered the top and sides. When disturbed by wind, or human contact, the dust floated into the air. It was a deadly cause of respiratory problems, especially for the very young.

There was no hiding from the fact that conditions here were much worse than on the other side of the river. One had the feeling of being trapped in a place that had little future. Across the river, people were poor too but the area itself offered more hope.

People there seemed to be building with a purpose. But I could not afford to allow myself to entertain such sentiments. Anyway, as yet, I hadn't met any of the people.

Owen came to the parish on the day that I arrived there. Over a cup of coffee, at the kitchen table, he encouraged Louis, the parish priest and me, his new assistant, to work together. At the same time, he made it abundantly clear who was in charge.

'It's alright to talk things over but we all know what we have to do. As parish priest, Louis, you have the final word.'

Louis was just a year older than me. A good conversationalist and well-read. Among the wider group, he was not seen as leaning towards our side. But I felt he was the kind of person one could get along with. It helped too that he had a good sense of humour.

For my part, I was determined to pull my weight, carrying out the traditional work in the parish: masses, sacraments, funerals and all other requests were great opportunities for meeting and getting to know people. Of course, I was very interested in what could be done outside that space.

The church in Villa Maria was the hub of parish activity. Neighbours in the other two barrios lent us small spaces where we celebrated Sunday Masses. Chatting to people afterwards, both adults and young people were expressing a desire to be involved in some way. I saw it as an opportunity to set up some groups. My new boss had no interest in that kind of pastoral activity.

A group of adults called the *Hermandad* or Brotherhood already existed in Villa Maria. Normally, the main focus of this kind of traditional organisation was the preparation and running of the feast of the patron saint of a parish, but this all male group was also involved in the politics of the *barrio*. The members had approached Louis and asked him to attend their meetings. It was something he liked to do.

On many occasions he accompanied a small delegation to the offices of the Mayor of Lima. The latter had his own political party and some of the delegates belonged to it. Due to the condition of the terrain, the installation of services like water and sewerage was an enormous challenge. Help from the highest level was welcome.

Built on mountains of rubbish, the place shook at the passing of a car. Trying to build houses in that situation was a nightmare. The walls cracked and the foundations constantly tilted. The sewerage and water pipes ran into enormous trouble. Even without the passing of the odd truck, delivering supplies to local shops, they were liable to break. Every other day there was a crew digging on a street.

From my earliest days in Peru, I was deeply impressed by the ability of the poor, not only to weather the daily grind of poverty, but to stubbornly refuse to remain there. They spared no effort to move forward with courage and enthusiasm. I asked myself the same question, over and over: 'How do these people manage to survive, and overcome the greatest of obstacles, the way they do?'

It was not until I had got to know a few families in my new parish better that I came to appreciate the vital role that the 'extended family' played. Tightly knit together, across generations and branches, these big families pooled their survival efforts, often under the same roof.

Take the Flores family, for example. They lived near the rubbish dump itself, on one of the narrow, ash-covered streets. When I first got to know them, their home was like most of those around it, a construction made of boards, bamboo and cardboard. As there was practically no rain in Lima, the roof was made of boards and plastic. Later they would get some sheets of asbestos.

Keeping the dust controlled was a constant effort, but the street outside, and the dirt floors inside, always looked as if they had been recently watered and swept. Water was bought by the barrel. In the heat of summer, it began to go off if left there for more than a few days. At the best of times it had to be boiled before it could be drunk.

The pervading dust on the streets, and in the air, was a serious health hazard. Many people, especially small children, suffered from bronchitis and asthma. But, remarkably, people in general seemed to be able to keep a rein on this constant threat. They relied on their ages-old herbal remedies and only fell back on western medicine in desperate circumstances.

Thirteen people lived in the Flores household, including six children between the ages of two and ten years and their parents. The grandparents, on mother's side, in their 70s, were still deeply involved in the family welfare. An uncle, mother's brother, who was paralysed from the waist down after being hit by a car, also lived there. They had two teenagers, a nephew and niece of father's, staying with them while they studied in secondary school.

María, the mother, in her mid-30s, was the hub of energy and purpose around which the whole group functioned daily. Early each morning, she went to the local street market and bought food and vegetables for the day. After getting the children ready and off to school, she began her income-earning activity, preparing lunch for workers in one of the factories in the industrial zone. I often met her as she pushed or pedalled her tricycle, determination and urgency written on her face.

Ever since he lost his job in a textile factory Emilio, the father, had been unable to find any permanent employment. He now worked on a temporary basis at the central market for Lima, where he helped unload and load trucks as they came and left. His day started at 5.00 am and lasted well into the afternoon. Pay was woeful and the work back-breaking.

José, the granddad, had turned his hand to many jobs in his time. He had been a fisherman and a taxi driver, among other occupations. Now he earned a little money selling biscuits, bread rolls, minerals and the like, in his kiosk at the local street market. It was a mobile affair and each morning and afternoon he pushed it to his spot and back.

Grandma Rosa was busy too. She had the small ones to care for. After school, she received the older brothers and sisters, with their main meal of the day at the ready. She was there in every emergency, like the time when Jaime, the oldest of the boys, had gone up onto the burning rubbish heap and seriously burnt his feet. Rosa, like her neighbours from the *sierra*, the highlands of the Andes Mountains, had a few *savila*, aloe vera plants, growing in pots, for all such emergencies. The aloe vera juice is truly miraculous for cuts and burns. You would never know how serious the boy's injury had been.

Uncle Jaime, though immobilised, could use his arms and hands. Under his guidance, Granddad had built a work bench that could be wheeled onto the street beside the house. There he mended shoes. The sign, brightly painted by the student nephew, read: 'Shoes Good As New'.

Maria regularly attended the meetings of the local Mothers' Club. There she learned useful, family-oriented skills but, most important for her, she also learned to analyse the situation around her and to speak in public. With husband Emilio, she had begun to attend the open-air general meetings in the *barrio*, and express her opinions on what might be done to solve, or alleviate, some urgent problem.

Increasingly, over the decade of the 1960s, women in the *barrios* had begun to participate in their local organisations. This no longer caused any surprise or negative reaction on the part of men. It was one of the success stories that had taken place in the shantytowns. When I had arrived in Peru, less than a decade before, women rarely participated in their community organisations. Few of them attended meetings and rarely spoke in public. Now they were even taking on leadership roles.

The poor in the shantytowns got nothing for free – light, water, sewerage, garbage collection – all had to be paid for. They were aware of that, but they also knew, from experience, that most often nothing was done until pressure was brought on the municipality or the relevant state body. When promises of starting dates were repeatedly broken, the size of the commissions going to the public offices increased. Often a bus load of residents had to be mobilised.

For the people in the parish, like those in the other shantytowns which were springing up around Lima, community work and solidarity were second nature. Back in their villages in the highlands, life was built around community. They shared the tilling of common land, sowing and harvesting. The community celebrations held in honour of their patron saint were especially joyful times, often going on for days.

The decision to move from their villages in the Andes was traumatic and involved a huge uprooting. But living conditions had become unbearable. There was no future there, especially for the young.

Lima was the destination for the vast majority of the poor who left the highlands. The other cities on the coast received large numbers of the migrants too, but in total only a small percentage compared to that of the capital.

Lima's population exploded. And it has continued to do so. In 1950 it had under a million people, by 1970 it had almost three million, and today it is home to about one-third of Peru's total population, some nine million people. How they went about tackling and overcoming almost insurmountable obstacles – to form homes, communities and entire districts – is a most inspiring, and yet unfinished, story.

When migrating from the *sierra*, people did not venture out blindly – there was a strategy. They followed in the footsteps of others who had gone before them. Before leaving they were in contact with their relatives. They also kept close to their *paisanos*, the friends, neighbours and acquaintances from their own districts or provinces. The bond they formed was powerful and decisive for the survival strategy in the capital city.

Newly arrived in Lima, they settled for a time in the *callejones*, the inner city slums. These were one-roomed huts that lined both sides of narrow passage ways. Neither the government nor the municipality had a central plan or the resources to provide support for the continuous arrival of the thousands looking for homes. With no houses, loans or facilities available, the poor had to come up with their own solutions.

Time was not wasted. They formed their own organisations and planned the 'invasion' of the most suitable waste land available. The northern sector of the city was the first to be taken over. They settled along the rugged foothills of the Andes. These were rocky, dusty desert places. All would require enormous effort in order to make them in any way habitable.

The danger of having to face eviction by the police was ever present. Pitched battles, between the 'invaders' and the forces of order, took place frequently. Sometimes a mysterious 'owner', from the rich side of the city, appeared and staked a claim on the land. Depending on his power to influence, the case in the courts could go on for years.

The poor became adept at defending themselves, within the labyrinth of the bureaucratic, and often corrupt, legal system. If there were no legal battles, and no problems with the police, then they quickly implemented the mapping out of streets, individual family lots, and public areas for schools and other services. Had they picked on a place too close to a public facility, like an electric power station, they would have to relocate. Otherwise, the government usually turned a blind eye to the situation.

The operation mostly took place on a weekend and was conducted with military-like precision. Under cover of dark, people began to arrive, using every available means of transport. Tricycles, as in so many situations in the *barrios*, played a crucial role, carrying huge loads.

Only the most essential things were brought along, just enough to survive the early days and nights. Bamboo matting, some stakes and a few tools were a priority. So too were some cooking utensils, sleeping mats and water containers.

Speed of action was a necessity, so the hut that each family erected was basic. When morning arrived, people travelling north or south out of the capital could observe the then familiar sight of endless rows of new makeshift homes dotting the foothills, the golden coloured bamboo contrasting, in the morning sunshine, with the sandy grey of the hillsides. It was a sight that gave testimony to the 'never-say-die' spirit of a people for too long marginalised in their own country.

ON ARRIVAL AT MY NEW PARISH, I was intent on building on the experience of my previous few years. One of the core elements of the new pastoral approach was working with small groups. It was in that close, more personal setting, above all, that people began to think, act and grow as persons.

I concentrated on setting up a youth group and an adult one in both Mirones and El Planeta. We used to meet mostly in the evening. It is amazing the effect that people's energy and drive can have on a place. Though their surroundings were dismal, their enthusiastic attitude towards life was contagious, and made me almost ignore the rest.

Often, walking back to the parish house in the moonlight, after a meeting that had often lasted well beyond midnight, my thoughts and feelings flowed freely. Indeed, down the years, in my dreams I have travelled that same path many times.

The whole *barrio* was silent, asleep and resting before an early start. The odd dog barked or let out a low, lingering howl as I went by. A quiet sense of satisfaction always came with me, no matter how scattered the meeting might have seemed. Those who attended were in a process of learning to think and grow as persons. It was palpable. I could see and feel it. As I made my way home, my inexperienced shoulders felt a growing responsibility for those sleeping people.

Conditions of great poverty and delinquency are no strangers to each other. Our area was no exception. My new friends were protective towards me, but once the meeting ended I was allowed to walk all the way back to the parish house, about a kilometre, on my own. Sometimes I wore a soutane and more often not. But I was never molested in any form. Those dusty, bumpy streets and lanes were becoming my new home and those at the meeting seemed to sense that too.

It was one thing to be talking passionately about changing the direction of our pastoral work, in line with the ideas of the Second Vatican Council, but the big question was how to go about implementing that vision. We were discovering that speaking about new ideas, on its own, would not be enough. The very nature of education itself had to be delved into. It wasn't difficult to see that if we continued to just talk about the new ideas, the result would be less than what was desired.

We had to try to come to grips, at a deeper level, with what the role of an educator involved. Once again, the Alvarez Calderon brothers, Carlos and Jorge, came to our assistance. They introduced us to two complementary methodologies: one used by the Young Christian Workers Movement (YCWM), and the other by Paulo Freire, the great Brazilian popular educator.

Both methods were based on the principle that our deepest values and ideas are all learned from life. There was nothing new in this. We all knew that the lasting lessons, the ones we would never forget, had been learned from our own personal experiences. The sayings, 'We learn from our mistakes' or 'Ideas are not learned, they are suffered' rang true. But this 'learning from life' was, most often, not a very conscious process. Rather, it was something we became aware of later.

What was new for us was getting to know about a method that made learning from life the centre of the educational process. People not only received information, but there was an emphasis on stimulating them to think for themselves.

There were three simple steps in the YCWM education process: See, Judge and Act. Initially, it was a matter of stimulating people to speak. The educator's role was to ask the appropriate questions and to get discussion going.

At the first step, 'See', members of the group were encouraged to observe the problems in the *barrio*, or in their group, and then choose one which they were more interested in working on.

Step two, 'Judge', meant the group reflected on the problem and tried to discover its causes. The ability of the group to analyse would grow with time, and local problems would be seen to be part of the wider problems of society, part of the bigger picture.

The last stage, 'Act', was where it was decided what action would be undertaken by the group. Especially at the beginning, it didn't really matter what the action chosen was: the emphasis was on the learning process itself.

Then the objective or purpose of the activity was reflected on by the members, guided by a question such as, 'What do we want to achieve with this activity?' Again, for a newly formed group, the objective could be something as simple as 'To be more united in the group.'

Next, it was time to examine how it would be achieved. We called it looking at the Means and Calendar – all the actions required, along with dates, times and responsibilities (individual and sub-committees) were agreed and shared out.

After the activity was carried out, we had an Evaluation. This was kept simple – what were the good and bad points of the activity? A final question would provoke reflection on the Christian dimension of their action – what would Jesus think of what we have done?

We priests were called *asesores*, or advisers, and we used the method with a variety of groups. The poor felt at home learning from life. Starting from their own experiences suited their practical approach. They just loved doing things. Don't we all? Or is it the farmer's son coming out in me again?

Paulo Freire's thinking and methodology had a major influence on many of us. The curious thing was that he was not offering any short cuts or easy solutions, which could have made his approach attractive. In fact, he did the opposite, showing that the road towards liberation for the poor would be slower than we would have wished.

In his book *Pedagogy of the Oppressed*, Freire showed why those individuals and groups who approached the poor in a big hurry, with clear instructions in their heads – as to what they would tell them to do – were doomed to fail.

Like Marx, he too saw there was a 'dominant ideology' in every society. It was supported, spread and controlled by the groups who held power. Values such as individualism, competition and 'freedom' were at the core. But the poor, who were the oppressed in society, had come to accept these values too.

'The dominated thinks like the dominator,' Freire stated, the poor internalise the idea that the present society is normal and the only one possible. He went on to show that the non-critical conscience of the poor, with all its prejudices, beliefs, naïve explanations and resistance to change, was where all education of the poor had to start. If this was not done, the naïve conscience of the poor would remain intact. Indeed, it would be reinforced daily by radio, press, television and their surroundings.

In a general way, from my time with Michael and Gerry, I was aware that it was important to use the language of the poor when trying to communicate. But from Freire, we learned that gathering the words, expressions, myths and experiences of the people was not something that would happen of itself. One had to make a conscious effort and do it in an organised way.

Once this task had been done, we noticed that it was indeed easier to get the people's attention and interest, whether it was giving a sermon at mass, addressing an audience or in a small group. Using their own experiences, we were able to present the reality of their lives in a way that opened the door for reflection, for example, by pointing out an underlying conflict or contradiction in a particular problem. It could be the problem of the municipality not collecting the rubbish – while in the wealthy parts of the city it was collected every day.

A pitfall to be avoided was the presentation of change as a total break with the present. People would get frightened and this created resistance. The roots of the future society were to be found in the present. It was vital to emphasise the dynamic elements of the people's culture, such as 'their never-say-die-spirit', their solidarity and ability to organise. This way, the poor could see change as a continuity of their own history.

After some years working with the poor, it was easy to see that the naïve or non-critical conscience was no fiction of the imagination. It was especially noticeable that, for a number of years after the founding of a *barrio*, there would be widespread enthusiasm and solidarity. But once the most pressing problems, like installation of water, sewerage and light, had been solved, participation dropped considerably. Leaders in the *barrios* found it more difficult to get people to come to meetings or help out in community activities.

From my own journey, I was keenly aware that it was never easy to let go of deeply rooted prejudices and ideas. Fear of change was common to us all. I had often asked myself the question, why have many Columban colleagues not embraced the opportunity for change? But I was in a hurry and not inclined to search for an answer.

Looking back, I am conscious that the Columban missionaries I knew in Peru were honest, faithful, follow-the-book people. Indeed, I can say the same about those men and women of the many other missionary organisations that I had contact with.

I have the clear impression that in the case of the Columbans, priests felt distinctly uncomfortable about going outside their own organisation to look for orientation on pastoral issues. Many were never to do that. They looked to their own leaders to show the way.

If the Superior had invited a pro-reform speaker to address the whole group, that would have been different. Even if the meeting was to stir up heated debate, it would have been acceptable. The initiative had come from the boss. That had been done once, when Miguel had invited Jorge Alvarez Calderon to give a talk in the centre house. It was not repeated.

The Columban leadership in Lima and in Ireland turned its back on change. They saw practical attempts to implement the recommendations of Second Vatican Council as a deviation from accepted practice. Those of us trying to do so were 'marked' men.

Instead of openly discussing the issues, within the whole group, the message that came down was 'business as usual' and a dictatorial approach was shown towards dissenters. For an organisation built around obedience to the Superior, this was the opposite of what was required.

Like many of his colleagues, Louis, my new boss, was not one for going outside the Columban fold to look for guidance or inspiration. He shouldn't have had to. In these circumstances, our attempts at dialogue were bound to stumble and falter. In an attempt to start a conversation one day, I said, 'Louis, what part of the Council documents do you think we might be able to use here in the parish?'

'Those documents are all general statements and stuff. As far as I am concerned, they change nothing for us here in El Montón.'

'That's a very sweeping statement, Louis. The Council was mainly oriented towards pastoral issues and pointed out a new way forward.'

'Oh, I know you *discipuli* are trying to pick out what suits you. Ye are making a big thing out of working with small groups, as if this were the great solution. Well, for me it's a waste of time, and it's not what we should be doing anyway.'

'Well, that's your view. But, in these small groups, people can begin to express themselves, think things through and mature as people and Christians.'

'You spend most of your time in meetings with these people and what is there to show for it?'

'Sure, the numbers of baptisms, first communions and marriages are easy to count and show results. It is not as easy to measure the progress of people growing and maturing as persons. But, that doesn't mean that it is not real.'

'Ye guys talk a lot about Christian community, as if it was something new, but that is nothing new for Catholics. That community spirit is expressed by people coming to Mass.'

'Now you know, as well as I do, that coming to Mass can be a habit or just to fulfil an obligation.'

'The answer to that is to teach them more Christian doctrine, prepare them better, so that they know why they are coming. What we need to do is prepare catechists. The only group I would have is a good group of catechists.'

'And what do you think of the Council saying that we should value the culture of the people?'

'It's a lot of words, that's all. We're not anthropologists, and we are not supposed to be. Treat people well and that's it.'

We did not see eye to eye on pastoral issues but, so far, my work with groups, outside the church building, didn't seem to bother him. I hoped we could keep it that way. Our different approaches to pastoral work ran the risk of sending out a confusing message to the people. We were in a similar situation to that in other parishes, run by Columbans, and other missionary organisations and native clergy at the time.

6.

BBC's Panorama Comes to Town

NEWS OF THE STRUGGLE between the conflicting pastoral approaches in Lima had begun to arrive at other Columban mission fields around the world. We pro-reformers were not the best propagandists for the cause. In truth, we were totally taken up with survival and at the same time trying to move forward.

As I write in 2012, Panorama, the BBC's current affairs programme, has been in existence for almost six decades. In the 1960s, already in its second decade, it had regular audiences of up to twelve million. Their main foreign affairs reporter, and documentary producer, was James Mossman. He had covered the Cuban missile crisis, the Vietnam War and many other hot spots around the world. His style of interview was ahead of its time. Up to then television interviewers were deferential, especially to those of the political class. Famously, he had put the English Prime Minister, Harold Wilson, through the mill for his support of President Johnson during the Vietnam War.

Shortly after the end of the Second Vatican Council, he had made a programme on the Catholic Church. It was called 'A Changing Church'. Interestingly, even at that early stage, he had sounded a warning: the papacy of Paul VI was putting the brakes on the process of reform. It had already begun to put 'power and unity before radical reform.'

Once more the BBC had decided to send the Panorama team on another searching mission. The impact of the successful Cuban revolution had echoed far and wide around the countries of Latin America, where millions of peasants lived in abject conditions. Fearing the advance of communism and that of Protestant organisations, the Catholic Church had sent thousands of missionaries into the sub-continent, where the over-whelming majority of people were nominally Catholic. The committed journalist, and his team of two, chose Peru as their destination, and our parish in El Montón as one of their main areas of focus. He would write later: 'I went to Peru to make a film about the struggle between Christian reform and communist revolution for the allegiance of the poor.'

Up to that time, I had a workable relationship with my parish priest. It had not yet deteriorated. Avoiding 'dangerous' topics, we were getting on quite well. Having studied journalism, he had an eye for news, be it from the Columban world or the wider Peruvian scene. My visits to the Society centre house were few then. He must have told me that the star reporter and his team were in town. However, as I recall events, there was no prior notice of their intended focus on our parish, so it was a total surprise when James Mossman appeared on our doorstep one morning.

The tall, slight, soft-spoken reporter somehow didn't seem to fit the picture I had of a veteran from war zones and trouble spots. That was until we had chatted around the table for a while. He had done his homework on the socio-political situation in Peru and indeed in Latin America. Though he didn't say so, he must have known of the division over pastoral approaches in the Peruvian Church. Now he wanted to delve further. In particular, he wanted to find out what people like Louis and I were trying to do. His plan was to follow each of us priests around for a few days.

He was a likeable, earnest man. On a number of occasions, he returned to the parish and I walked the *barrios* with him. Both Louis and I had, to some extent, got used to the smell, the wretched living conditions and the disease. As we walked and talked, and sometimes stopped to film, I could see that he was moved. We would return to the presbytery for a cup of tea and continue to chat. The sharp, sensitive journalist was asking questions that struck a deep chord with me, questions that I had begun to ask in the early days of my arrival in Peru.

'What is the point of the Church, people like you, trying to just lessen, and put a patch over all this misery? Why are you not driven to challenge the whole rotten structures that allow this injustice to go on?'

I confided in him my own search for answers and how a group of priests, foreign missionaries and native clergy had been so fortunate to have two Peruvian priests, the brothers Carlos and Jorge, to lead and inspire us on our journey. He had seen no signs of a big project or any buildings that we had constructed. Early in our conversations, his question was direct:

'What exactly are you trying to do here?'

'Well, James, the short answer is, we are trying to empower the poor. This is a process. Firstly, we try to help them break free of a mindset that tells them they are of little worth and that cruel poverty is their lot. This thinking is reinforced daily from the very top of society – they are portrayed and treated as second class citizens.'

'How do you go about doing that?'

'We have a simple method that comes down to learning by doing.'

James was interested in my explanation but had another question.

'Yes, but how slow is that process?'

'Well it is slow. We concentrate our efforts on small groups, where people can interact with one another and grow together. You can see it happen before your eyes, and there can be nothing more inspiring than witnessing a marginalised people begin to walk tall.'

He was listening intently, and it was easy to see that, apart from being a fine professional, he was touched emotionally by what he was seeing and hearing. The separate interviews with Louis and me were filmed, out on the plaza, on the last day. As we bid farewell, I was keenly aware that I had had the privilege of sharing the ideas and motivation behind my commitment with a special person.

The programme was aired on the BBC and it did show the differences in the pastoral approaches. In answer to a question about what I thought of the danger of communism spreading in Peru, I had said something to the effect:

'That is not our problem. The poor people, and the workers, have every right to choose the social system, and form of government, that they consider best.'

Given the preoccupation of the official Church, I was told that the above statement had raised more than a few eyebrows. But my reply would not have surprised nor bothered the valiant journalist: we had talked for many hours.

A short time after the programme was aired, James Mossman wrote an article for the Columban Magazine, *The Far East*. In it, he told of how the visit to Peru and El Montón had affected him. Even when going out for a meal, the images of desperate poverty would crowd his mind and he wrote: 'I am thinking about the millions, even hundred of millions, of people all over the world who have no supper to go to ...'

The title of the article was 'Intruding on Another Man's Agony'. He went on to tell how he had felt like an intruder filming some of the scenes of misery and sickness, how he questioned whether it was right to film people's suffering and then leave. His conclusion was that only if the film moved people to think and act would such intrusion be justified. A few years later, I was to get news of his death. He had taken his own life. In shock and sadness, I gave thanks that our paths had crossed. I was the richer for it. The words of the poet Antonio Machado went around in my head:

> Traveller, the road is only
> Your footprint, and no more;
> Traveller, there's no road,
> The road is your travelling.

7.

PEOPLE PRESSURE

EARLY ON, I BECAME aware that there was a lot of distrust and division between the three *barrios* that made up the parish. It meant that there was very little contact between them. The distrust went back to the formation of the most recent one, El Planeta.

The land it now occupied had been an extensive brick-making business, mainly adobe, the unburnt, sun-dried type. It bordered on El Montón. The communities of Villa Maria and Mirones had had their eyes set on it; the ground was solid for building on.

But it was staunchly defended by the 'owner' who claimed he had title deeds going back to the Spanish conquest. It was a matter of good timing by the organisers of El Planeta. The business was coming to an end, and they had found out that the said titles were not what they were claimed to be. They took over the land, fought a long battle in the courts. It was still going on.

The people of Villa Maria, especially, felt hard done by and jealous of their new neighbours. After all, they had arrived in the general area a number of years before, and had to settle in the worst of places.

It was not difficult for the people to see that allowing the bitterness to continue to fester was not Christian. It didn't make any sense either from the point of view of the struggle to improve their living conditions. There is strength in unity. So, with less persuasion than I had anticipated, the leaders of the groups in the three *barrios* agreed to meet.

Building up community spirit to gradually replace the negative feelings became a priority at that first meeting. After teasing out ideas about what practical thing they could do, they had decided to organise a big *paseo* or outing. At subsequent preparatory meetings they were clearly eager and determined to make a new start. I let my parish priest know what was afoot but he showed no interest.

In itself, the prospect of enjoying a day in the sun, out of the dreary Lima winter, was highly attractive for people in the *barrios*. The organisation and carrying out of the event would serve to get the leaders working together and for people to get to know one another. They were planning excitedly. The decision was taken: we would travel some forty kilometres into the Andes, along the river Rimac valley, to where there was sun all year round.

One of the preparatory commissions was responsible for getting transport. They brought me along on their search. Soon there was good news to relay: the municipality of Lima and the army, between them, had agreed to supply the buses. A small contribution per family would be made to cover tips for the bus drivers and prizes for the sports events.

About a week before the day of the outing, everything was prepared. A small group was named to meet the parish priest and formally invite him to join them on the big day. No one was prepared for his reaction. He called the whole operation off. It was not a parish event and he would not participate. Neither could I.

However, he had seriously miscalculated the depth of feeling and commitment the project had awakened. Without letting me know, a committee was formed. People rustled up some transport and headed for the Columban centre house. Owen was informed that they intended to camp there until the ban was lifted. The stalemate lasted for a full day. It ended when they were informed that the activity could go ahead as planned. The commotion caused around the society headquarters was major.

This whole episode was momentous for a community just finding its feet. Up to that point, people probably put the differences between their two priests down to personality traits. Perhaps they thought that each of us was doing what we felt most comfortable with. Now, the gap between two opposite and opposing lines of pastoral work became visible for all to see.

At one level, I felt sorry for Louis. He had made a terrible mistake. I felt he had not taken the decision on his own. He would have received advice from the top. Our relationship grew tense and I found it impossible to talk to him, except for trivial conversation. Though he never said so, I felt he did not believe me when I told him that I had nothing to do with the people going to the centre house. For both of us, this was our first experience of people pressure within the Church. We were among Catholics but 'Peruvian style'.

Unlike what we had grown up with in Ireland, the people here did not appear to be awed by the power of the priest or the Church. The fear of being socially ostracised, for having ruffled clerical feathers, was not something that bothered them.

They were not domesticated Catholics and did not feel fettered by many of the rules and regulations from Rome. Around the whole issue of sex, which so obsessed the official Church, they felt much more at ease. An incident that took place, when the archbishop of Dublin came to Lima, speaks for itself.

He stayed at the Columban centre house and was being shown around the shantytowns. In one parish he was scheduled to visit a 'Mother's Club'. Their meeting place, a modest room built of bamboo sheets, was cleaned and decorated with care. They spared no effort to prepare for the visitor. The mud floor was sprinkled and cleaned. Pictures were hung on the wall, a bunch of flowers adorned the table and, of course, sandwiches and coffee were on a side table. In due course, the distinguished guest was seated at the table, with his Columban escort beside him.

As the latter looked across the room, his face flushed. On the wall in front of them was a picture of the Sacred Heart, that iconic image of Jesus. Hanging beside it was a calendar, displaying a scantily clad, buxom lady. In an opportune moment, at the coffee break, the escort expressed his concern to some of the women. He was to discover that his suggestion regarding the inappropriateness of the presence of the provocative calendar was his problem. The women could see nothing out of place:

'What's the problem, Padre? What planet do ye live on?'

After their decisive intervention to save the outing, the organisers must have realised, like me, that a watershed on our path of personal and collective growth had been reached. The realisation of the importance of what they were doing seemed to grow.

Logistically, the event was a big undertaking. The members of the different groups looked after the practical details, even down to making sure we had a few mechanics in the group. That wasn't a problem. Some men in the *barrios* made their living keeping all kinds of second hand vehicles from the US ticking over, long past their sell by date.

Whole families, carrying provisions for their picnic, joined us on the day. Excitement, expectation and singing whiled the journey away. We were in the valley, between the steep mountains, with green grass, trees and flowers to enjoy for the whole day. Sheer joy and happy voices filled the air. It would be impossible to exaggerate what it meant to the people or the satisfaction it brought to their leaders. The privilege to be able to share that place and time was mine to treasure.

Back home in the parish, I was spending a lot of my time working with the youth and adult groups in Mirones and El Planeta. However, as we lived in Villa Maria, there were many opportunities to meet people there. Not long after my arrival, I was made aware of an underlying, deeply rooted resentment.

The first priest to come to work in the area was a Frenchman, Padre Gerardo. He had come to even worse conditions than we were living in. On parish ground, beside the presbytery, he had built a simple meeting room for the youth. It was administered by the youth club which he had founded, *Los Misioneros*, the missionaries. When some of the members had sized me up, they revealed their predicament.

Before moving on, their fondly-remembered priest friend had been given a state-of-the-art stereo set, which he handed over to the club. They played their LP discs on it. It was a prized possession and was now the symbol of their discontent. It was indeed just that, a symbol – the outward expression of a sensation of being ignored and mistreated.

They told me how their relationship with the priests in the parish had changed drastically some months before my arrival. Mario was the parish priest then and Louis was his assistant. For whatever reason, both of them decided to take drastic action – perhaps the music was too loud for their liking. They changed the lock on the door of the club premises and removed the stereo. Ever since, it had sat in our sitting room.

From the outset, the club members accepted that there was very little I could do. My parish priest was not for re-considering and the problem dragged on. Meantime, I enjoyed playing football with them. But a resolution was to come several months later and it came about in a most unexpected way.

It was the occasion of the Confirmation ceremony in the parish. Children from twelve years up had the opportunity to make a solemn renewal of their faith. The ceremony was to be performed by the Archbishop, Cardinal Landazuri Rickets.

On the evening before, he arrived to celebrate a special Mass. To my complete surprise, Owen showed up, accompanied by the former parish priest, Mario. It certainly crossed my mind that their presence was not gratuitous. After the uncomfortable lifting of the ban against the outing, it was probably a show of support for Louis, I thought. Mass ended and we had something to eat in the sitting room. When the meal was over, I excused myself to do something in El Planeta.

I was returning to the house, convinced that the Cardinal would have long since departed, and rounding the corner at the plaza I saw his tall figure in the twilight, beside the church. He was surrounded by a dozen or so boys from the *Misioneros* club. They had obviously been waiting for him as he came out of the presbytery.

Distrust and suspicion were rife on both sides of the pastoral divide. I instinctively recoiled from the possibility of being seen by His Eminence as in any way part of a conspiracy. I made an instant retreat and visited a family in the *barrio*. The youth had taken a bold step and it was bound to have consequences. The odds were stacked against me. It was an eerie feeling coming back to the house that night, and I feared for the worst next day.

The ceremony was due to start around midday. We didn't expect the Cardinal until about half an hour before that. Out of the blue, his chauffeur-driven car pulled up in front of the church, over an hour ahead of schedule. No, he wasn't confused about the time, he wanted me to take him around the parish and to meet people.

We had a Volkswagen beetle. His six foot plus frame, and all his regalia, had to be squeezed into the passenger seat beside me. We drove down the bumpy, dusty streets of El Montón, past the Heap itself. As always, some people were sorting rubbish by the roadside. A little further on there were a number of make-shift enclosures where pigs were reared.

In Mirones, I knocked on a few doors and soon we had a small group of people, all as dumbstruck as me. In spite of his impos-ing figure, standing tall in his red robes, he was a simple man at heart. Maybe it was his formation as a Franciscan but people were soon chatting freely. The members of his order, founded by St Francis of Assisi, were committed to a vow of poverty and service of the poor.

He wanted to know what we did, where we met. This kind of close contact with the poor, experiencing their living conditions, would not have been usual for him. As Archbishop, his official visits to parishes were formal affairs. Now, here he was, early in the morning, listening intently and eager to learn.

We said our goodbyes and made our way to El Planeta. There was the same surprise and incredulity at first, then the listening-dialogue. He examined the humble abode where we held our meetings and celebrated Mass. It was time to head back to Villa Maria. Word had gotten out and there were a few more stops to make. Now, on our own, my illustrious passenger was silent. I would have given anything to know his thoughts.

Back in the presbytery, Owen and Mario were present again. The lengthy ceremony ended and we clerics all came into the sit-ting room. Without any delay the Cardinal let us know what was on his mind. The improvised meeting he'd had on the plaza the previous evening worried him. He said:

'I cannot leave the parish like this. The relationship with the boys from the club next door is bad. It is not Christian and we cannot leave it like this.'

Turning to my parish priest he continued: 'Louis, go out and find the president and secretary of the *Misioneros* club and bring them back here with you. When you come back, I want you and Mario to apologise, shake hands and tell them the past is over. That is the Christian thing to do.'

Louis duly returned, followed by the two lads. The Cardinal, flanked by the four of us clerics, spoke of forgiveness and asked the parties to shake hands. Then he announced: 'I am appointing Lucas (that was me) as adviser for all youth groups in the parish.'

One could have heard the proverbial pin drop. There were some awkward moments of leave taking and the two club members lifted the hi-fi set between them and departed.

This was an extraordinary turn of events. The Cardinal was relying on the Columbans to run a growing number of parishes in the shantytowns. Nevertheless, he had told their boss that a mistake had to be put right. But much more importantly, he was telling him that he believed in the line of pastoral work I was following. Owen, Mario and Louis were dumbfounded. They must have been certain that His Eminence had got it all wrong. But he had spoken and that was that.

By nature, Cardinal Juan Landazuri was a man who hated situations of conflict but he could, at times, take some risks for what he believed in. This was the man who later brought Gustavo Gutierrez, as his theological expert, to the Latin American Bishops' Conferences – the proponent of Liberation Theology was not at all popular with many of their lordships.

The totally unexpected direction of the Cardinal's intervention in the parish affairs must have been devastating for Louis. Within the month he had asked for, and received, a transfer to another parish. As for myself, I was relieved, but more than anything else, I was amazed that the work I was trying to do had been vindicated in the way it had. It was also a boost for the line of pastoral action our group was implementing.

But there was sadness there too. Louis was about my own age. I asked myself whether the whole experience would embitter him. Some years later, we would find ourselves on the same side of a dividing line – both outside the clerical institution, raising our own families – but, in the meantime, there was not much time or space to linger. Life would move on.

8.

NO TURNING BACK

MY NEW PARISH PRIEST was appointed without delay. Given the circumstances, I was not expecting any favours. But the Cardinal's intervention must have influenced Owen's decision to appoint Leo, one of the few Australian Columbans in Lima at the time. He was not identified as belonging to our group but was known as someone who was tolerant. I would not have to keep looking over my shoulder all the time. That was a huge relief.

On the wider Columban scene in Lima, developments that would shape the years ahead had been taking place. A number of young Columbans from Ireland, US and Australia had come to Lima. In spite of being forewarned about the danger of associating with the reformists, they had joined the ranks. Shortly afterwards, we had an official visit by the top man of the Society, the Superior General.

Jimmy had been a professor at the seminary before getting the big job. I had studied under him. He was a traditionalist and one could not imagine him thinking outside that mould. A gentle, bookish, retiring man when I knew him back then, now he had taken on his new role with zeal.

One by one, we were questioned. What Church were we following? Of course, the question was to the point. In fact, we no longer followed the same one that he did. We were not nearly strict enough for his liking – not putting pressure on people to receive all the sacraments, nor putting enough effort into teaching the catechism. In short, we were not turning out traditional practising Catholics.

Jimmy represented the dual history approach of the pre- Second Vatican Council Church. As he understood it, our job was to occupy ourselves with the salvation of souls and keep on the sacred history trail. The secular world was a different history, on a parallel rail, and was not our domain.

Too much of our time was taken up with things that, as he saw it, had little or nothing to do with the Church. We were involved in community organisations, promoting awareness of the rights of the poor and, according to him, instigating protest. This was an unacceptable involvement in politics, an unacceptable deviation from our role as priests.

Of course, each of us argued that being committed to the raising of awareness among the poor, of their dignity and rights, was only carrying out the teaching of the recent Council. It was something a priest should do. Furthermore, the witness given by every Columban had, inevitably, political implications. If he avoided all mention of the rights of the poor and concentrated on their heavenly destiny, his message was equally political.

After coming out of my session with Jimmy, I was rattled. He still had a lot of power. I wondered about how he might decide to use it. But, at the same time, I felt a certain satisfaction. I had been able to defend myself with confidence. A few short years before, this would have been unthinkable. Fear, and a feeling of inadequacy, would have paralysed me.

We were all told, in the clearest terms, that we were on the wrong path. We were involved in a dangerous line of pastoral approach, in clear disobedience if we continued. This was not the end of the matter and we would be watched.

However, Jimmy's visit was to achieve little, except a hardening of positions. His efforts had come too late in the day. At that time, we were no longer an isolated group. We were integrated into what was in fact a small but growing movement. It extended beyond Lima to the provinces, especially those of the southern Andes, where some of the poorest people lived.

For the first time, an organisation of priests, independent of the hierarchy, had been set up. It was called the National Office of Social Information (ONIS). The leaders were Peruvian priests and it had many members of foreign missionary organisations. Regularly, statements on the social and political situation in the country were distributed to the media and communities in the parishes. In addition, periodic national meetings and seminars were organised to review pastoral work with the poor.

Another important reality was the influence Cardinal Landazuri had on things clerical. He was not one for intervening at every turn, but he could not be easily used by the traditionalists either. In fact, in a few years he had become an important figure in the Peruvian Church. He was not a Helder Camara, that outspoken, prophetic bishop of Recife, in the poor North East of Brazil. Nevertheless, he showed leadership qualities. In his own quiet way he encouraged and promoted commitment with the cause of the poor among clergy and bishops.

On the Latin American scene, Landazuri was to play an important role in the preparation of the historic meeting of Bishops in Medellín, Colombia, in 1968. That event broke with the Church's tradition of prioritising its own internal interests. It concentrated its reflections, and recommendations, on the glaring poverty of the poor, and on the unjust and 'sinful' structures that held them in virtual slavery. Inspired by the life of Jesus as portrayed in the gospels, a majority of the bishops proclaimed a 'preferential option for the poor' as the centre of the Church's work. The option was not an exclusive one: the Church was to work with all sectors of society in each country to promote awareness of the unjust situation and of the need for reform.

From the early sixties, the Latin American bishops had put in place structures that were advanced for the time, structures that facilitated the consultation of laity and clergy and had their suggestions represented at national and international meetings. Right through the Second Vatican Council, they were meeting in Rome and planning the implementation of its recommendations in South America. Influential, reform-minded cardinals, bishops and theologians led the way. Their organisation, CELAM, was well ahead of other hierarchies around the world.

THE CONCLUSIONS OF THE Bishops' Conference in Medellín were inspired by Liberation Theology, which was developed in Latin America in the 1960s. Theologians from different countries had begun to meet and share their concerns about how to give witness to the gospel in a continent where the vast majority of people lived in dire poverty. They had studied their theology in European universities. Some of the best known names are Leonardo Boff, a Franciscan from Brazil; Jon Sobrino, a Spanish Jesuit who has worked all his life in El Salvador; and Juan Luis Segundo, a Jesuit from Uruguay. Gustavo Gutierrez, a Peruvian priest, is regarded as the founder of Liberation Theology.

During my years as a cleric, Gustavo was a friendly and inspiring presence at many of our meetings. He worked in a poor parish as well as teaching at the Catholic University and acting as advisor to UNEC, the National Union of Catholic Students. He had a special ability to put complex ideas in simple language. His book, *A Theology of Liberation*, published in 1971, is considered to be the fundamental work on the subject. It provided a coherent biblical and theological basis for work that had been carried out by members of religious organisations, lay leaders and diocesan clergy at the grass-roots for a number of years in Latin America. In Basic Christian Communities, he had contributed his own reflections and witnessed how small groups used the See, Judge, and Act method of reflection and action, and grew as persons and Christians. He had watched other groups, in freedom, study the Bible and discover they were made in the image of a loving God; they too grew in awareness of their dignity and rights. This new theological approach was 'a critical reflection on the praxis (of the Church and Christians) in the light of the Word of God.' Unfortunately, there was to be no warm reception for it in the centres of power.

Over the following two decades the Vatican elite became increasingly alarmed. It was to level many accusations against Liberation Theology, such as being a political interpretation of the Bible, using Marxist analysis, supporting temporal messianism and promoting class conflict. But I find one accusation most interesting – the new theology was promoting class conflict within the Church. The Basic Christian Communities, out of control, would sooner or later reject the hierarchy itself!

For another two decades the commitment, made at Medellín, was to be lived out by many in the Church, at all levels, across the length and breadth of Latin America. But it was done at great personal risk and cost in so many cases. The upper classes could not accept the need, or the inevitability, of change. They continued to rely on cruel military dictatorships to enforce the status quo. The latter were backed by successive administrations in the United States. The powerful neighbour to the north had its own interests to protect: many American companies worked in Latin America and the danger of 'communist' regimes coming to power had to be closed off.

So, during the 1970s and 1980s, as the situation in Peru grew increasingly troubled and uncertain, those of us committed to the cause of the poor also kept a close eye on the dramatically deteriorating situation in Central America.

In 1969, just a year after the Bishops' conference in Medellín, Liberation Theology came under scrutiny by the US government. Nelson Rockefeller, who was Secretary for Inter-American Affairs under Richard Nixon, after a tour of Latin America with his advisors, wrote a report which identified Liberation Theology as a threat to the national security of the United States. It endangered US interests.

Another meeting of Latin American bishops was held in Puebla, Mexico in 1979. Though the orthodox bishops were in the majority, and some of the 'Liberation Theology' theologians were barred from attending the actual conference, their influence with the liberal bishops was notable. Once again the conference committed the Church to a 'preferential option for the poor'. It was no coincidence that a committee of advisors to the in-coming Reagan administration produced a document which singled out Liberation Theology, stating bluntly: 'US policy must begin to counter liberation theology as it is utilised in Latin America.' The Reagan administration, 1981-'89, responded both militarily and ideologically. Its main targets were the countries of Central America, especially Nicaragua and El Salvador, where the old order was under threat from the growing grass-roots movements for change. Imbedded in these movements were Christians inspired by Liberation Theology.

In Nicaragua the Somoza dynasty had held power for forty-two years. It was a cruel dictatorship, backed militarily and economically by the U.S. The Somoza family owned 30 per cent of the country's arable land and controlled 40 per cent of its economy. But the dispossessed had after many years of division formed a united front – the Sandinista National Liberation Front – and fought an armed struggle, seizing power in 1979.

All US aid to the country was suspended, an embargo imposed, and support to the counter-insurgents, the 'Contras', along the borders with Honduras and Costa Rica, was authorised. The Reagan administration was not able to overthrow the Sandinista regime by military means, but the economic sanctions, combined with the costs of the prolonged war, devastated the economy. Sandinista popular support fell and they were defeated in the elections of 1990.

In El Salvador, the cruel, US-backed military junta was involved in a dirty war to suppress a popular uprising. An estimated 3,000 people a month were being killed by the military's infamous death squads. Many priests and laypeople backed the peasants and workers in their struggle. But the bishops were a conservative group.

Oscar Romero was one of the latter. In fact they had chosen their reliable colleague to head the Bishops' Conference. But an event was to take place that would radically change him. One of the priests of his archdiocese, Rutilio Grande, a Jesuit, was assassinated along with two parishioners. Grande had been targeted because he defended the peasants' right to organise farm cooperatives. The night Romero drove out to view Grande's body, and those of an old man and a boy, was to be his moment of awakening. In a packed country church, facing the silent pain of the peasants, he must have heard them ask, will you stand with us as Padre Rutilio did?

He was powerless to stop the violence. On the diocesan radio he broadcast weekly homilies to the whole country and told the suffering poor that they would survive the awful time.

Then this slight, ascetic man with a great heart took another step. At the end of his radio homily on 23 March 1980, he addressed the ordinary soldiers of the army, for they too were peasants. He began: 'Brothers, you are from the same people, you kill your fellow peasants.... No soldier is obliged to obey an order that is contrary to the will of God.'

Then his voice grew louder: 'In the name of God then, in the name of this suffering people, I ask you, I beg you, I command you in the name of God: stop the repression.'

The next day the Archbishop was shot dead while saying Mass in the cathedral. The brutality would not stop there. At his funeral, snipers from the rooftops shot down about forty mourners as they scattered and trampled on one another outside the cathedral.

Some eight months after Oscar Romero's assassination, three nuns (two Maryknoll and one Ursuline) and a lay volunteer, all US citizens, were abducted, raped and shot. At the opening of the grave the US ambassador and international media were present. There were calls for an end to the economic aid to the junta. But it was to continue for another decade until another barbaric slaughter by a military death squad raised concern in the corridors of power.

Under the cover of darkness twenty armed men burst into the Jesuit residence at the University of Central America in San Salvador. They shot the six priests, including the Rector, Vice-rector and their housekeeper and her young daughter. The priests were well-known intellectuals and members of the Liberation Theology movement. The pictures of their mutilated bodies lying face down on the yard beside their modest home became one of the most haunting images of that dirty war. This horrific event forced the US administration to end it long-standing support for the military. It also stirred the United Nations to intervene and broker a peace agreement in 1992.

As the twentieth century ended, the School of the Americas, which was run by the US army and trained military and police from Latin American countries in commando operations and 'counter-insurgency warfare', could boast that it had 'helped to defeat Liberation Theology'. It had certainly spared no effort. But there were two other causes that explain the slowing down of that movement.

The first was the role that the Vatican and successive popes have played. Church leaders of known conservative ideas have been consistently appointed ever since the early 1980s. The best known proponents of Liberation Theology have been threatened and silenced.

There is another reality which may help to explain why Liberation Theology is much less in the public domain. The political face of Latin America has changed dramatically over the last couple of decades. All the military dictatorships have been replaced by democratic governments. Many of the latter have specific policies of 'social inclusion' of the poor. There is a long, hazardous road ahead for many countries in the region. Economic growth side by side with glaring inequality leads to social conflicts. The poor of each country are pressing for better working conditions and a fairer share in their country's wealth. But today, unlike in the days of the military dictatorships, they can make their voices heard.

As I recall the struggle of the poor in Central America, I realise it had a deeply sobering, yet inspirational, effect on so many of us in Peru. From time to time our lives are influenced by extraordinary events in faraway places, by heroic gestures and images that stay with us for ever. Many portrayed enormous courage and commitment, often in the face of the darkest powers. Such was Oscar Romero on the radio, calling on the peasant soldiers not to shoot their own.

MY ONWARD JOURNEY WAS moulded and influenced daily by circumstances and events much closer to home. I was back in my parish, about to start a new phase. Jimmy, the Superior General, had left us and I was getting to know my new boss.

Leo had a way of putting one at ease in his company. This fair-minded priest was at heart a poet and an artist. Though several years my senior, I felt from the beginning that age was not an issue for him. He did not feel comfortable about getting involved as adviser, or facilitator for groups, but he was sympathetic towards what I was doing.

I always remember a particularly touching gesture that this caring and proud Aussie used to show me. As usual, on most nights, I returned late from meetings in the *barrios*. Leo was always waiting up for me. He had whiled away the time reading a book, painting or writing some poetry. We sat and chatted for an hour or so. He often prepared a nightcap, from whatever liquor was available, and listened with keen interest to what had gone on at the meeting.

His companionship meant a lot to me. By now, I was totally taken up with the pastoral work. But Leo was showing me how important the smaller things in life were, and I was grateful for that. I wasn't as sure of some things as I might have appeared. It was comforting to know there was someone watching out for me. An event was to take place that showed me how important that was.

The youth of Villa Maria had little space to play their favourite game, football. They mostly used the side street that came off the industrial Argentina Avenue. The only public space in the *barrio* was the dusty, pot-holed plaza. At one end stood the church and, at the other, the school. Small children played there all the time.

There must have been a dozen or so football clubs in the *barrio* but all had to travel outside to play. Led by the *Misioneros*, they formed an association of clubs, with the objective of building a sports ground on the plaza. Their plan was to use about three-quarters of the area, leaving the part in front of the church free. It would be used for other sports like volleyball and basketball too, and for community meetings and celebrations.

Right from the start, the plan was opposed by the *Hermandad*, the traditional all-male group whose members were conscious that they wielded influence in the municipality. Their argument was that it would be the wrong use of the plaza and spoil its 'aesthetic look'. A more typical park, with trees and benches, was their preference. Whether a tree could ever set it roots in the rubbish was another matter.

The *Hermandad* members had, from the time Louis was parish priest, an inside track with the mayor of Lima. Consequently, the newly formed commission of club representatives would never get any official approval for their project. But they did find a way to make a breakthrough, and I was to be part of that conspiracy.

The boys asked me to accompany them to the municipality. They had found out that Don Julio was the man they should talk to. A civil engineer, he was not the head of the Public Works Department, but had a reputation for getting things done. In his mid-50s, his stooped back, and weather-beaten face made him look older. Before coming to Lima, he had spent many years working on roads in the *sierra*. He was known as a man who was sensitive to the needs of the poor and understood their struggle.

From the first moment of our encounter, he struck us as *simpatico* or likeable. But he was also a man used to resolving problems. He promised to get the materials, one way or another and the youth were to supply the labour. It was a refreshing experience. This unlikely bureaucrat somehow survived within the system and could get things done.

We never knew, or asked, whether the mayor was aware of the project. In quick time, Don Julio arrived with a couple of trucks and the process of removing some of the surface began. It seemed like a token gesture, for the rubbish was metres deep. But it let us all know that the work had begun in earnest. There was great excitement and no shortage of youth to help out.

All the materials promised arrived, including seating and wire mesh for the perimeter. Under the experienced eye of this wily engineer, the building went ahead, amid the banter and toil of the youth. Brightly painted, with its proud sign arched above the entrance, 'Unity Is Our Strength', the grand opening was approaching.

The building process had gone swiftly, but the opposition had not gone away. It seemed not to matter that all the youth, including some from the opposers' own families, and the majority of adults, were buzzing with excitement. The minority was vocal and had let their opposition be known at the municipality. I was seen as one of the main culprits.

Peruvians relish ceremony and celebration. No opening could go ahead without singing, dancing, some theatre and, of course, speeches. In order to avoid any embarrassment for me, Leo insisted he would do the blessing and give a short speech.

It was the perfect solution but one I couldn't have asked him to take on. In his own quiet way, in a short time, he had gained the trust of the people, including the youth. As I watched from the crowd, amid all the excitement, I was deeply touched by his protective gesture.

In the weeks and months that followed, the sports ground was a hive of activity. A tournament was organised with all the soccer teams of the *barrio* participating. Several preparatory meetings were held with the delegates from all the clubs. Strict rules of conduct were agreed.

A few of the teams wanting to participate had dubious reputations. They were known even to carry weapons while playing. The event proved to be of great entertainment value, and passed off without any serious problem. It was an especially gratifying moment for the organisers when the prize for best conduct went to the team that would have been least expected to win it.

Living in El Montón I had rarely had any health problems. Playing football a few times a week stood by me. The Peruvian food was second to none. Those stuffed avocados, or the large juicy mangos, were a real treat. My Mother needn't have worried. She would write, 'Remember, you are of no use to anyone sick, so make sure you eat well'. During my time in the parish, I can only remember being ill once.

In bed with a fever, I had piled on more blankets, thinking that the shivers were due to a cold or flu. Things weren't improving and we got the doctor from the parish clinic to examine me. My diagnosis was thrown out: I had a stomach infection and needed ice treatment to bring down the temperature. Self-diagnosis, I had learned, could be a dangerous habit.

But soon, life would remind me that health is indeed a treasure, one that has to be appreciated and protected. It was towards the end of his first year in the parish, when Leo began to have breathing problems. Over a number of months, it developed into asthma. He had a particularly difficult time after getting up in the morning.

It was obvious that the dust, and the very high humidity in Lima, especially in winter, had affected him. He never complained and tried to struggle on. Then, doctors told him that he would have to move to a more congenial climate. Before his departure, an experience we had one evening, with its serious and light sides, seems to sum up those eventful couple of years we shared.

Sometimes, people visiting Lima came to the parish. One evening we had a special guest, Dan Berrigan. A Jesuit priest, poet and writer, he was also an anti-Vietnam war activist. He and his brother Philip, also a priest, had participated with others in the burning and destruction of army draft files in Maryland.

It was probably 1968 and Dan was very much in the news in the US. In fact, I realise now, that he was probably on the run, having received a jail sentence. After returning to the US he was apprehended and served three years in jail.

He had arrived in the afternoon and we showed him around the *barrios*. About tea-time, it had started to rain heavily, something very unusual in Lima. Every few years, we might have a half day of rain, and that always created emergency situations for the poor. Their rustic dwellings were not prepared for a downpour.

We had been in the sitting room of the parish house, engrossed in conversation with Dan, for several hours. At one stage, Leo drew my attention to the bulge that was forming in the mud and bamboo roof over our heads. 'It has happened before, but that's as far as it goes,' I said, drawing on my experience, in the hope of allaying his worries.

We continued our conversation, but the bulge grew bigger. Then, all of a sudden, it burst and emptied its contents on top of us. We scrambled from the disaster zone to the kitchen amid fits of laughter. Dan had got a particularly bad wetting. After getting him some clothes to change into, the chat continued in the kitchen.

Our slight, gentle and courageous visitor bid farewell next morning. Afterwards, I followed his involvement in anti-war, peace and human rights movements. As when, in 1980 he founded the Plowshares Movement. For trespassing on a nuclear facility in Pennsylvania, and damaging warheads, he was jailed once more. I cherish the memory of that rainy night in El Montón.

The time had come for my first visit home since arriving in Peru. Leo offered to remain in the parish until my return. Once again, I was lucky he was there the evening of my departure, or I surely would not have got out to the airport on time.

Farewell visits to the parish house had been going all day. Then the *Misioneros* club arranged their own goodbye close to departure time. It dragged on and finally my parish priest had to rescue me, and we were on our way in the Volkswagen.

Buses and smaller transport, carrying friends from the parish, followed us. At the departure area there was singing, cheering and long, emotional hugs. With a lump in my throat, I made my way to the boarding gate and to my seat in the plane. Passengers near me wanted to know what all the fuss was about.

'Ah, people I worked with in the parish,' I said, in an offhand way. How could one begin to try to explain what it was all about?

On my arrival in New York, I had to go to visit my aunts, uncles and cousins in Philadelphia. At the bus station, I carefully placed my two bags on the floor beside me, as I phoned my cousin Mary. Immediately, she cautioned me, 'Watch your bags there.'

I looked down and they were gone. People were moving rapidly, one way and the other, but the culprit was nowhere to be seen. I was embarrassed. That wouldn't have happened in El Montón, I thought. I would have to smarten up, for I was in the developed world now!

After the emotional shock, my brain began to function. The precious few presents would be of no value to the thief, and he would dump the bags somewhere in the airport, I told myself. I called my cousin, Aunt Bridgie's son, John. He was a cop and that evening we paced the station for several hours, vainly hoping. But it gave me time to put things in perspective. At least I was safe and homeward bound.

I DROVE UP THE BOREEN to our house in Ballyroe, wondering about the state of my parents' health, for it had been all of six years since I had last seen them. The over-grown ferns and branches of pine trees were telling a tale. The reek of turf was not nearly as tidy as of yore.

Both my parents had indeed aged more than I had expected. They were living on their own now, and their health had worsened. Dad had suffered a few minor strokes and his movement was slower. Mom had suffered for many years from diabetes. Her sweet-tooth cravings were generally too strong to resist. From time to time she had to go to hospital.

Farming was reduced to the minimum. There was no more sowing of crops or rearing of pigs, just some cattle and sheep. Though there was no real need for a horse now, for sentimental reasons Dad still kept one. Having some hay was a necessity for winter fodder. So hay-making was one of the things I could give a hand with. So too was the mending of fences, which were in a poor state.

Both my parents loved to go out and that is what we did most days. We did things we would all enjoy remembering. This precious time was ours and we went wherever the spirit moved us.

We retraced some of Mom's childhood steps in places around her childhood village of Crossard. She wanted especially to visit the ruins of a fifteenth century Dominican monastery in Urlaur. It was there that a yearly festival was held. Her parents had taken her there many a time. Now, in the shadow of the abbey, by the quiet lake shore, she could recall all the music, singing, dancing and fun as if it were yesterday.

'Let's hit for Westport today,' she said one morning. So we headed west. Croagh Patrick too was on her mind. Over twenty years earlier she had brought my sister Ann and me on the annual pilgrimage on the last Sunday in July. Legend had it that St. Patrick had spent a long fast at the summit of the mountain.

We recalled how, joining the many thousands of other pilgrims, we started our climb after midnight. In the driving rain, and dark, we made our way following those in front of us step by step. Mom was overweight and the last stretch tested her will and endurance. The stones were loose and slippery and the climb was much steeper.

'But we made it,' she said, gazing up at the holy mountain, a kind of wistful expression on her face.

'The cold at the top was something else. I've never felt anything like it,' I recalled.

'But, that was the sweetest cup of tea that we got up there. You remember?'

There was time to visit Dad's brothers and sisters, nieces and nephews. Time to pull into a hotel or pub for a bite to eat and a chat. Probably, the time of the day that my father enjoyed most was the evening in a pub, with a pint of Guinness and a musician or two performing. My mother would keep time with her hands, a relaxed smile on her face.

If life hereafter were anything like those days and nights, I would have settled for that, without a second thought. My parents would have too, I knew. We would have to count on those memories. It was time to part once more.

'Write when you get to Aunt B's in Philadelphia and give our love to them all. And don't forget to write immediately when you get to Lima. We will be waiting on your letter. God bless you Luke,' Mom said. It seemed to me she looked less sad now than on other occasions of parting.

'Don't worry, son, we'll be alright,' my Dad was able to mutter as I drove away. Our letters back and forth and the golden memories of those precious days were to be their peace and comfort in their autumn years.

9.

SHELTERING THE WORKERS

WHEN I RETURNED FROM my holidays, Leo was ready to leave for his new mission. He had decided to go to work in the rainforest of Peru. His parishioners would be tribal people who lived in villages that sprawled along the banks of the river Huallaga, one of the many tributaries of the Amazon. The hot, rainy climate would suit him healthwise. And the poet and artist in him would enjoy getting to know a new people and their culture.

Before Leo had left for his new mission, there had been a change at the top of the Columban organisation in Lima. Owen had finished his term of office and, for the first time, we priests were allowed to express our preferences about who the next leader should be.

Juan was a popular choice. Unpretentious and out-going, he had arrived in Peru just four years ahead of me, but was one of the 'elders' of the mission.

On pastoral matters, he was seen as someone who was sympathetic to the new approach to pastoral work. His experience had been mainly in the St. Martin de Porres parish. There he had been faced with a difficult situation, which he had resolved successfully.

The priest prior to him had laid the foundations for a huge church. It took several years and many fundraising efforts, including calling on the support of rich families in Lima, to see the job through. Finished, it looked more like a cathedral. The people called it *El Templo*, the Temple.

Undoubtedly, Juan had a natural gift for building a bond with the people. He enjoyed their fiestas and seemed to carry the clerical status lightly. Equally, he was good at relating to colleagues on either side of the pastoral divide. As the new boss, he did what came easy to him – to be tolerant. The centre house became a place where guys like me could begin to feel more comfortable.

A native of County Kerry, Juan had a number of expressions from the land that, for some clerical ears, could have too earthy a ring. Memories of a bunch of us sitting around having a beer bring back some of his trademark sayings, like 'a farting horse never tires'. We had found a superior who could break the tension and get guys laughing, with his irreverent quips.

At the parish, I found myself in a new situation. Before Leo left us, Juan told me I was taking over and Mickey would be my assistant. A volunteer priest from County Limerick, Mickey had a retiring manner and was most at ease in one-to-one conversations. But behind the unassuming exterior was a man with a sharp mind and a great capacity for attention to detail. This was a quality we were to need very soon.

Several years earlier, in Mario's time, the parish had taken on the responsibility of being treasurers to get electricity installed in Villa Maria. People brought their regular quotas to the parish office in the evenings. They paid as they could, and the process had taken a long time to complete.

It fell to Mickey and me to prepare a final report to be presented at a public meeting in the *barrio*. But a problem presented itself immediately. Where were all the records of payments that had been made?

Mickey began a systematic search. Pages and bits of paper began to appear in drawers in the office and the parish house. He stuck at the task of preparing a credible report for weeks on end. His desk was a proverbial jigsaw of bits and pieces of faded and crumpled paper.

'Everyone has a role and a contribution to make,' I would say to myself, happy for Mickey and very glad he was on the team. He did indeed produce the report and presented it himself on the evening, fielding all questions. It passed with flying colours.

One evening, not long after Mickey's arrival in the parish, Ana, a woman who was active in the neighbourhood organisation in El Planeta came to us very upset. She worked in Texoro, a textile factory on Argentina Avenue. For several months, the workers, mainly women, had been unpaid and on strike. Now, the company had locked them out of the premises.

Desperate, they were determined to continue their struggle but needed to get news of their situation out into the public arena. Ana had come to tell us they planned to occupy a church building in one of the Columban parishes.

Sympathetic to their situation, we suggested that our little church and its location was not likely to draw much public attention. Instead, they should think about the *Templo*, the St. Martin de Porres church across the river which our Superior Juan had managed to finish.

Next day, the impressive building was harbouring many scores of women. A banner asking people for their support and solidarity was draped across the main door, now closed. As neighbours went by, to do their early morning shopping at the nearby local market, some, in groups of twos and threes, paused to read the placards on the lamp-posts and take in the significance of the new reality.

The only access to the church was through the parish house. There, Tom and Peter were to be found in animated discussion at a table, as women came and went, preparing and bringing refreshments to their companions.

Both priests were Columbans: Tom from County Meath and Peter from my own county. They had arrived in Lima some years earlier and were following the line of pastoral work that promoted the rights of the poor. Though there was a big age difference between them, and they had different personalities, they made a good team.

They gestured to me to get a mug of tea and take a seat. Very practical details were on their minds. The provision of water, food and bedding, were all priorities, as were arrangements such as having Mass celebrated on the steps outside the *Templo*, and getting loudspeakers installed there.

Tom's route to the missions had not been straightforward. For seventeen years after ordination, he was in charge of discipline in the seminary. It was a job that very few, if any, would have wanted. A gentle man with an engaging smile, he let the code of honour work most of the time: we were expected to report our own misdemeanours.

Inevitably, though, there were occasions when one was caught in a most unseemly gait – chasing along the corridor towards the chapel, ends of the soutane in both hands, in a useless attempt to beat the final bell. Coming to a sliding halt, the soutane was let drop to its full length, and the offender walked sheepishly past the guardian of clerical decorum.

Pranks, too, were not unknown. One always got the impression that Tom was never really surprised, and half expected this from young men, even seminarians. On a Columban's day celebration, after the meal, a few of us brought a turkey carcass to another classmate's room and stuffed it in the wardrobe – an innocent practical joke, carried out by young men who had bonded as they prepared to work for a 'splendid cause'.

Some days later, Tom was visiting our rooms, checking on general tidiness, especially how the occupants had made, or not made, their beds. It must have been the peculiar odour that provoked him to investigate until he found the source. We owned up, and got a bit of a lecture. But behind the serious outward appearance, one could almost see the head of discipline chuckling away silently to himself.

From the closed, protective environment of the seminary, Tom had come to Peru in his 40s. But despite his age, in a short time, he had got a good grasp of the language, identified with the poor, and developed a deep appreciation for their culture. The traditional songs and dances of his parishioners, migrants from the highlands, were dear to his heart. I can still see him, going around the parish house, humming a tune to himself: 'Yo *soy Huancaino por algo.'* The statement roughly translates, 'I'm from Huancayo and proud of it.'

Now, he was standing shoulder-to-shoulder with Peter, supporting the struggle of these brave women, in a whole new experience. Peter had arrived right after ordination. Sharp and witty, he was also a natural leader. No better man to tell a yarn, which grew with each telling.

My new companion in the parish was reluctant to get involved in mentoring groups, but felt totally at ease supporting the cause of the women as they occupied the church building. He seemed to enjoy being part of their struggle.

The women occupied the *Templo* for a number of weeks. They got publicity in the press and on radio. During that time negotiations between their union and the company continued and a solution was worked out. Most importantly, once the priests had accepted and supported the workers, the police had respected the church as a place of sanctuary. This had not been the case some months earlier when the priest, in a city centre parish, had called in the police to remove striking workers from the church building.

Some time after the women textile workers had left the *Templo*, the miners from the southern town of Marcona took refuge there and were equally welcomed and supported by my two friends. They stayed for a longer time, until they had got a solution to their demands. The impact of these events echoed across the land, sending out the message that part of the Church, at least, was for standing firm in defence of workers' rights.

Our meetings to discuss pastoral matters used to take place in a run-down, colonial-type building in the centre of the city. One day in October 1968, someone came rushing into the room, all excited. He turned on the black and white TV set. We watched in amazement as the head of the Reformist Military Junta, led by General Velasco Alvarado, announced that the oil fields, *La Brea y Parinas*, in northern Peru, were at that moment being taken over by the Peruvian army. Until then they had been an enclave of the American-owned International Petroleum Company.

Just five days earlier the democratic government, led by President Belaunde, had been ousted. Belaunde was coming to the end of his term, but it had not been an easy ride. Without control of the congress, he was in constant tangles with the opposition. Even a tepid agrarian reform didn't get through. Then, there was the dispute with the International Petroleum Company over the contract to exploit the oils fields. It boiled over when a page of the said agreement went missing. This was the catalyst that allowed the armed forces to take over.

The Junta called itself the 'Revolutionary Government of the Armed Forces' and stated its objective of pursuing justice for the poor. This was breaking the mould. Most Latin American countries had right wing military dictatorships. Traditionally, in Latin America, the military had been the allies of the rich and powerful. In foreign policy, the new government went further and pursued a partnership with the Soviet bloc and Cuba.

On the home front, in quick succession, the military government implemented far-reaching reforms. It nationalised entire industries, expropriating companies in mining, fishing, telecommunications, electricity, steel and others. Government control of the economy was increased.

In agriculture, the reform was the most radical attempted in Latin America. The big *haciendas* were expropriated, given over to the peasants to be run as cooperatives.

All these reforms were to set the groups which traditionally held power in Peru on a course of radical opposition to Velasco's government. Indeed, he was disliked for racist reasons too. To them he was a *Cholo*, a term used in a derogatory way to refer to someone of mixed native Peruvian ancestry.

The language of revolution, and the attempts to radically change the unjust social and economic structures, became everyday topics in the media and in private conversations. For those of us who were working in popular education in the *barrios,* these were days full of great excitement and hope. The millions of poor peasants stuck in grim poverty in the highlands, clung to Velasco's promise:

'Peasant, the landlord will no longer eat from your poverty.'

10.

ON THE WAY OUT

AFTER RETURNING FROM MY visit home, I had begun to think more about what my commitment to working with the poor really implied. The government of the military junta had made a lot of radical reforms in most sectors of the economy. It had created great expectations among the poor. But it was easy to see that the way ahead would not be fast or smooth.

Already, the junta was beginning to feel the pressure from opposition within the country – from the traditional parties, from groups whose economic interests had been hurt, and from left-wing organisations that accused it of trying to impose reforms from the top down, without real participation of the workers. On the external front, because of its alignment with the Soviet bloc, it was being squeezed for credit and pursued for foreign debt.

The country had become quickly politicised by the radical discourse from the top. But parliament had been closed and elections ruled out. The idea that it would indeed be a long, drawn-out process seemed to follow me around.

In my own, very private thoughts and feelings, I was questioning my ability to continue indefinitely as a celibate. I was feeling the need for a female partner, someone with whom I could share my commitment to the cause of the poor. However, for some time, I was unable to express my sentiments to others, not even to my best priest friends. We had been formed to distrust and repress our emotions, and never talked about them. Although we spent our day-off each week together, I never brought up the subject.

So, without consulting anyone, I had taken the decision one morning, walking back to the presbytery, to leave the clerical priesthood, get married, and with a companion at my side continue our commitment. I had no idea how I would go about leaving the parish. It would be a sad time for us all and would have to be done in as sensitive a way as possible. But there was no need to hurry.

A new social worker came to the parish a few months later. We didn't need someone in the traditional mould who would only attend to the most serious cases of families requiring support with food or medicine. Rather, we needed someone who would also work with the women's groups, along the lines being used with other groups in the parish.

Carmen was recommended to us. She had worked in other *barrios* in Lima and in the training and formation of peasants' and community leaders.

It wasn't love at first sight, but from early on I was impressed and took notice. She was good-looking, vivacious and capable. I introduced her to groups in Mirones and El Planeta. On special occasions, like the anniversary of the *barrio* or Mother's Day, I was invited back. There I would see her in a relaxed atmosphere. She had bonded with her new friends.

Sometimes, before going to her meetings with the women, she dropped by the parish house to chat to Mickey and me. Full of enthusiasm about the way the groups were evolving, she wanted to know what was afoot in the wider *barrio*. Not knowing of my decision to leave the priesthood, she was enjoying our chats. For me, they soon became more than just that. I was fast becoming attracted to her.

Years later, at family reunions, I have been known to give a slightly tongue-in-cheek version of how our romance blossomed. At times, I would have been known to say:

'There was I, keeping my head down, going about my business, and then this beautiful girl, in a mini-skirt and red poncho, came on the scene. What was a lad to do?'

Even at this late stage, I must say it wasn't quite like that! Or more correctly, not at all like that. Carmen is a hoarder of books and papers. Down the years she has carefully kept our correspondence, back and forth, from that time. The evidence is there.

She was not the girl that tempted the unfortunate priest, causing him to betray his vocation. And she would reject any insinuation that might be construed as giving the slightest credence to the Church's portrayal of a woman as some kind of temptress, even if made in a jocose manner.

An unforeseen event that forced me to take time off, leaving me with many hours to reflect, coincided with this crucial juncture on my journey.

As they had done many a time before, a group of lads from the *Misioneros* club had invited me to play football one Saturday morning in early January. To avoid the summer heat, we had agreed to meet at 6.00 am in one of the pitches that belonged to the University of Engineering. It was in a working class area and the boys felt comfortable there.

The pitch had not been watered for many a day. The hard, dusty clay surface was bare, except for odd clumps of stubborn grass scattered here and there. We had just started the game in the cool morning air when, without any time to warm up, I had raced after a ball that had nestled beside one of the grassy mounds.

Unfortunately, it was covering a pot-hole and I went over on my right knee. The pain was severe and I had to hobble off. After getting back to the parish on the scooter, I foolishly decided to carry on doing all that was planned for the weekend.

My football pals brought different remedies to rub on the affected knee. By Monday morning the pain was unbearable. It was Juan, I think, who recommended I go to a clinic run by a group of German nuns in the city. A surgeon, known for his skill in treating traumatic injuries, worked there.

On examining my knee, it was clear to him that I had worsened the problem by continuing to walk around on it since the accident. All the ligaments on the inside of the knee had been severed and badly separated. After the operation, I awoke to find that there was a cast the whole length of my leg, and it would remain there for many months.

Before leaving the hospital, I had a few chats with the eminent surgeon. Robert Temple was of English extraction, gentle and easy spoken. When I asked him for the bill, he smiled and said, 'Ah, if you can get your hands on a bottle of genuine Paddy's Irish whiskey that will do fine.' He appreciated the work I was involved in and my belonging to an organisation like the Columbans didn't hurt either. I was keenly aware that for future emergencies I would not have that protective mantle.

During my recovery I sought out the company of an old friend. When Juan was elected superior, he had brought Gerry back from 'exile' to the Holy Cross parish, where we had started off together. It was there, in those memory-laden surroundings, that I came to weigh up the depth of my feelings for Carmen. I was falling in love with her. The imposed rule of celibacy no longer held me in its grip.

IN MY TIME AS A PRIEST I had known some genuinely happy and fulfilled celibate clerics. They were men whose commitment, obvious happiness and easy smile seemed to shine from deep within. Celibacy lived out like that, freely and humanly, is indeed a special witness.

Equally, I always had the impression that many of us priests who were working among the people carried the rule of celibacy more as a burden, we had to grin and stoically bear it. We had gone through a long period of training and conditioning. It was supposed to have moulded us for ever. But, could any amount of training compensate for the lack of the gift of celibacy itself?

A few years ago I had the opportunity to read what Dermot, a resigned Columban, had written on the same subject. I was enlightened by his research and fascinated by the time at which he had first done it. Though he was some years after me in the seminary, and we haven't met in over fifty years, I can still remember him as gifted and witty – ready like us all to face out into the unknown.

After ordination he had spent five years studying scripture. His first missionary appointment was to teach at a seminary in Fiji. He tells how he loved his work as a priest but had fallen in

love with Betty, his future wife. For three years he read, spoke to
people and wrote – all with the purpose of trying to understand
celibacy, unable to 'walk away' until he had done so. From the
notes and papers he had written at that time he put together an
article he shared with resigned Columbans and current members a few years ago.

He wrote: 'I would say that most of us in the seminary – not
only Columbans, of course – thought of celibacy as the price we
had to pay for the privilege of being in the priesthood. It was a
form of asceticism, a continual spiritual warfare.'

That understanding of celibacy, he was to discover, had no
biblical basis, and it could be misleading and harmful. Celibacy
was not something to be suffered; neither was it a struggle or a
cross.

Its true meaning was totally different – it was a gift to be lived
fully and joyfully. As with all gifts (teacher, administrator, artist),
'Training, hard work and experience can all be used to develop
the gift, but no amount of application can make up for its absence.'

In the Apostle Paul's time 'a charisma was a gift that one had
received which rendered one particularly capable of performing a task or ministry in the community. This special expertise
or ability was regarded as a manifestation of the presence of
the Holy Spirit and was therefore for the benefit of the whole
Church.' People had different gifts or charisms, such as the power of healing or working miracles; others, for example, were ex-
traordinarily gifted teachers or administrators.

The common notion of priestly celibacy, centred on abstinence from sexual activity and marriage, has no biblical basis.
The essential element is something very different. 'The gift con-
sists in a God-given sensitivity to the values contained in the
New Testament idea of the Kingdom of God: sensitivity to the
values of a life such as Jesus lived.'

As I reflected on the above, the abysm that existed between
our thinking in the seminary and the real meaning of celibacy
dawned on me – the price we had to pay for joining the priest-

hood versus a special God-given sensitivity for living out the values of the Kingdom.

'The Kingdom of God was the central idea in the preaching of Jesus....This Kingdom was to be the gathering together of all creation under the sovereign rule of God. Jesus proclaimed that this process of gathering was already moving inexorably towards its completion. His followers were commissioned to form a community, which would be a sign to the world of the future fullness of the Kingdom.... In a sense, Christians are to live the future, to try to realise, in the present world, the values of the fullness of the Kingdom ...'

'Love one another as I have loved you,' Jesus said. All Christians are called to live by values such as compassion, solidarity, forgiveness and simplicity of lifestyle.

We live in a world where the dominant culture is fuelled by a soul-less brand of capitalism, where goals such as wealth, status, power, ruthless competition and disregard for the common good all bombard people right across the globe. Against all the odds, we Christians are called to show by our daily living that this world and these values too are passing.

Those Christians with special gifts will each give a special witness. Celibacy is one of those and it is bound to the Christian ideal of elected poverty.

'Poverty and celibacy are so closely linked that a lack of poverty entirely negates the witness of celibacy. To proclaim by one's celibacy that the values and institutions of this world are passing away, and at the same time to show clearly by our possessions, and lifestyle, that we have a considerable stake in the preservation of these values and institutions, is a crazy contradiction.'

As I prepared to leave the clerical institution, like so many of my friends who took the same decision, I was aware that celibacy and priesthood were not essentially connected. It was a man-made law. Several of the apostles and their successors were married. There is a thousand years of tradition for a married clergy, up until the Latern Council in 1139. But that knowledge would provide slight consolation and would not shield us against being banished by the Vatican.

After his long biblical research, my friend Dermot writes: 'When I committed to celibacy I had no idea you could even think about it in those terms.' So many of us could empathise with those words.

❧ ❧ ❧

I WAS IN THE PROCESS OF FOLLOWING through on my decision to leave the clerical priesthood, a decision that had involved not nearly as much searching or analysis. I was about to move on, absorbed mostly by mixed feelings of joy, sadness and concern about the immediate future. In Lima, I had often heard the saying, 'True friendship has no price'. Now, it was taking on a deeper meaning for me. I had great friends, some of them priests, and many were people from the *barrios*. That bond was to be tested. This would be new territory for us all.

Gerry and Mickey were the first to whom I opened my heart. As they listened to my sketchy plan for continuing my commitment of working with the poor, they were sympathetic but genuinely worried for me. Wasn't it an idealistic dream that had very little chance of succeeding?

Shortly after my operation, I had told Carmen that I had decided to leave the clerical priesthood and to get married. However, I wasn't able to express my real feelings for her. Perhaps my lack of experience in such matters may have led me to believe that she would pick that up herself! It is much more likely I didn't have the courage to tell her just then. Back in El Montón, with my crutches, I was looking for an opportunity to talk to her. We didn't have the space to do so freely.

The long months of imposed inactivity, and personal reflection, had passed. The cast on my leg was finally removed. My physiotherapy started, and on an afternoon when Carmen came by the presbytery I handed her an envelope. It contained an invitation to join me for a bite to eat after my next physio session.

We met in a coffee shop, on the corner of Colmena and Tacna Avenues in the city centre. It was closed some time later, but that spot has been the object of nostalgic visits by both of us from time to time.

After soup and a sandwich, I asked for a double *pisco sour*. Carmen asked for a *café con leche*. When I had finished my awkward expression of love for her, for a few moments she wore that infectious smile that I had become so attracted to. Then she grew more serious, saying:

'You know Lucas (no Padre this time), even after you told me you were leaving, I still saw you as a priest. After tonight, it will never be the same again between us. But I will need time. Let me tell you something. I thought I was in love once before ...'

And then she confided in me. Though a number of years younger than me, she was not new to a relationship, having broken one off a few years earlier. It had hurt deeply and she was not for rushing into anything.

But, in the late evening, as I accompanied her to her home on the *micro*, sheer joy brimmed up inside me – I knew that she liked me too. Later she would say, I even put my hand on her knee.

We began to exchange letters. Until I re-read them recently, I had totally forgotten, or erased from my memory, the fact that Carmen had asked that we take time out to reflect for a month. Hoping to weaken her resolve with a bit of humour, I had written the following letter in the typical bureaucratic style we all knew so well in Lima.

Very Esteemed Miss,

I present myself before you with all due respect, to say that with reference to the 'agreement' made last Thursday, regarding the suspension of talks for one month, I wish to present a prior motion for the following reasons:

1. The said agreement seems to have been made in a hasty manner and without due consideration.

2. It would appear that neither party took into account that one month has 4 weeks and 30 days, each with 24 hours.

3. Others, which do not occur to me now or that, most likely, have nothing to do with the present case.

*For all the reasons expressed above, and those to be mani-
fested, I ask for a breather. In other words, I am proposing
the suitability of a café con leche to reconsider the said
agreement. Trusting my petition will be listened to, taking into account your altruistic spirit and because it is a
humanitarian request.*

On behalf of the Consumer Society, Lucas.

The girl of my dreams did relent and wrote back some days
later. We would continue to write and meet over the following
months.

As we got to know each other better, we were aware that each
of us would be moving forward and building our future on personal histories that were very different in many ways. But, crucially, we also had a recently shared experience of commitment
to the struggle of the poor. We had witnessed each other's efforts
to live by the same values.

At the same time as we were deepening our relationship, we
were talking too about how best to manage our departure from
the parish. It had, in a way, already begun. We had been letting
the news go out.

I had been talking to Gerry until late one evening, when Juan
arrived. It was well after midnight. He had come to tell us that he
had decided, of his own accord, to come to work in the parish after I left. It was most welcome news, a great gesture of friendship
and a vote of confidence in our work. However, his wish would
not materialise.

The priests' organisation, ONIS, anxious to promote its
sphere of influence, saw there was greater need for his presence
in the *Cono Norte*, or Northern Sector.

Acceding to persuasion from the same organisation, I accepted a suggestion to go to the city of Chimbote, north of Lima.
There, for a week, I listened to all the arguments for changing my
decision. After returning, I wrote to my Love:

*Dearest Carmen, I understand your worry regarding the
danger of being influenced by other people. Now, after my*

visit to Chimbote, it is clearer for me. Most likely, I went to please the friends in ONIS. The visit has helped me to realise that we have to build our own future. On the way back, I was thinking about how the organisation is paramount for them: it is much more important for them than individuals like us. Jorge Alvarez is the exception. Probably, at this time, we cannot expect more from them.

This evening, Eleazar, Genaro and Pablo each dropped by the parish house. They are relaxed. And so am I: profoundly happy and immersed in our love and our commitment. Sometimes, I wish we were in that future we have planned, but we both know that this time, with its joys and sorrows, is so precious.

Until tomorrow, My Love.

One morning I had a visit from the secretary general of ONIS. Alfredo, a Peruvian diocesan priest, was a profound person. As a young man he had spent some years living a contemplative life, as a member of the Little Brothers of Jesus, in the Sahara desert of Algeria. They were followers of Charles de Foucauld's path of Christian witness. He was a man of compassion, and had a strong commitment to the cause of the poor. His mission on that morning was to plead that I reconsider my decision. But I sensed no pressure coming from him. Some months later he was to take the same route as me. Afterwards, until his untimely death from cancer, when he left behind his heart-broken wife Estrella and his three young children, the only work linked to the struggle of the poor he would be able to find was with a Protestant organisation.

A prominent leader of the Theology of Liberation movement asked to see me. He put it bluntly: 'Listen Luke, there are guerrilla fighters in the jungle who never see a woman from one year to another, for years. Now, if they can do it, why can't we? Celibacy is not the problem.' Somewhere, it seemed, I had heard that before!

It was widely known that the observance of celibacy was indeed a problem for Peruvian clergy, especially those in the *sierra*.

Priests had women and children 'on the side'. Of course, official-ly, and in public, all showed support for the Roman imposition.

There was a standing joke at some clerical get-togethers about a certain high-ranked cleric, a Canon, who at meetings with his peers used to wax strong about celibacy being the 'jewel on the crown of the Church'. All knew of his female partner and several children.

Quite clearly, I was getting the message that the organisa-tion, and the movement behind it, were much more important, for some of my former colleagues, than any personal decision or need of mine. By putting my own needs and interests first, I was letting the side down. Well-intentioned and committed as they were, they were still clerics at heart. They were holding on to, and utilising, the flawed structures of a Church that was essen-tially patriarchal and undemocratic.

Many a time then, and since, I have asked myself how pro-reform clerics could hope to build a new society without ques-tioning the warped structures of the Church institution itself.

Only some priests showed they understood – my commit-ment as a Christian had every right to be human and personal; in fact, it was essential that it be such and be respected. If the man-made rule of imposed clerical celibacy made this impossible for me, then I had every right to get married, without any sense of 'betrayal of the cause'.

When I had made my decision to leave the clerical institu-tion and get married I had written to tell my parents. Now, from the other side of the Atlantic, my mother was writing, asking me to come home quickly, and think things over. Like many an Irish mother of her time would have done, she got the new archbishop to write to me. He hailed from our parish in Knock.

MY PARENTS WERE WORRIED for me. How I wished that life was not so complicated. If only they could meet Carmen and see how much in love we were. But that, I knew, could not be for some time yet, not until we had put some foundations down for our new life together. More than was usual for me, the memories of warm, safe days from my childhood came rushing back.

The village of Ballyroe bordered on three lakes. From our house we had a view of two of them. A third was visible from another field on the farm. They marked the landscape and were witnesses to many happy hours of our childhood.

The boys of the village used all three lakes as their fishing grounds, in all seasons except winter. Frequently, after Sunday Mass, we assembled, with our gear and box of worms, and decided which lake to fish. We knew all the good spots and by evening we all had a string of perch to show for the care-free hours spent.

The dipping, scurrying action of the floating cork was the clue. When a particularly active spot was found, all of us fishers moved in. We were often too close for safety.

One windy afternoon, as I swung my line, the hook caught John's right eyelid. It was stuck there. When I recall what followed, I still shudder. With our dirty hands, a number of us struggled to get the hook out. Finally, the opening in the skin was wide enough to get it loose.

We had tried our best to keep the point of the hook away from his eye but it must have suffered a lot of bruising. Surprisingly little blood came from the wound. I can still see my brave companion rubbing that eye and wincing. After a brief pause, we all continued to fish. He had no infection or any other problem afterwards. In those days, our mothers had their own remedies for mishaps like that.

My siblings and I got a sense of adventure out of setting the night line for pike. We had our lucky place on the lake shore; a small perch or a frog were the favourite baits.

Next day, with excitement in the air, we checked the line. If there was a strain on it we knew we'd had a bite. Bringing in the catch was high drama, especially that first sight of the fish breaking the lake surface. As it came close to the shore, I never ceased to be awe-struck by those huge bulging eyes and that enormous mouth, full of sharp teeth. We had to be careful.

They were all big fish to us and got bigger in the telling at school next day. With our catch hanging from a pole, which one of my sisters and I carried between us, we made our way home in triumph. We could already savour the meal Mom would prepare.

The lake nearest our house bordered on one of our fields. I had learned to swim during my first year in secondary school, not very well, a sort of doggy paddle. That summer I passed on my little knowledge and primitive technique to my sisters and brother. Patsy was the most adventurous and surpassed me quickly.

Mother always cautioned us to be on the look-out for her call. When our fun-time was up, she stood at the gable of the house and sent her verbal message to us, across the warm summer air, 'Come on home now!'

We could just about hear her but we could see her waving. There was always the temptation of another swim or two, before we set off, tired and at a lazy pace. On the odd occasion, Mom's patience had run out and she waited for us with the sally rod in her hand.

We lined up and, as we passed her by, each of us got a re-minder for our misdemeanour on the back of the legs. I cannot remember it ever hurting that much but, as the sally was put back in its place beside the horse tackle in the kitchen, we all knew we had passed the line.

Dad never lifted a hand to any of us, but he, and we children, seemed to know that, at times, someone had to show us enough was enough.

One summer's afternoon, Dad and I were harvesting oats in the field that overlooked Cullentra Lake. Ann and Patsy had gone for a swim there and we were keeping an eye on them.

All was well, until we saw Ann gesturing frantically to her sister, who was swimming farther off-shore than usual – no, she was heading across the lake. With no possibility of reaching them quickly, we could only look on. After many long minutes, Patsy reached the opposite shore.

Then we couldn't believe what we were seeing. After tak-ing a breather, she started to swim back. To our great relief and amazement, she finished her challenge, hugged her sister, and raised her arms in triumph, for the benefit of the relieved pair in the harvest field.

The elders in the village had always warned us of a dangerous undercurrent in that lake. I am not too sure if any of them had attempted the crossing or even knew how to swim. Anyway, on that summer's evening, we had witnessed an adventurous girl, in her early teens, challenging that belief and putting it to rest. After all, maybe the warnings were only our parents' way of helping to keep us safe.

THOSE MEMORIES FROM MY childhood seemed to serve as a comforting and steadying influence for me during my last days in the parish. The reaction of the people to my leaving was very different from that of some clerical colleagues. While sad to see Carmen and me leave, the former were happy for us and wanted to see us doing what we were planning. Their understanding and friendship had no conditions attached. Individually, and in small groups, they began to come to the presbytery to chat and wish us well.

Carmen and I had decided to start anew in the *barrios* of the southern sector of the city. I had already gone there. In the *barrio Ciudad de Dios*, City of God, I had spoken to the Maryknoll priests who worked in that area. They were friendly and helpful, telling me that the nun in charge of the *Colegio Fe y Alegría*, Faith and Joy School, was looking for someone to help organise a parents' association.

Sister Rosa gave me a two month contract. We knew one another from seminars on pastoral work we had attended. She seemed happy to give me my first bit of work. After our meeting I had rented a room in the *barrio*.

There were many leave-taking sessions in each *barrio* of the parish. All of them had that life-giving mixture of joy and sadness that was, in its own way, uplifting. The last get-together was in the parish house in Villa Maria. It was crowded and subdued and we shared a final Mass together.

Next day, I moved with my few belongings to the Columban centre house. My intention was to rest and say my goodbyes. Just a few months earlier, the central administration in Ireland had appointed a new Superior, one who was not sympathetic to the the reform movement. On my third morning at headquarters, he approached me to say:

'Luke, I would appreciate it if you moved out.' Never once did he ask me if I had any money in my pocket, never enquired about where I was going to stay or what I intended to do.

True, we were on opposite sides as regards pastoral approaches, but I was shaken by his coldness and lack of humanity. The traditional Columban charism of hospitality and kindness seemed to have been swallowed up, and over-ridden, by his understanding of what it meant to be the Superior at that time. I got my bag and took a bus, on the first leg of my journey to my rented room in *Ciudad de Dios*. There was full and plenty in the centre house. He was not going to want for anything. I was on that crowded mini-bus, with little in my pocket, but I was in love, and shared a dream that nestled deep in my heart.

Until recently, I had never broached the event of that morning with my former boss. The occasion arose at a Columban's day celebration in the centre house a few years ago. Late in the evening, a group of us were reminiscing about days gone by. I reminded him about the way he had treated me at that most vulnerable time in my life.

He had mellowed over the years and appeared to be genuinely surprised by my intervention. 'Oh, did I?' he exclaimed. Could it be possible, I asked myself, that he had forgotten? Wasn't it more likely that the cleric in him had erased from his memory what it saw as just another forgettable piece of human drama?

On my next visit, a year later, to that memory-layered centre house, the former Superior made it his business to sit beside me. He told jokes and obviously wanted to make amends. For those few hours, after all those years, he showed me he could be human after all.

11.

BANISHED AMONG THE PEOPLE

BACK IN MY SEMINARY DAYS, a phrase often repeated to us students had to do with what being a priest really involved. We were told, 'As a priest, you must be all things to all men'.

I had often tried to make sense of it. But it was the practical impossibility of living it out that always struck me. If anything, it pointed the way towards an impersonal, robot-like approach to priesthood, one that did not take into account the gifts and qualities of the individual.

Anyway, from now on, there would be no need for me to try to work out that conundrum. Having spent the first night in my new *barrio*, I awoke bereft, in practical terms, of clerical status. My goals were going to be much more modest and realistic now.

I wrote to Carmen:

> *My Love, I got to my room just after midnight. The barrio was quiet but some people still had lights on. That gave the place a homely feeling and made me feel more secure on my first night.*

> *This will be just a short letter to share with you my great joy at seeing our dreams on the road to fulfilment. At times, I feel like standing back and trying to appreciate more the blessings that have come to me at this special time.*

> *I had dreamed of meeting a girl like you: someone to love, to be my companion. We would live out together our commitment to the poor. Though not one of them, we would try to keep close to them, and somehow get work that would allow us to be part of their struggle.*

*Luke in pram with his cousin Eddie Molloy who was reared
with the family*

*Luke with his parents, William and Kathleen (nee Meehan),
before going to Peru*

At home in Ballyroe with parents, brother Liam and sister Mary

With sisters Ann and Patsy, both student nurses

Cutting turf with his father – nephew Joe joins the action

With Gaelic football teammates in the seminary

Arrival at Port of Callao, gateway to Lima

Shantytown of Villa Maria (El Montón)

Community of barrio 'El Planeta' build a meeting place and chapel

Before a soccer match on their day off, missionaries with workers,
members of the 'opposing team'

With members of Misioneros Youth Club before leaving for first visit home

Opening of the sports grounds on the plaza of barrio Villa Maria (El Montón)

A moment of celebration at a women's group in El Planeta
– back row Luke and Mickey, front row, second from right, Carmen

Carmen and Luke dancing the traditional Huayno on the streets of Huancayo
in the early morning, celebrating the 'Fiesta de San Juan'

By the shore of Lake Llanganuco at 3,850 metres, under the majestic Huascaran Peaks, almost another 3,000 meters higher

At front, Aunts Paye and Estela, and at back with sister Dori and brother Carli

Celebrating Civil Wedding, December 1971

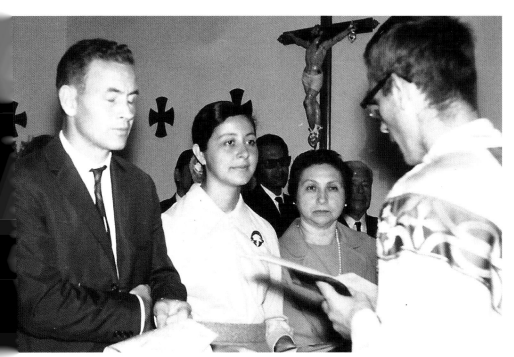

Religious Wedding Ceremony, July 1972

*With father on the farm, winter of 1973, I had come urgently
as mother was ill – Carmen's first visit*

Carmen and her father-in-law feeding the animals

Carmen's parents, Carlos and Dora (holding baby Kathy

With Carmen, Kathy and Grandad – all ready for a day in the bog

A birthday party in Carmen de la Legua – back row, Aunts Paye, Horten and Carola

Children growing up – with Kathy, William and Tony

Son William accompanies Dad recording in a barrio

...men reciting her poetry at the premises of the Association of Peruvian Writers, Lima

At the sixth century monastic site of Glendalough, first visited by Carmen in 1973, and some twenty years later accompanied by our family

With Des Kelleher and Noel Browne, outside his thatched cottage in Connemara – photograph taken by Sean Hogan, who also joined us for the visit

Recent family photograph – front to back and left to right: Baby Grace, Jack, Eva, Linda, Liam, Carmen Grainne, Tony, Luke, Dale, Kathy and William

Luke and Carmen with cousin Mary Killeen, our enthusiastic contact with the extended family in Philadelphia

With Michael Shannon (on a visit to Ireland) are Joe O'Grady,
Jim Kennedy and grandson Liam

José, now married with his own children, holds a photograph of Luke and himself
at his First Communion (taken on a family visit to barrio of Mirones)

It was a dream, and the path seemed full of obstacles. But, last night, coming home on the micro I felt a great joy. Part of the dream was being fulfilled and we were where we wanted to be.

I was surrounded by workers. They were in their work clothes and tired. But I could feel their comradeship and strength, as they chatted and joked.

We both know that the road ahead is uncertain. Clerical friends are not exactly rushing to say, 'there might be a possibility of work here or there.' We are out now and ploughing our own furrow. But we have the friendship and good wishes of so many people from the parish and we have ourselves. And like Mario Benedetti's wonderful poem-song says:

> *If I love you it is because you are*
> *My love, my accomplice and everything.*
> *And on the street, side by side,*
> *We are much more than two!*

Last night I slept wrapped up in the warmth and security of your love.

Until this evening, with all my love. Lucas.

Even though my work at the Faith and Joy school was for a very short time, it provided me with my first lesson. Sister Rosa was enthusiastic about the prospect of having a Parents' Association. I had talked to her about how she saw its involvement, and thought I understood – mainly the physical improvement and up-keep of the building, but the parents' ideas would be welcome too.

On my second evening she sat in to observe proceedings. After the meeting she told me that she did not want the association interfering in the running of the school. I think I had mentioned something like delegates being able to report to management on sub-standard performance by a particular teacher.

Sister Rosa was a progressive woman but she had to see how things would work out. She had a school to run. I wasn't in my parish now and would not be able to make assumptions. My years of working in parishes had accustomed me to not having to report to anyone. As long as I had not committed some public 'scandal' I could continue to make my own decisions.

The work at the school was in the evenings, and while it lasted I had time to search for my next job. It actually came to me, in the person of Don Julio, the fondly-remembered engineer who was so instrumental in helping us get the little stadium built in Villa Maria.

He had found where I could be located and got a message to me. We met in a café across the street from the Municipality of Lima. With his usual cup of black coffee and cigarette to the ready, he could hardly conceal his excitement. The Municipality had taken over a boys' orphanage in the southern cone, not far from where I now lived. They needed a person to take charge of the children's formation.

He gave me a brief history of the institution and, before we parted, insisted that I accompany him to meet the head of department with responsibility for the appointment. I left with an application form in my pocket.

When Carmen and I visited *La Ciudad de los Niños* (the City of the Children), it had fallen on hard times. Just two years earlier its founder had died from injuries he suffered after being knocked from his bicycle by a car.

But, Padre Iluminato, an Italian Capuchin priest, had seen a lot of his beloved project realised. In 1955 the Association City of the Children was officially recognised as a non-profit organisation for abandoned and vulnerable children. The government gave the priest a large area of desert land on the south of the city. In those days the old Pan-American Highway used to pass by there.

With his long white beard, he was a familiar figure to people leaving the city for the beaches on summer weekends. He used to stand on the side of the road with his collection bucket, looking for support.

A few years before his death, a new motorway had been built and diverted traffic away from the orphanage, depriving it of cash donations. Then the earthquake of 1970 had badly affected the place. It was now a series of run-down buildings. The workshops, like carpentry and metal work, had no professional teachers. It was obvious that the whole project needed a big cash injection and on-going support.

The boys had three meals a day and the younger ones went to primary school on the grounds. But there was a serious lack of staff. We picked up a pervading sense of loss and insecurity from the children.

It was not a difficult decision for Carmen and me. I applied and was given the job and would start in about a month's time.

Carmen and I were about to start a special stage on our journey. Our relationship had blossomed in a short time. Just ten months earlier I had gone to her parent's home on the occasion of her birthday. I had arrived with my crutches. At that time, she didn't yet know of my true feelings for her. I was treated by everyone with the deference shown to a *padre*.

Over the following months, as our relationship grew, Carmen had found pretexts for me to get to know her family.

They lived on the other side of the city, in Miraflores. This district, in another period, had been home to the upper classes. Now it had many areas that were middle class, with many old, run-down colonial style houses.

Carlos, Carmen's dad, had been able to purchase one of these houses and overhaul it. He worked in administration for the International Petroleum Company. It had been nationalised by the Velasco government and he was made redundant shortly afterwards. Kind and gentle, he was also a gifted musician, who had taught himself to read music. Seated at the piano he used to lead the party playing all the popular songs and dances.

One of twelve children, he had grown up on a *hacienda* in the north. After an injury that left his father unable to work, his mother had been the driving force for the family. Education was her top priority and as the older children finished primary school she found ways to get them enrolled in secondary school in Lima. When the opportunity arose, she moved there with the whole family.

As was typical everywhere, in those years, long before women's liberation, the boys on both sides of the family were given the opportunity of higher education, and most of them became professionals or tradesmen.

Carmen's mother, Dora, also came from a large family of nine children. She was a retiring, caring woman who always seemed to be thinking of others. Her grandmother was of Italian descent and granddad was of mixed Spanish Peruvian ancestry. He had held the position of director of the finance ministry in the 1930s. They were from Lima.

Both parents were traditional Catholics. At first, they must have been jolted by our obviously developing relationship. For some time before this, they had come to accept Carmen's work with the poor so the path we were planning to follow may not have been such a great surprise for them.

But any initial concern soon seemed to melt away and I felt accepted in my new family. Simplicity was a way of life with that loving couple and they were to be more understanding and supportive than I could have ever expected.

Carmen had two siblings: an older sister and a younger brother. It must have been easier for them to understand and accept what was happening. Dori was reserved, but she did have her small circle of friends and was very loyal. Since finishing secondary school, she had been a bank employee. Their younger brother, Carli, had just started to study at the university. He was outgoing and enthusiastic and we quickly became friends. The three were very close.

Work at *La Ciudad de los Niños* was due to begin in early January. It meant that I would be living on the premises. Carmen wanted to be involved too, in a voluntary capacity. Our courtship had been short but we felt secure in our relationship. So, we decided to get married. To do so in a Church ceremony required the completion of a process called 'laicisation'.

We had already set that process in motion but it could take any length of time, a year and more. It was not that long since I had left the clerical institution but I already felt distanced from it. I was a Christian and believed in Jesus and His message. But

I no longer felt fettered by regulations issued from Rome. They could deal with my request whenever they wanted to. Some years later they slowed the whole process almost to a halt, in an attempt to diminish the exodus of priests from the clerical institution. We decided to seal our union in a civil ceremony.

At the simple ceremony we were accompanied by Carmen's extended family and friends, and by leaders and friends from the *barrios*. A few priest friends also joined us. From the Church perspective, we were doing things the wrong way round.

The party at the family home brought together people from different social classes. I was apprehensive beforehand, but needn't have been. Several of the uncles and their families, on both sides, had worked and lived in the provinces, in places far removed from Lima. They didn't share that closed class mentality, prevalent among the upper classes in the capital. Our friends from the *barrios* were made to feel at ease.

In the afternoon, with rice raining down on us, we made our way, through the cheers and hugs of family and friends, to the street and a waiting taxi. It would leave us at the bus station and we were on our way to Ica, some 300 kilometres south, for our short honeymoon. Family and friends had made this possible. It was 18 December and we would return a few days before Christmas.

Our arrival at the orphanage, the City of the Children, happened quietly one evening. Jorge, the administrator, had given us the key to our room, which was adjacent to his. That small space was to be our kitchen, bedroom and sitting room.

Next day, we had breakfast. Carmen's mother had ensured we brought some provisions with us. Afterwards, there was a knock on the door. Two of the older boys had come to 'suss us out'. Seated on the single bed and the only chair, we had our first conversation.

Our answer to their first question, 'how long are you going to stay?' could not have been reassuring for the boys. 'That depends on the Municipality,' we said. Ever since the founder, Padre Iluminato, had died, they had seen people come and go. The overall state of the place had deteriorated. Over the next few hours we listened mostly, as our visitors gave us an invaluable insight into the life and atmosphere within the orphanage.

There was a big age difference between the boys. Some were only six years old, while a few others had been there nearly from the beginning and were nearer twenty. It had always been the way that the older boys, in turns, took on the responsibility of cooking, washing and mending clothes, and general cleaning.

In the founder's time, there were always volunteers coming in to help out. They did things like organising games and helping out with school lessons. Some of them had been involved in the building of an outdoor amphitheatre, which lay abandoned, along with the dreams of its builders.

Now, all that volunteer effort had dried up, leaving a huge void in the boys' lives. It was not a happy place any more. What they had seen, since the takeover by the Municipality, had not been encouraging. People seemed to keep their distance. They felt no one took a real interest in them.

After having a few similar chats with other boys, the road ahead for us was very clear. We needed to make a special effort to connect with our new charges; they would have to feel that we cared.

There was a large, unused room that soon became the centre for our work. With help from the older children, we painted and decorated the walls. The tables and chairs needed a face-lift too.

Working with youth, especially the older boys, was something I liked to do. It had been a large part of my experience in the parish. The method of 'Formation through Action' had stood the test before, and we would use it here too.

But this would be a new experience, very different from that of *Padre* in the parish. There, I had made great friendships, but a lot of the time I felt I was on a pedestal and treated differently. Married now, and outside the clerical structure, I neither expected, nor would I get, special treatment. It was a great feeling of liberation. And Carmen was at my side. Her contribution to our joint effort was to be vital. She brought not only her skills, but a whole feminine dimension to it.

In the afternoons, small groups of children began to drop into our humble abode. Carmen always seemed to have at hand some *arroz con leche*, the typical rice pudding, or *mazamora morada*, a delicious dessert made from purple corn and fruits.

Of course, it was also an opportunity to do some formation. Crowded around the little table, I can see her explaining a thought-provoking cartoon to them. It was called *El Burrito con Anteojeras*, the Donkey with Blinkers. The story told how the animal saw everything so differently when the blinkers were removed – it was just like what happened to people, when they began to learn how to think for themselves.

From that unlikely 'classroom', they took their plans to the more spacious meeting room. Over a number of weeks, and with Carmen's guidance, they produced a dozen drawings, which they hung proudly around the walls.

Once we had formed a good relationship with the boys, we formed several groups according to age. The method of 'See, Judge and Act' fits all sizes and ages. Not surprisingly, the lack of sports was a problem that manifested itself in all groups. The boys took on the challenge of preparing a soccer pitch – there was no lack of space in which to do so.

Another yearning that all the boys had soon came to the surface. It was summertime and naturally all wanted to enjoy a day at the beach. We used the preparation for the event as a learning path for the older boys especially.

Transport was supplied by the Municipality and we had a generous supply of sandwiches and soft drinks on board. From mid-morning until late afternoon those children were carefree, as they played with the sand and splashed about on the seashore.

Exhausted and elated, we arrived back at base. Carmen and I had just refreshed ourselves, when a group of the older boys came in. They were carrying a bucket full of shellfish, which all had helped to gather at the beach. Carmen added a few ingredients of her own, and we shared a mouth-watering soup to end a memorable day. Our relationship with the boys was on a solid footing.

We were about three months at the orphanage when Jorge, the administrator, moved to his own house in the city. Presumably, it was considered sufficient that Carmen and I were living there.

With the room adjacent to us now vacant, we got permission to open a doorway in the dividing wall, and use it. It was coming up to Carmen's birthday and the bigger boys took on the job of renovating our dwelling. As well as putting in the door to our new bedroom, they painted the whole place. In an especially moving touch, they made a fine double bed for us in the carpentry workshop.

On her birthday, I was at the Municipality and wrote a card:

> *My Love,*
>
> *At last, they say they are going to pay us at 2pm. It has been hectic here but I will be able to get you the radio. So much activity these days and today I had hoped for more calm. But amidst all the frenzy, and the boys fixing our little place, we are building our life along the lines that we wanted.*
>
> *You must be exhausted. But I know you are happy and I am too, at your side.*
>
> *By the way, I think the children may have a surprise planned for you.*
>
> *Enjoy your day: it only comes around once a year. May the Lord keep you well and give us strength in the times ahead.*
>
> *With all my love, Lucas.*

Quicker than we anticipated, our work had become much more than a job. A bond had developed between the children and ourselves. They were feeling comfortable in our presence and speaking freely. We were available to chat at any time.

But the situation was to change radically for us all. The Municipality, in an attempt to bolster the financial situation of the orphanage, appointed a new director. Victor came from a business background and, as we would soon find out, had little or no interest in a Formation Programme as such.

At our first meeting, he laid out his philosophy and plan. He recalled how he had grown up among the poor in the northern sector. The clear implication was that he should know what poor children needed. The best formation, to his mind, was having children do physical work. So, the time given to formation would be cut drastically – all the children would work.

The Municipality had been experimenting with a sewerage treatment plant nearby. It purified the water so that it could be used to irrigate some of the desert land that the orphanage owned. All sorts of agricultural produce could be grown and pigs and chickens reared; the boys could turn the wasteland into a productive oasis.

Carmen and I would have had no difficulty with the smaller children learning about growing crops, rearing chickens or doing a little work. However, what was being proposed seemed totally unacceptable to us.

Over the next several months, we argued in defence of the children's right to have a reasonable amount of time set aside for their personal formation and for play. But we were fighting a losing battle. Victor had powerful backing.

My contract was coming to an end and, originally, at that stage I was to be given permanent employment. Instead, I was told that my services were no longer required.

Frustrated and impotent to do anything about it, Carmen and I had to prepare to leave. To make matters worse, there was less than a week to go to Christmas. The boys would feel the separation even more.

When word got out, they came around. To our surprise, though very sad, they were bearing up. Life had already dealt them many knocks. I liked to think that our short time together had also helped them to mature a little.

Many of them were asking us for a personal memento. We got copies of our wedding photos and dedicated each one with a personal message. We spent most of the day prior to our departure, and the following morning, writing our farewell messages. It kept us all busy and seemed to soften the pain.

We had hired a small pick-up truck, and the first thing to be put in there was the double bed. It was their loving reminder of a mutually enriching experience, and would follow us on our future travels. Brave boys, they wouldn't show their hurt and actually cheered us out the gate, as we fought back tears of admiration and affection.

The experience we were leaving behind, though cut short and apparently limited in what it had achieved, would always mean very much to us. It was our first as a couple. Without saying so, I think we were both conscious that we had given and received in a way that would not easily be repeated in any workplace.

Some months before we left the orphanage, I got word that Cardinal Landazuri wanted to see me. I met him in his office, beside the cathedral, on the *Plaza de Armas*. Carmen waited in the corridor outside. My 'defection' must have hurt him. Nevertheless, I did not hear a word of any kind of rebuke from him. He was friendly but it was obvious that he had some important matters to get through.

To be honest, when I was completing my part of the laicisation process, answering the questions and signing the papers, it had not fully struck me how draconian and demeaning the whole affair had been. Now, his Excellency was to remind me by reading the document to me, translating from the original Latin to Spanish, as he went.

There it was in the clearest terms: I was a living, walking source of grave scandal, so my future activity in the Church had to be drastically curtailed. I could not preach, give out Communion, hold any pastoral office, teach or hold a post in any institute of higher education controlled by the Church. Neither could I teach theology, or teach/hold a post in any lower level institution run by the Church. The document ended by saying that a work of 'piety or charity' should be imposed on the laicised person. When completed, this should be reported back to the Sacred Congregation. This document, called a 'Rescript', remains largely unchanged to the present day.

Finally, the Cardinal showed me a letter that I would have to sign. It was a solemn promise that I would keep far away from my former parish. It actually mentioned a specific distance.

I was a very different person to the one he had last met. I felt free to ignore the absurd imposition contained in the letter. But the memory of that early morning visit to the parish, by the big man, and his later intervention that same day, weighed with me. I signed the letter. Relieved, he put it in the drawer of his desk, where it would remain under lock and key, he assured me.

There was, for him, still one tricky problem to be solved: our religious wedding ceremony. At that point the Cardinal called Carmen in. He insisted on doing the ceremony himself, in his private chapel in the cathedral. Only Carmen's immediate family could be present.

When neither of us was for accepting this request, he pleaded repeatedly with my spouse. 'Carmen, I am offering to do your wedding in my own private chapel. It is quiet and beautiful. Why won't you accept my offer?'

I had a soft spot for the good man, and he was looking after his flock by protecting it from my scandal-giving presence, as laid down by the Roman Curia. But we were not for relenting. He had done his best and reluctantly had to accept our decision. Mickey, our loyal friend, officiated at the Mass during which we exchanged vows again, surrounded by our family and friends.

It used to amaze me back then that grown men could go to such lengths in an effort to avoid a non-existent danger of scandal. What he, and other high-ranking clerics, surely wanted to avoid was the possibility of people seeing resigned, married priests live normal and committed family lives. They feared that the rule of clerical celibacy might be exposed, even more, for what it is – a law imposed by a patriarchal and power-hungry Church.

It was a simple conclusion to come to. For these men, it was never about what the people thought. Rather, it came down to what the clerical institution dictated. We, who were seen to challenge its power and control, were betraying the cause, and had to be banished.

12.

'THE REVOLUTION' CALLS

AFTER LEAVING THE ORPHANAGE, we stayed with Carmen's parents. We had been looking for work for a few weeks when we got an offer and accepted it. It was to involve travelling to Chimbote, some 400 kilometres north of Lima.

Despite its mistakes and weaknesses, we were impressed with what the Velasco government had been trying to do. We would take the opportunity presented to us and try to make a contribution.

Some well-known, left-leaning professionals were close advisers of the regime. They had come up with the idea of a state-run organisation that was to give organisational and technical support to the diverse sectors of the working class and the poor. At the same time, it was to create awareness around, and support for, the reforms of the revolution.

It boasted an ambitious name, 'National System of Support for Social Mobilisation', known as *Sinamos*. Carmen was contracted to work in the training department. There, with two colleagues, she had the task of organising workshops for all the staff on leadership and community development. Always more comfortable among the people, some months later she asked to be transferred to work in the *barrios*.

My role was to recruit and head a team of people who had some experience of working in the shantytowns. The latter had been given a new name. They were officially called *Pueblos Jóvenes* or Young Towns. To the poor, they were still their *barrios*.

The original name of *Barriadas* had a derogatory connotation, implying that their inhabitants were mostly lazy and of dubious reputation. The new name was positive, and it acknowledged their proven qualities: their desire and capacity to contribute to the development and progress of their new communities.

I had encouraged two friends from Lima to join us. Olga, committed and always eager to learn more, had been in a youth group in my first parish, with Michael and Gerry. Esther, enthusiastic and determined, had been active in one of the first parishes run by the Columbans in the northern cone. For them, as well as for me, this was going to be a totally new, and challenging, experience.

As one entered the port city of Chimbote, the sight of the *Pueblos Jóvenes* looked no different from what we had become accustomed to in the capital: row after row of bamboo huts, stretching for miles. One would never suspect that vast wealth had been generated there, up until the very recent past.

The fishing boom had lasted right through the 1960s. Now, it had collapsed. The most important cause was over-fishing. Not even the apparently unlimited quantities of anchovies could survive – catches of over ten million tons a year for a decade.

There was a lesser cause for the disappearance of the anchovies. The plankton, on which they fed, floated in the cold waters of the Humboldt Current, close to the surface. But the phenomenon of *El Niño* in 1972, as it usually did, meant that warm water drifted over the cold, lowering the depth of the plankton.

At the peak of production, it was the largest fishing industry in the world. There were over 150 plants producing fishmeal and Peru had 40 per cent of the world supply. Fishing accounted for up to 30 per cent of total export earnings.

When we arrived in Chimbote, some factories still worked round the clock producing fishmeal. It was exported around the world mainly as feed for pigs and poultry.

An all-pervading stench hung in the air day and night, as the smoke billowed into the already polluted sky. It was accepted as an inconvenience, a reality that was impossible to get used to, but something one had to learn to live with.

The failure of the fishing industry not only rocked the city of Chimbote but the government also. Together with the serious fall in agricultural production, following the reform, it added to the country's serious financial problems.

The 'good days' had also ended for the fishermen who had flocked here from towns and cities along the coast. While the boom lasted they were reputed to have earned a lot of money. But they were classified as temporary labourers, were paid by the ton landed, and had no pension. Living amid insecurity seemed to be at the heart of the fishermen's culture at the time – eat, drink and be merry, for who wants to think about tomorrow. Chimbote had more than its fair share of brothels and bars.

Now we had come to a very subdued and rattled city, and were beginning to find our way in a brand new organisation. Already, after just a few weeks together, our team of promoters had made a habit of playing soccer. I had just togged out one afternoon when a colleague from the office came to tell me that word had come in, through the Columbans, that my young brother had died and the burial had already taken place.

I sat numbed on the cement-covered playing ground and cried. After some minutes, I composed myself, got up and joined my companions in the game. It was what Liam would have wanted me to do, as he watched on from somewhere. He was only thirty-two and in his short life had experienced his share of personal turmoil.

❧   ❧   ❧

FOR THE PREVIOUS TWO YEARS before his death, my brother had been at a good stage in his life. He had returned from London, with his wife and baby boy, to take over the farm from my parents. On the fatal morning, he was alone in his car, driving to Castlebar, on his way to hand in his resignation at a local hotel where he worked part-time. At a curve on the road he had hit a stone wall at speed and was killed instantly.

As I came to grips with the shocking news, I was immensely grateful for the memory of our last meeting in London, some three years earlier. I was on my first visit home from Peru and still a cleric, though thankfully not the same one he had known.

We had gone out together and were able to talk easily, in a way that I had not been able to do in my last years as a clerical student. I was no longer interested in passing judgement on him and I knew he sensed that.

His family situation at that time was difficult. His lovely wife, Marguerite, was suffering from some form of post-natal depression, which was stubbornly hanging on. On her own, she was struggling to take care of their year-old baby.

In spite of the conflicting realities in Liam's life, sadness mixed with great joy, he was determined to keep doing his best, and was hopeful for the future. He then had two loved ones to live for. His path through life had not always been so clear.

My sisters Ann and Patsy, and he, were all born in quick succession after me. There were just four years between him and me. Growing up on the farm, we had made little of our age differences, doing our chores and playing together.

My going to boarding school was a physical separation, which we had to try and make up for during vacation. By the time I had finished secondary school, he had started his daily, almost twenty miles round trip bicycle journey, to St Colman's college in Claremorris.

It was my time in the seminary, especially during the latter years, that put an emotional distance between us. Liam had finished secondary school, done a few courses, and got his first job.

Sociable and entertaining, he was a frequent visitor to the pub, where he began to drink too much. He had several serious car crashes, fortunately with no fatal consequences. He needed the help of a counsellor, but back in 1950s Ireland this wasn't considered an option.

During my fifth year in the seminary, Liam was still living with my parents. Through my mother's letters, I was aware that they were under constant stress. My mindset then was of no help to my brother. One day, I judged him and found him guilty. Angrily, I had told him, 'You are making a right mess of your own life, and of our parents' lives too, wake up and cop on,' and we had parted.

Deep within, I too was torn apart. 'This can't be right, there must be another way,' a little voice whispered. But I was not free to listen. I was a cleric in the making, one who knew a lot about laying down the law but very little about how to recognise, and listen to, my younger brother's cry for help.

Soon afterwards, Liam moved to London. For a time I carried around a feeling of guilt for my judgemental action, until I wrote to him and apologised. We made up and began to exchange letters.

ৰ্ঝ   ৰ্ঝ   ৰ্ঝ

IN THE DAYS AND WEEKS following the news of my brother Liam's death, the memory of our last meeting served to give me some consolation. But, as I silently grieved over his untimely departure, I was surrounded by workmates eager to face a reality full of challenges. Life moved me forward.

Oscar was our boss and leader. A dynamic man in his forties, he had been appointed director of the recently formed *Sinamos* in the region where Chimbote was located. In fact, he was the only civilian to hold such a post, the others being high-ranking military officers.

For the briefest moment on meeting him, the fact that he had lost his left eye caught one's attention. We would learn later that it had happened at a political rally when he was a young man. But it was the ready, winning smile, and the hearty handshake, that told you who he was.

Our boss was about to undertake a huge political challenge – to try to make this brand-new state institution relevant and meaningful for the restless poor, amid growing opposition from political forces on the right and left. Parliament had been shut down and political parties felt, and were in fact, sidelined. Increasingly, they were to see *Sinamos* as trying to usurp their role.

Most surprising for us at the time was the opposition to the Revolutionary Government from the left-wing parties. After all, it had taken on board most of their dearest causes. It was only later that I came to some understanding of that opposition. The experience of having the military lead a revolution was totally new in Peru's history. In addition, it was an experience led from the top down, something that was ideologically impossible for the more radical left-wing parties to accept: revolution had to come from the poor and the workers. The contradiction was, of course, that the leaders of those same left-wing parties, most of whom were from the middle class, had no problem with taking unto themselves the representation of the poor and workers.

The revolutionary government had, over the previous four years, shown itself to be on the side of the weakest in society. It had broken the historical record of the military as allies of the wealthy classes. But, the initial enthusiasm of the poor was waning, and the government was being hit by harsh realities – internally by the consequences of natural phenomena, political opposition and its own mistakes, externally by isolation and lack of credit.

We were both taken by our new boss. He was sharp, witty and politically astute. Carmen had been involved in politics as a student in the university, but working within the political arena was new to me. I would have a sharp learning curve.

Oscar was not a man of many words but he was effective in getting across what he considered to be the important ideas. He motivated us to develop an atmosphere of comradeship within the office; there was to be no insistence on hierarchies. He showed the way by example, moving around and talking to people.

But alongside this easy-going manner he was a man with a great sense of urgency, which he also transmitted to us. In hindsight, I realise that he must have been aware, even then, that the revolution of the armed forces didn't have time on its side. Above all, he motivated his staff to listen to, and be at the service of, the people. We should also, of course, learn to be aware of political undercurrents.

All of this was in stark contrast to the inertia and self-serving that we were accustomed to from the bureaucracy in the capital. There, in the pre-revolution days especially, a document rarely passed to the next desk without somebody's palm being greased.

It was refreshing to see how professionals like lawyers, engineers and architects attended meetings in the *barrios* after work, or took off to work in the *sierra* for a week.

However, the enthusiasm and dedication of all was to be tested more than we could have imagined. We were working in an area that had been struck by two disasters: the end of the fishing boom, resulting in tens of thousands of people out of work, and the consequences of a disastrous earthquake.

The latter had happened on a Sunday afternoon in 1970. It had measured 7.9 on the Ritcher scale, and the epicentre was some 35 kilometres out in the Pacific Ocean, off the coast of Chimbote. The effects had been felt even in neighbouring countries.

On the day of the worst disaster ever recorded in Peru's history, I was with a group of people, sitting expectantly in the parish house, in Villa Maria. We were about to watch the opening game of the 1970 Soccer World Cup held in Mexico. Though some 400 kilometres away from the epicentre, Lima shook for a never-ending minute. El Montón rocked and swayed but incredibly survived.

Two days later, the Peruvian national team played their opening game against Bulgaria. People said they had been spared the dreadful news. Despite going two goals down, they won the game by three goals to two. They were to go on to have a great performance in the tournament. Their achievement brought some joy to a suffering nation.

In Chimbote, the cost in human life was enormous. Over a thousand people were killed in the city, mostly by falling buildings. That same quake brought immense destruction to the towns and villages of the Huaylas Valley, which stretched all the way into the very heart of the Andes. Over 70,000 people perished.

Some months before we arrived in Chimbote, when the city was still recovering from the earthquake, prolonged heavy rains caused the local river to overflow. Flooding seriously affected buildings and basic sanitary conditions. Even the central plaza was not spared.

The massive unemployment, plus the suffering caused by the natural disasters, had created an atmosphere of widespread discontent. It was noticeable that the attitude of the people here was different from that of the people in the *barrios* of my former parish. As I look back now, I realise that the latter worked at a multitude of different, badly paid jobs and often had to change and look for others. The vast majority of the former were tied to the fishing industry. They had become accustomed to relatively good wages during the boom, were convinced that it would last forever, and had just seen the bubble burst before their eyes. They had crash-landed and seemed shell-shocked as to what to do next.

The first task of our team was to help to revitalise the community organisation in the *barrios*. Each member was responsible for two or three *barrios*. During the day, the promoters visited the people to get to know their situation, listen to them and set up meetings. In the evening I accompanied one of them to a meeting.

It was important that we were honest with the people and explained exactly what support we could give, limited though it was. As a consequence of government rhetoric, expectations were high.

In spite of the traumatic and unstable situation in which we found ourselves, we were welcomed by the people. At least, on a personal level and in small groups, we sensed no animosity. The same could not be said about the reception we got from another quarter.

In our team of promoters, there were some who had been, and probably still were, members of left-wing parties. While they were not totally confident in the military-led process of change, they knew it was having a profound impact on the whole country, and believed the opportunity should be availed of. They used it to create awareness among the poor about their right to have their basic needs met, to organise and have their voices heard.

Manuel was the oldest and most politically aware of the promoters in our team. It was from him that I was to learn most about the dividing lines between the left-wing organisations. Back then, dogmatism and sectarianism seemed to be generally accepted as inevitable, even somehow normal. Manuel was also the first to tell me about the anti-*Sinamos* sentiment among the steel workers in *Siderperu,* and the pending strike.

A radical left-wing group held sway there. They were opposed to the Velasco regime. No real revolution could be led by the military. The labour area of *Sinamos* was trying to get a foothold in the strategically important industry. This drew a response – a strike was organised.

That morning we were all in the *Sinamos* offices. By mid-day the workers had begun to march by. The slogans on their banners and placards, and their chanting gave a clear message – '*Sinamos* Get Out'. The situation looked like getting out of hand. We left the building quietly, in ones and twos.

Our team decided to take refuge in the apartment that Carmen and I had rented. On the way there, some of us were recognised and had abuse hurled our way. Ironically, our abode was the upstairs apartment, at the home of a steel worker!

Huddled together in the small room off the kitchen, we made cups of coffee and tried to take in what was happening on the streets.

'We were lucky we weren't physically attacked. That was so frightening. You'd think we were their enemies,' Olga had complained as she slumped on a chair.

'The way these guys think, anyone who is seen to be collaborating with the Velasco government is an enemy. They are following a radical political line. It's as simple as that,' Manuel tried to explain.

'What is their objective? What are they hoping to achieve?' I ventured.

'Do you mean a realistic plan for replacing the present regime? No way. They just want to make their presence felt and gain a bit of political space. The last thing we should do is take any of this in a personal way,' Manuel added wisely.

For most of us it was a first experience of being on the receiving end of the workers' anger. Politics were complicated and none more so than on the Left.

The owner of the house was known to Carmen and me as a jolly man who was prone to having a jar too many. Just to add another touch of unreality to the day, unannounced, he opened the door. Obviously in a merry mood, he looked hazily around the crowded room and attempted to make a head count. Then he retired, repeating approvingly to himself, 'All is well, everything is in order.'

Shortly after that sobering experience on the day of the steel workers strike, Carmen and I had travelled along the narrow valley of the *Callejón de Huaylas*, the Huaylas Valley, to the city of

Huaraz. There we attended a workshop for *Sinamos* staff. On the return journey, we had time to take in the sheer majesty of our surroundings. The whole area was sometimes called the 'Switzerland of Peru'.

The valley lay between two of the highest mountain ranges of the Andes, the *Cordillera Blanca* or White Range and the *Cordillera Negra* or Black Range. The latter was without snow or ice. It blocked the warmer air from the coast from reaching the White Range and melting its snow caps.

Side by side with the extraordinary beauty that surrounded us was the evidence of the enormous difficulties, and dangers, that faced the people trying to make a living there.

Travelling in itself was a hazardous adventure. The narrow road, in many places, was cut into the side of the mountain, at a dizzy height. Especially in the rainy season, there was always the danger of falling rocks and mud slides.

But it was the stubborn tenacity of its people, in the towns and villages along the valley, which was admirable above all. Time and again, they had recovered from the destruction wrought by enormous landslides. Such was the history of Yungay, after the 1970 earthquake. It had been a town of about 25,000 inhabitants.

We were standing in an eerie place, with perhaps some fifteen metres of mud and rocks under our feet. Only the very tops of the palm trees, which once adorned the main plaza, stuck out. All around us, the whole area of the town had been smothered and buried by the raging avalanche turned landslide.

Barely a few hundred people had been saved. They had been on higher ground, at the cemetery, the football pitch and the circus. On that lazy Sunday afternoon, as some people rested while others watched the coverage of the World Cup of football in Mexico, there had been no time to escape.

The landslide fell several thousand metres and travelled some sixteen kilometres at over 300 kilometers per hour. It reached and engulfed the town in minutes.

We stood in the cemetery and looked out on the scene of destruction. Our gaze went back up the mountain, following the visible trail the landslide had left. It was silent and lifeless, as if nature wanted to erase the memory of a people.

The dirt road up to Lake Llanganuco, at the foot of the mighty Huascaran peak, was still intact. In places, the sliding mud and rock had sped down, just metres away.

One of our companions was Eduardo, an engineer with years of experience working in the *sierra*. He was at the wheel of the jeep and carefully negotiated his way up the mountain until we got to the shore of the majestic lake.

Almost unbelievable as it seemed to us on that sunny day, this was where an estimated hundred million tons of rock and ice had come crashing down from Peru's highest mountain. The resulting landslide had reached Yungay in some three minutes.

It was so quiet and peaceful now. The recent tragedy could well have passed off for a horrible nightmare. Those greenest of green waters were calm and crystal clear. Towering above was that tallest of Peru's mountains, with it sparkling glaciers. All was at ease, resting in its stunning beauty. It was no wonder that its people couldn't contemplate leaving their land.

The new Yungay would indeed be built, with government support, in a safer location. But the town's survivors, and the people of the valley, wanted to make sure the next generations would never forget. They already had plans to turn that once vibrant community, turned cemetery in a flash, into a rose garden – a place of remembrance. There all, natives and tourists, could reflect on our intertwined and sometimes precarious relationship with Mother Earth.

We had been almost a year in Chimbote when word arrived that my Mother was in a coma in hospital. Her diabetes had got out of control again. As we would soon be due our annual vacation, and had saved some money, we were able to travel to Ireland.

Shortly before leaving the parish, I had taken out Peruvian citizenship. Now, it was to actually complicate things for us. In Lima, we were going through the red tape to get our papers in order for the journey. It was already the second day, and when I got to the counter, I was told, 'Come back tomorrow' – the ever so familiar *mañana*.

After explaining to the employee about my mother's illness, he stepped to one side of the window and returned with an empty envelope. 'Join the queue again and come back in half an hour,' he told me.

It was the first time that I had really felt cornered in that kind of situation. I put a little money in the envelope, joined the queue and handed it over. Again, the same employee stepped out of sight, returned with my paper signed and stamped and, with a smile on his face, wished me a safe journey.

As we stepped off the Aeroflot flight in Shannon, the cold March air bit our faces. Only in the *sierra* of her homeland would Carmen have felt that same sting. It was winter and she quickly would have to learn to cope with the change, but now we were focused on getting to Castlebar.

At the hospital, we found Mom still in a coma and Dad by her side. For some minutes I had whispered in her ear, telling her we had arrived. To everyone's surprise she woke up, opened her eyes and was soon able to speak. Her first words were directed to Carmen: 'Carmen, come here and give me a hug. You are so welcome.'

It was a deeply emotional moment for me. Just as I had always imagined, if only my Mother could meet Carmen all her doubts would vanish. Her recovery was remarkable and a few days later we all walked out of the hospital, arms linked. My sister Mary, her husband Ned, and their family lived in the village of Knock, close to the church. We all stayed with them

There have been moments of extraordinary grace in my life and this was one. In the background, I had the privilege of watching as Mary and Carmen cared for Mom. It was especially moving to see how easily my Mother and Carmen, with her less than perfect English, got on. In front of my eyes, all those negative self-judgements about being the mother of a failed priest were falling away.

At times, as my mother enquired about Carmen's family or the attitude in Peru to priests who had left the clerical institution, I was called upon to translate. 'As long as you and Luke are happy and doing good there, it doesn't matter to me anymore what the priests and the Church here say,' Mom assured her.

The farm had to be looked after so Dad and I went over each morning to tend to the animals. He still had some cattle, sheep and a donkey. Mom made sure to remind us to look after her hens, ducks and geese.

It was in the late mornings, over cups of tea in the kitchen, that I began to grasp, at a much deeper level, what Liam's recent passing away had meant to my parents. Their whole world had been turned upside down. Liam had come home with his wife Marguerite, now much improved, and his young son Anthony. Now, not just a son, but a whole family, and its promising future, had been swept from their lives. Their daughter-in-law, and their adored grandson, had returned to London to live with her parents.

With his hand on my shoulder, Dad had led me to Liam's bedroom. There, hidden in a drawer, he showed me some of their grandson's special toys – joyful memories burnt into my parents' souls, but too painful now to be out in the light of day.

After a couple of weeks, Mom was much better, but she would never be well enough to live on the farm again. In fact, for some time before her latest illness she had been living with my sister Mary and her family. Carmen had begun to accompany us to look after the animals.

It had snowed one night and next morning she was ecstatic with excitement and child-like joy. We built a snowman, complete with one of Dad's old caps and a pipe. Muffled up against the cold, with Carmen proudly sporting her wellingtons, we accompanied Dad on his round of feeding the animals. His faithful dog was at his side. A few of the sheep had little lambs and, perfectly at home among them, the geese stood tall against the glistening snow.

As the day of our departure came close, I had been telling myself that spring was around the corner. Nature would burst into life and Mom would surely be out in her flower garden. Though frail, she would be with her inseparable companion again, and my sisters Mary and Ann would be at hand to brighten their days.

True to her Latin American character, Carmen had little difficulty in expressing herself. During our visit, she had endeared herself to my parents and could make them laugh and enjoy small things.

'Come on Love, let's show your Dad and Mom how we dance in Peru,' she might say, as she put a tape in her portable tape-recorder and led me on to the floor to do the traditional *huayno* of the sierra or the coastal *marinera*. Her red poncho was always at hand for an impromptu moment like this. And though stitched and mended, it is still part of her wardrobe to this day.

The final parting was emotional and tears flowed freely. But there were smiles too, as we reassured one another. I knew I wasn't alone in feeling, among the mixed emotions, an immense gratitude for that precious time together.

❧ ❧ ❧

BACK AT WORK IN CHIMBOTE, something that I was conscious of, but had not given much thought to, began to take on more importance. Despite enjoying the work and the camaraderie among the staff, in one aspect I wasn't entirely comfortable.

There was a big difference between the work in the parish and that in which we were now engaged, and I was feeling a bit out of my depth. Back then, I was aware that trying to bring the Christian message to the poor was always going to have political consequences.

If people were encouraged to accept their lot as God's will, put their hopes in the next life, and direct all their efforts towards that goal, that line of pastoral work would have one type of political consequence.

On the other hand, if the Christian message focussed on the dignity of the poor and their rights, it would in fact be a 'subversive message' for the powers that be, with very different consequences.

To those of us on the side of radical reform, it was clear that wherever the Catholic Church worked, it was either domesticating people to accept the status quo, or liberating and empowering them to challenge it – all in the name of Jesus.

The situation we were working in now, however, was different. We were in the arena of party politics. The organisation we now worked for, *Sinamos*, was not a political party, but it was the instrument the government used to gain support for its reforms. As such, it was being closely watched by all political parties, most of which were critical and in opposition to the government.

I knew little about the different parties. My knowledge came mostly from hearsay. Likewise, the categories they used to analyse Peruvian society were not much more than phrases bandied around. For the first time, I was entertaining the idea of taking time out to study.

Carmen had done a couple of years of social studies after graduating and could easily understand what I was feeling. She encouraged me: 'There is never going to be a right moment for you to study. Now is as good a time as any. We have no family yet and I will get a job. Afterwards, we will have many years to work with the people.'

So we decided to leave Chimbote. As we got our things together in preparation for our move, I felt good about the experience. Although we were leaving our work with the poor after only a short time there, we had a plan to continue and had learned a lot.

The overall impression I was coming away with, I think, was that of the great complexity of Peruvian society. From the fishing boats, now mostly lying idle in the bay, to the towns and villages of the Huaylas Valley, precariously and laboriously connected with the coast, the whole reality was so extensive, geographically challenging, and divided in socioeconomic and political terms.

What kind of party, or group of parties, could ever effectively represent this vast country, which had different races, cultures, and classes, and above all varied and deeply-embedded socioeconomic problems? I wondered, and would remind myself that it was this same terrain and country, though in very different times, that the Incas had made their own, in the most admirable of ways.

Though it would have meant different things to the different sectors and social classes, all sang the national anthem with gusto and pride. On all sorts of formal occasions, the red and white flag flew over the homes of the poor and the powerful alike. But I sensed that during the recent years, the millions of poor had started to sing the anthem much more as an expression of their birthright to a fairer deal in their Peru.

The country had been shaken to its roots by the reformist efforts and the revolutionary language of the Velasco-led government. It would be no exaggeration to say that it would never be the same again. Politics on the Left had seen many new groups and organisations spring up. It was a very challenging time and one that I found difficult to navigate.

I had been out of the clerical institution for a few years now and had not had much contact with my friends within. It was, I suppose, a necessary separation, a space that I had needed.

At times, I had missed meeting up with individual Columbans and other priest friends. With them, I had spent many meaningful and happy years. The exodus of people like me, in such large numbers, had left deep, unexpressed, emotional scars in many of those who remained. In some cases these feelings would be un-expressible for years.

Just recently, in a formal dialogue between some current Columbans and others, like myself, who had left the clerical institution, it was brought home to me how raw an issue it still is for some of the former. Pat, also a Mayo man and a year my senior, became all choked up as he tried to express, for the first time, his sense of loss and hurt.

In the few years since I had left, I had drifted away from the clerical institution, and come to see it more and more as a flawed system, one that needed radical reform. Also, I was more comfortable away from the adulation which was so often shown to the priest.

Once Carmen and I had taken the decision to leave Chimbote, we did not want to stay around. It wasn't easy telling Oscar, but we needn't have worried. He was understanding, and was even able to joke as he wished us well: 'Don't get into trouble down there in the big city, now. Who knows, I may soon have to pack the bags myself.'

13.

A Time to Receive

WHEN TRAVELLING BACK to the capital, our idea was that Carmen would try to find a job. I would study and do some part time work. We planned to stay with her parents initially.

However, shortly after our arrival, we got confirmation that Carmen was pregnant. Over a year earlier, she had a miscarriage at an early stage, and already there were signs that all was not well. She would have to rest completely for several months. The new situation obliged me to revise my plan.

Looking for work, I spoke to Michael, my friend and companion in that first parish. By this time, he was director at an English language centre. He had resigned from the clerical priesthood some months before me.

Living with my parents-in-law, we had calculated that we would be able to get by if I had four hours work a day. But, in order to be able to attend classes at the university, I wanted the earliest teaching hours in the morning and the latest at night. Michael was still his confident, outgoing self:

'Brother, there is no problem. You know, these times of the day are yours for the asking. It is not always easy to get enough teachers at these hours.'

'Great, but you must give me the classes for beginners and I don't have an American accent.'

'No problem there either. You know, we guys from Mayo and Galway speak English with exceptional clarity, much better than in Dublin and away ahead of London, not to mention New York,' he said with a wink and a broad smile.

In order to save time on journeys, I got myself a second-hand motorbike. The traffic situation would demand extra care, but the little machine was to become my reliable companion.

It was September 1973 and I had registered to start studies in sociology at the Catholic University the following year. I was at the cafeteria, when word began to spread like wildfire among the students – there was a military coup in progress against President Allende in Chile.

They were bombarding the presidential palace. Crowded around a portable radio, we were listening to what would be Allende's farewell speech to his people, as the bombs rained down on the historic building.

It was hard to believe what we were hearing. The intervention of the CIA in the truckers' strike, in an attempt to bring down the democratically elected socialist government, was public knowledge. But the utter savagery of what was happening, and the events of the following days, were frightening and depressing in the extreme.

We learned how the Allende supporters were rounded up in the national football stadium in Santiago. There, many of them were tortured and murdered. However, the brutal killing of Victor Jara had the widest impact.

He was a popular Chilean singer/songwriter, an educator and a political activist. As one of the promoters of the New Chilean Song Movement, his popularity had spread around Latin America. Having given concerts in Lima, he was well liked here too.

The manner of his death would be etched into the consciousness of all who dreamed of a better life for the down-trodden across the continent. Myth has now been mixed in with reality, but witnesses tell how he had led his fellow prisoners in song at the stadium. Having refused to stop, he was taken away and tortured. Three days later, his machine-gunned body was left on a road on the outskirts of the city.

Like so many others, as the days went by my disbelief and sadness gave way to a sobering realisation – the road to political participation and mobilisation of the poor, to achieve better living conditions, was a rocky and dangerous one. It would be opposed by ruthless forces from within and from outside. Democratically elected governments had no special immunity.

Several months after that chilling experience, I had started my studies. Because I had no previous diploma or degree to show, I had to do a year of general studies. I was among students who were trying to figure out what exactly they wanted to study. At times I did ask myself: what am I doing here?

It was both exciting and somewhat daunting becoming a student. On the one hand, it was the opportunity I wanted, and it was a good time for me to study. There was no problem with motivation or focus. However, although I was used to being around young people, it was mainly as a mentor or guide. What would it be like trying to fit in as a student, I wondered?

It was a private university for mostly middle and upper class students. But it did take in some students from the poor areas. There was a scale in place which took into account a student's financial circumstances. I was put on one of the lower paying levels.

Two circumstances contributed to making my transition more enjoyable than it might have been. While within the clerical ranks, I had got know some of the professors. They had been speakers at seminars I had attended. They were closely identified with Liberation Theology.

Quite by chance three of my Columban companions had also enrolled to study sociology around the same time. Wally was from the US and had been at the Holy Cross parish, practically since the scattering of us rebels. He had resigned from the clerical priesthood about a year earlier and started his studies. Noel and Mickey, both still within the ranks, were about to start. We would have many a cup of coffee after class, when we talked about anything and nothing.

These sessions certainly helped us ease our way into university life. It helped also that there was a friendly atmosphere, and a buzz about the place. The professors were accessible. Their analyses of the situation in the country came down on the side of radical change.

I had finished my first year at the university and begun to study sociology. After my years of receiving and giving since arriving in Peru, I was eager to get a more scientific, overall view of the social and political situation in the country I had come to love.

I remember, early on, being intrigued as we examined the issue of objectivity in the social sciences. Was it possible? Could the subjective element be avoided? Not really. It all depended on what theoretical framework one started off from. This was very logical and borne out by the many and varied socioeconomic and political analyses going the rounds. But it was a discovery for me then.

At one extreme, for example, was a general acceptance of the status quo, and that all that was needed were some minor changes to the system in vogue. At the opposite end, the premise that only a system that had the State in control of the means of production could bring social justice and real integration for the poor. In between, there were many other starting points and combinations.

I believe it was a Peruvian politician who once said that it made no sense to be a conservative in his native country: what was there to conserve of the economic and political system? We were already into the sixth year of the Revolutionary Government led by the military. Radical change and how it was – or was not – being achieved was on the minds of the great majority of the teachers and students.

The reforms, their strengths and weaknesses, were closely monitored and examined. In those classrooms, freedom of thought was in the air. We were introduced to the main socioeconomic thinkers like Smith, Keynes and Marx. I was enjoying the experience, which had come my way at the right time.

In those years at the university, we heard that the theory of neoliberalism was being muted at the Chicago School of Economics. The most prominent of the so-called 'Chicago Boys' was Professor Milton Friedman. What he and his colleagues advocated was so blatantly just a way to allow the super rich to accumulate much more wealth it was dismissed by all.

It was unthinkable back then that a system that wanted the 'market' to be king, to be let loose with minimum controls to pursue its reckless path of profit and greed, could soon be adopted by countries around the world. And irony of ironies, after several decades of governments abandoning the defence of the common good of their peoples to gambling capitalism, the system has collapsed. And the ordinary people pay the price!

As I studied and worked that first year at the university, Carmen was keeping well. By avoiding physical activity, and resting as much as possible, she was close to completing her eight month of pregnancy. During those months her help with typing assignments for the university had saved me many a time. When she wasn't occupied at that, she was knitting 'for the baby', though we had no idea of its gender.

Then the growing excitement in the household was to be greatly tempered by two events. First it was Dora, Carmen's mother, who, feeling unwell had to go to hospital. It was decided to operate on her a few days later, and Carmen and I were shielded from news of the result. A day later, news arrived that my mother had passed away.

I was numbed, but felt consoled by those cherished memories of our recent visit. We had already said our goodbyes. Now, without doubt, she would continue to be present in our lives, but in a new way. Wasn't this one of those special coincidences again? She was telling us that this was the cycle of life, one life ending and another about to begin, that our sadness would soon be overtaken by joy.

Two days after receiving news of my mother's death, we were sitting around on a Sunday afternoon, when Carmen began to feel pains. Her two aunts, Tita and Paye, both single, were in no doubt.

'You should go up to the attic and bring down that small, brown travel bag and we'll get it ready,' they urged.

Smug in my inexperience, I stuck my head out over the newspaper: 'Let's not get over-excited. There is another full month to go. I'm sure the pain will go away.'

'Tell me, just how many babies have you ever seen delivered?'

'Well, when I was in the parish, on a few nights I brought mothers in labour, and their partners, to the hospital in the back seat of the Volkswagen.'

'I can tell you that you'll be taking another ride, as soon as you get that bag down here. Now, leave that paper and get busy.'

There was no mistaking the urgency or finality in the tone of her voice. It was all hands on deck, and Carmen and I were in a taxi on our way to the hospital. Aunt Paye had phoned the obstetrician who had previously told us he would assist at the birth.

As I sat in a waiting area, near the delivery theatre, a nurse came to tell me that my wife was indeed in labour and it would not take long. The accuracy with which Tita and Paye had read the signs amazed me. Of course, I should have realised that they must have shared the experience of the births of their sister Dora's three children – one of them being the young woman now about to give birth. Though that had been many years before, clearly it was not something one ever forgot.

It was 1974, and a man being allowed to witness the birth of his child was not all that common. The doctor had come out of the theatre, and was leading me to a nearby room.

'Put on this coat and try to look the part. I have told the nurses that you are a medical student.'

In shock, I followed the doctor and found myself by Carmen's side, holding her hand. The delivery, at least in my memory, was swift. After hearing her first cries, and then seeing and holding our baby girl, we could let our emotions of joy and relief flow – the doctor had assured us that she was well.

However, our joy was tinged with sadness, for Carmen's parents were not with us. Dora was still in hospital, recovering after her operation, and only arrived home a week after we did.

There was no hiding the fact that her health had seriously deteriorated, and we could not be protected from the terrible truth any longer. Dora had terminal liver cancer, Carmen's sister Dori told us.

It was such devastating news. This gentlest and most caring of people was just fifty-six. Why her? The sentiments expressed by the great twentieth century Peruvian poet, Cesar Vallejo, seemed to express the desolation of Carmen and her family:

There are blows in life that are so hard
I don't know, like the wrath of God!

And yet, life had to go on. Baby Kathleen, or Kathy as we called her, would lighten the gloom that hung over the family. Her grandmother, for the month or so that she was able to sit up in bed, used to hold her in her lap. Those precious moments seemed to momentarily suspend the pain and her face lit up.

My father-in-law, Carlos, though broken-hearted, was determined to fight to save his soul-mate of so many years. For a few hours each day, stubbornly hoping to find some life-saving information, he would go out and talk to friends, consult doctors, and often arrive back with some herbal remedies.

But, as Dora's condition continued to worsen, her pain and discomfort increased. We decided we should move out. It was our dear priest friend Jorge who helped us get that first place of our own. Like an older brother, he was always attentive to the ups and downs of our on-going journey.

Carmen was quite an emotional person. She could laugh and cry easily. But she also had a surprising strength of character. Despite her middle class up-bringing, she could climb onto the crowded *micros*, walk the dusty streets, and in their humble homes, empathise and share with the people in the *barrios*. Now, I discovered that she had an inner strength she could call on in times of crisis.

As the long months of her mother's agony wore slowly on, she became that steady, reassuring presence for the whole family. It was as if, more than any of us, she could accept the final outcome, and see beyond the end of the suffering, to that better place, where her mother was going.

There would be no more Sunday afternoon family get-togethers with Don Carlos at the piano. No more playing with her granddaughter. We all knew life would be very different; she was going to leave a huge void.

But Carmen seemed to have been able to let her mother go, even willed her to go to her resting place, in the certainty that she would continue to look out for us all in a new way. We would have two mothers, and Kathy two grandmothers, watching out for us.

When the end did come, it was Carmen who prepared the moving farewell ceremony in the house, before going to the church. She led the singing of her mother's favourite songs and hymns, as we carried the coffin down the steps from the house, and out onto the street. As we made our way, I noticed Jorge wipe tears from his eyes. It occurred to me that I had very rarely, if ever, seen a priest cry.

In her quiet, unassuming way, Dora had been a sort of centre of gravity, not just for her own family, but for the whole extended family – her own siblings, five sisters and five brothers and their children. She was a shoulder to lean on, a presence that radiated welcome and understanding at all times. Her home was where everyone felt at ease.

In the months after her passing away, she was sadly missed by all. Her sisters Horten, Paye, Estela and Carola all lived together now. It was inspiring for me to observe how, in a natural kind of way, they continued the tradition, and their home gradually became the uniting and energising centre, on a new part of their collective journey.

For Carlos there would be no easy way to move on. The decision to sell the family home must have caused him to have mixed emotions – so much effort put in, so many good memories. And yet, it could never hold the same place in his heart again.

Carmen received a small inheritance, and without thinking twice about it, she exclaimed: 'Let's go and see your Dad. It will do him good to see his granddaughter.'

'Are you sure? We could get a bit of a car or something with it.'

'No, nothing is as important as seeing your Dad. We can go when it's summertime over there.'

≈   ≈   ≈

IT WAS A LAZY, SUNNY AFTERNOON in July when we arrived in Ballyroe. Dad was nowhere to be seen. Then our neighbour Tom, his face and clothes all speckled blue from spraying the potatoes to protect them against blight, shouted from the nearby field: 'Welcome home Luke and Carmen! You'll probably find Willie over by the lakeside. Most fine days, he wanders over there. He tells me it's what he enjoys doing most of all.'

As we made our way across the 'lake field', with Kathy on my shoulders, memories and emotions welled up inside me, mostly of joy, but some of sadness too.

I felt that I knew exactly why Dad loved this spot by the lake's edge. It was here that he had seen his young family pass some of their happiest moments. He could still hear their shouts of joy and laughter, borne across the fields, on the light summer breeze, as he cleaned a drain or weeded the turnips.

Those carefree children had grown up all too quickly. Like so many Irish families in the 1950s, his had suffered the pangs of emigration too. But never one to curtail, he had encouraged each of us to follow our dream. Things might not have worked out as he had wished, but he had his priceless memories.

As we approached, he was sitting on a low bank with his back to us, clad in a light vest, the legs of his trousers rolled up and his feet playing in the water. By his side, his faithful canine companion was stretched out on the grass.

My sisters had told him we were coming, but he wouldn't have known the time, and anyway the lakeside was too tempting. We were up beside him before he noticed. His first reaction was to shake with laughter, like a small child caught playing one of his pranks.

After we had all recovered a little from our emotional encounter, automatically, we sat down on the bank. We travellers needed to share that space, to soak up some of that peace and quiet and feel the lake water on our feet. Kathy, meanwhile, splashed around in a shallow pool beside us.

We dearly wished to make that moment linger, and it would, for Dad was in a talkative mood.

'Look where we found you, and we thinking we would find you busy on the farm,' Carmen said.

'Well, love, a man must know when his days' work is done and begin to let it go, leave it to others. I love to come here, especially in the summer. A nap among the daisies does one the world of good.'

'Can well believe you, I like it already'.

'Have never been on an aeroplane myself. Coming all that way from Peru, must be very hard. Packed in like sardines I suppose.'

'It was sure great to have it over. But the stewardesses do their best to cheer us up. Plenty of cups of tea, you'd like that.'

'Crossing on the boat was no fun either. I remember when we ran into a storm in mid-Atlantic. Kathleen, God rest her, couldn't think of looking at food next morning. There were only three of us down for breakfast. But, tell me, how did the little one make the journey?'

'No problem at all. She went to sleep a few hours after we left Lima, and woke up only when we had touched down in Shannon. You know, you have another Kathleen now. Kathy, say hello to Granddad.'

Mischievously, she began to splash him with water. At first, Dad laughed heartily, but then, suddenly, he went silent, and his head dropped. Looking sideways, I noticed he was quietly weeping, and put my arm around his shoulders.

My first thought was that he was overcome with sheer joy. But quickly I realised that it might not be as simple as that. After what he had been through with his grandson Anthony, wasn't part of him aware of the danger of getting too emotionally involved and risking suffering heartbreak all over again?

'Don't worry son, I'll be alright. It's just so good to see you all.'

'The important thing is that, for the next month, we are going to be together and we'll have a great time,' I said awkwardly, all too aware of how fast it would fly by.

We did get over that moment and continued to while the afternoon away, until even the patient dog began to stretch and yawn. As we made our leisurely way to the house, I felt proud of my Dad.

In spite of all the loss and disappointment, he stood erect as he always had. He took a certain pride in that and in his as yet dark hair. I could joke about it. His step, though slower than of yore, was light too. Never one to expect pity, my old man was giving me a lesson about growing old with dignity.

Some of my fondest memories from what was to be our last visit with Dad came from doing the simple things on the farm together. He had cut down on all the extra work, like tillage and milking cows.

There was still a small herd of cattle and a flock of sheep. They all needed fodder for the winter, so hay-making was still a big job. Another important task was making sure there was enough turf to keep the house warm during winter.

Normally, the sheep were easy to look after, but in summertime they needed more care. In the warm summer days, the blue-bottle fly was active, and the eggs it deposited on the sheep's wool could hatch quickly into larvae. These maggots, if not removed, could eat into the skin of the animal.

There was one of the flock, which Dad's experienced eye knew needed immediate treatment. Rounding up the sheep was not something that he and his dog could manage any more. Judy was not a trained sheep dog, but she did her best to follow Dad's conflicting orders.

Indeed, the apparently simple task stretched the lot of us. Carmen and I criss-crossed the field, pursuing bouncing sheep, with no particular strategy in mind, much to the amusement of man, dog and, dare I say, those woolly friends. The latter finally seemed to have had enough fun, and idled along to huddle in the indicated corner, as if they had known how to from the start.

As for the affected animal, she was more than willing to be treated, and Dad's mobile clinic went into action.

'Poor thing, it looks very bad to me. See what they have done to her back,' I said.

'It's bad alright, but we have got to her just on time. We'll check again tomorrow.'

'Don't you ask one of the neighbours to give you a hand in this situation?'

'Oh yes. But at this time of year, you know, they are all busy. I did let it go too long.'

'I know, you were waiting for us to arrive!'

'You could be right there, son.'

For our inspection next day we more or less let the sheep do it their way. Before we got hold of our patient, Dad knew she was out of danger.

'See how she is not lagging behind on her own today. She is in among the others.'

The turf was no longer cut by hand. Like his neighbours, Dad had it cut by machine, which also laid the sods out in rows to dry. Before it would be ready to be brought home, now by tractor and trailer, there was another job to be done.

Early one morning, I helped Dad to put the tackling on the donkey and yoke him to the cart. The traditional wheel, with its wooden spokes and steel rim, had been replaced by my brother Liam for much more comfortable motor car wheels. They made easier work for the donkey too.

With Carmen and Kathy on board, we set out for a day in the bog. It was still the custom to stop and chat a while with people we met along the way. So the one hour journey turned into nearly two. By mid-morning we had reached our destination.

Mother and daughter were on a joyful journey of discovery. They began to stroll and explore, as larks above them glided effortlessly in the clear sky. The heather was in bloom and the flat bog land seemed to stretch out around us for miles with no trees to block our view.

Dad and I got on with our task of 'footing the turf'. To ensure that the sods would fully dry, they had to be put standing on one end, leaning against one another. There was no great expertise needed, but the stooped position did tell on one's back. It was the younger man who felt obliged to stand up and stretch most often.

Only the playful interaction of mother and daughter broke the silence. Then, all of a sudden, a hare bounced from its nest. It was right in front of them. Wide-eyed, both screamed excitedly. We all watched it scamper away for a short distance. But it was in no particular hurry, and sat upright on its hind legs. It looked back at us, as if curious, but not unhappy, at our visit. As for us, our furry friend had added another bit of magic to that enchanted place.

After a couple of hours, we were called to share the picnic Carmen had prepared. This was a rare treat indeed, for it wasn't very usual for women to come to the bog. At least, I can't remember Mom ever having done so. Dad chuckled to himself when he saw the time-worn table cloth, which once adorned the parlour table, spread out in front of us.

'Kathleen was proud of that cloth. I was actually with her when it caught her eye in a store in Philadelphia. She loved the design with the shamrocks.'

'Was it alright that I brought it today? Just saw it in the drawer and I fancied it too,' said Carmen.

'No problem at all, love. The fresh air will only do it good and today is a special day.'

Sitting around on sods of turf, we tucked into the sandwiches. Dad was in a pensive mood. I was considering how a feminine touch had added a bit of magic to our table.

We did another couple of hours 'footing', this time joined by Carmen and Kathy. Their original designs stood out proudly as we surveyed our work in the evening. We hadn't finished the job, so there would be another day. As we journeyed home, it was comforting to know that our labour of love had not ended yet.

In mid-summer, it barely gets dark at night. Dusk seems to drift hazily into dawn. We had all gone fishing late one evening. Conditions were better around sunset and afterwards. Fish were biting and I was catching, keeping the big perches only. We must have all been taken in by the serenity of our surroundings, broken only by the excitement of the dancing cork.

None of us seemed to want to be the first to propose to leave. It was near midnight when we made our way home. Dad had clearly enjoyed the evening. When we were growing up, he never seemed to feel he had the time to indulge in that pleasure or indeed go to football games.

I had missed his presence, especially when it came to my teenage years and Gaelic football. He never saw me play. Some lads had their dads at the games. But mine always had to be making hay or fixing a fence. He never knew how much I needed him there, to boost my confidence. I would ask him to come, but never knew how to tell him that I actually needed him at the game.

'We have a big game on next Saturday. If we win this we are in the final. Can you come with me this time, Dad?'

'Ah, son, you go ahead. This is a very busy time, with the hay and turf and all. You will be fine without me.'

'Come on Dad, just this time.'

'You know Luke, by evening time I am tired. I would have to change and get ready and then cycle all that way. You go and enjoy it.'

The day I needed him most was the occasion of the county minor (under eighteen) club final, between my team, Ballyhaunis, and Castlebar. We had a good team, with several of my friends from secondary school on it. I wanted to win that medal, with Dad there. However, he didn't make it. We lost by the barest margin, and I was convinced that I hadn't played with much confidence, not nearly at my best. Afterwards, I would often ask myself, 'What if Dad had come, wouldn't I have played much better?' For parenthood, I had learned a valuable lesson: being on the sideline, cheering, encouraging, or just watching, was indeed very important.

Inevitably, when recalling how I missed my father at the games, thoughts of what his own childhood must have been like would take over. He was only ten when the 1916 Rising took place, and he probably had never played for a team. In the turbulent years that followed he had to take the emigrants' boat all too soon.

As it happened, Peter and Noel, the two younger Columban friends with whom I had shared so much searching and learning, were home on holidays at this time. Noel had already visited us. We had gone out one night and enjoyed a good sing-song in the pub. When we got home, Dad and Noel had stayed on talking, and I think that it must have been then that the man of the house came up with the idea.

A few days later, Peter, Noel and Gerard visited us. The latter, a year younger than me and from nearby Claremorris town, had been on mission work in Korea. We were seated around the table in the parlour where Carmen had prepared tea and sandwiches. It was a pleasant and unexpected surprise, and we were chatting away when Dad changed the line of conversation.

'Luke, I have asked your friends to come because there is something I want to talk about. You know how the farm is getting to be too much for me anymore. I want to ask you and Carmen to stay at home and take it over.'

There was an awkward silence, and Noel intervened: 'Of course, the decision is up to you both. We are here because your Dad has asked us to come. But, we would ask you to consider what he is proposing.'

Peter and Gerard said something similar and, from their tone of voice and demeanour, it was obvious that they felt somewhat uncomfortable.

'You know, Dad, Carmen and I haven't come home with the idea of staying, but we will think about it and talk it over,' was all I could say.

Over the next few days, as we walked the fields, we did consider the possibility of remaining on the farm with Dad. Carmen was showing her courage once again.

'If you want to stay on here, love, it's alright by me.'

'But what would we do here? What would you do here? And we have so many plans for our life in Lima,' I replied.

'You know your own country, dear, and I will be happy with whatever you decide.'

'Love, the problem is that I don't know my country that well any more. You saw for yourself, when I was walking in front of the church the other day, how the parish priest left me with my hand outstretched and went the other way. Maybe he was absorbed in his own world.'

'I know it would not be easy. Do you think you could get a job teaching or something in education?'

'No, without retraining that would be impossible. After seven years in the seminary, studying philosophy and theology mostly, we never got a basic degree of any kind.'

'And what about the farm, could we make a go of it?'

'Well, that is the big question. Dad would expect me to do just that. I have told you about his burning desire, obsession even, to have a son continue farming the land. I am his last chance to ensure the family name continues. For his generation, it is a desire steeped in history. He says he made a solemn promise to his Uncle Tom, that he would do that. But, when we children had all left, except our youngest sister Mary, my parents had left the place to her. Now she is married and financially secure, so he probably feels she would have no problem with us coming here.'

'Yes, I know, dear.'

'But I don't know if we can do it. My heart and mind are somewhere else. You know where.'

It was probably the hardest decision of my life, one that has left me with a silent pain to this day. With recurring thoughts about how I might have put our plans on hold to look after my old man. About how our company could have comforted his lonely, last days and nights. But, at the same time, I am also aware that what he really wanted was more than that: a son to work the land.

We took a taxi to the train in Ballyhaunis. As Dad hugged Carmen, she cried out:

'We'll be back soon, dear.'

'It's a long, long way to Peru, love.'

I lifted Kathy in my arms and we all embraced that frail but valiant man. His parting words of resignation stuck in my throat.

Just a little over a year later, Dad passed on to his place of rest. After my mother's death he had gone back to live on the farm. He was in Ballyhaunis getting his groceries when he felt another stroke coming on. The owner contacted my sister Mary and she took him to the hospital, where she had given birth to all her children. There he died, as his older sibling, Luke, recited the rosary, that brother he had always looked up to, and for whom he had run messages as a boy, during the war of independence.

14.

Following Our Dream

After returning from Ireland, life in Lima, as usual, took on its hurried pace. I had to finish my studies, so my routine was the same: teaching English morning and evening and studying during the day.

Studying sociology was helping me to better understand the complex reality of Peru. I was learning to read the forces at work at important moments of the country's ever more unstable situation. There was, of course, much more to learn. The idea of continuing to study briefly crossed my mind but our commitment to working at the grass-roots was calling us on.

Kathy was still our only child. Carmen had had two miscarriages in the intervening few years, both at early stages of pregnancy. Each time, we walked out of the hospital, arm in arm, together in silent pain, nursing our shattered dream. Ever since, when I hear of a couple's loss, I am conscious that their grief is theirs, something very private. Only they can know the darkness of the loneliest hours.

The gynaecologist was a courteous and busy man. Like the other couples, we had our five to ten minutes in his office on each visit. Disillusioned, we heard of a different doctor who was known for putting patient care at the top of his priorities. On our first visit, he dedicated an hour to making sure he got Carmen's full medical history. She followed his advice, a combination of medication and rest, and would subsequently give birth to two boys.

More than a year before I finished at the university, we had been planning our way forward. We had decided to go to live in a working class area, on the left hand side of the River Rimac. It was located just across the river from my first parish, and some three kilometres down the road from my last one. The district was called Carmen de la Legua.

Before making our decision, we had made many visits there. I have clear memories of taking the bus, and returning late in the evening. We used to get off at *Plaza Unión*, that ever-busy hub of mini-buses and buses, full to over-flowing with weary workers making their way to their *barrios*. With Kathy on my shoulders, we used to pick our way along the crowded, hurried street to *Plaza Dos de Mayo*, and take another bus.

Carmen de la Legua's population had exploded in the 1950s and in the mid-1960s it had been made a district, which included the parish of Reynoso, of poignant memory – the place where we rebels used to meet, breaking Owen's 'curfew' and his heart.

Like the district of San Martin de Porres across the river, it had once been the dried up bed of the river. The main street, where the buses ran, had been built, but all the others showed the familiar rounded stones, betraying their origin from another time. Houses were in various stages of construction, having followed the familiar pattern of building bit by bit, as people could afford.

There was one *barrio* in the district that had been formed for just a few years. A large area, which lay directly behind a row of factories that faced onto Argentina Avenue, the city's main industrial artery at that time, had been 'invaded'. It was here that we were to try to make our contribution.

In the months before finishing studies at the university, in 1978, we had set up a non-government organisation, which would allow us to present projects for popular education and communication to foundations in the developed countries. Until such a time as we had a project approved, I continued to teach English classes early in the morning.

At the language school I used to meet Tom, my former dean of discipline at the seminary and, afterwards, companion of Peter in San Martin de Porres parish. Now, he had left the clerical priesthood and was teaching English too. He was in his fifties then and had married Rosario with whom he had worked in the parish. They had two lovely girls, Raquel and Bridget. Well into mid-life he had taken on the big challenge of rearing a family. But the responsibility seemed to rest easily on his shoulders and he was happy just to be one of the ordinary people. That was something I admired him for and fully understood.

The decade of the 1970s saw the beginning of a massive exodus of priests, religious brothers and sisters, worldwide. Peru and Lima were no exception. All foreign missionary groups, and the native Peruvian clergy, suffered big losses. I can think of ten Columbans who worked in Peru and left the ranks.

As I look back on our decision to go to live in Carmen de la Legua, I cannot remember any great discussions that Carmen and I had about what it would mean to try and rear our children, and live out our commitment there. We wanted to do it and had a basic belief that we could. Committed as we were we made light of possible difficulties ahead, things like our precarious financial circumstances and the ever-darkening political situation. My wife was excited about getting started. She was sure we were following our dream and would face the problems as they came up.

We had moved, and right away Carmen was busy putting her touch to the house, hanging and arranging her memories, and, as only mothers can do, making it a children's play-place. I turned my hand to the dusty, abandoned back garden. Water was indeed life. In a short time we had a little patch of grass, and even a withered old vine had returned to the land of the living.

We got to know our immediate neighbours quickly. A few came to welcome us to their *barrio*. With the family that lived directly across the street we were to build a special relationship.

Franco and Ada had six children, five girls and a boy. Though the economic situation had worsened with the imposition of austerity measures by the military government, Franco, who was the bread-winner, was managing to support his family. They looked healthy and neat when leaving the house for school. He worked in construction, most often taking on jobs on his own. He could do it all – bricklaying, plastering, plumbing, electricity, the lot.

Ada managed the household. Like all her neighbours, she had to be thrifty to survive. Her daily trip to the open-air market, in nearby Reynoso, meant she had to stretch her meagre budget, with the nutritional needs of her growing family in mind. She was a great cook. Many a time later, she would send over a dish, or invite us to her table. It always surprised me how the ingredients, purchased on that tiny budget, could taste so good.

The three older girls were teenagers then. It was moving to see how their mother had been able to instil in them the importance of continuing to study. Nelly was the oldest and would be finishing secondary school in a year. She was determined to go on to third level and would need to get a part-time job and start saving some money.

Carmen and I were about to become involved in community development work in *Villa Señor de los Milagros*, Villa Lord of the Miracles. We needed someone to baby-sit when neither of us was home. Our young neighbour was delighted with her new job and so were we. She did go on to study engineering for the fishing sector. Whenever she couldn't come over, she asked one of her sisters to stand in.

On a number of occasions, when returning to Peru with our grown-up children, we have visited that fondly remembered family. Apart from the painted walls, decorations and curtains, we were in that same kitchen-cum-dining room, around that same big wooden table. There, we have re-kindled the bond that had been formed, when our two families, both of very different backgrounds and at different stages on their paths, had helped each other to walk more securely into the future.

Four or five blocks from our house was the main square. On one side stood the parish church. Padre Miguel, an American priest, had been there a number of years and was known as a doer. He had lobbied government offices to get services for the people. Beside the church, he had built a parish school. It was there that Kathy would go to kindergarten.

Two nuns, also American, worked in the parish too. They lived in a simple house in the *barrio*. We became good friends and often talked about the situation in the country and the Church.

When Padre Miguel left the parish a year later, his place was taken by Felipe, a Peruvian priest, a leading member of the Liberation Theology movement, and a professor of theology at the Catholic University. He continued to teach there by day. Both Carmen and I knew Felipe. She, from her time in the National Union of Catholic Students, I from my time as a member of the priests' movement, ONIS. We were good friends, and from time to time would meet up for a chat.

It was time to introduce ourselves in Villa Lord of the Miracles. Having chosen a name like this for their *barrio*, one might think that these people were very religious. They were, but in their own way. Their faith was not expressed in daily or weekly attendance at Mass or other rituals. Rather, it centred on the feast of their patron saint, and the main Christian feasts. It was popular religiosity and was not clerically controlled. Indeed, it was viewed by most clergy as not at all up to scratch.

Prior to our going to the *barrio*, the atmosphere in the poor and working class areas of Lima had dramatically changed. General Velasco, leader of the revolutionary junta, sick and incapacitated, had been ousted by the military, and his prime minister, General Morales Bermudez, had taken over. The latter had initiated what was to be a turbulent five years of rowing back on the main reforms of the revolutionary government.

Frustrated by the change in direction of the new regime, and above all by the steadily worsening living conditions, the poor were more open to the messages of the left-wing parties, and were taking part in large scale mobilisations.

These political organisations were actively competing against each other in order to increase their presence, and eventually their control, of the neighbourhood organisation in each *barrio*. They followed orientations that originated either in Moscow or Peking. Sectarianism was rife and the road to unity was still only a dream.

For their part the people in the *barrios*, especially the leaders, were more wary of any offer of help from 'outside'. We were not representing any State or Church institution and had to be frank about our background, and what we believed we could offer.

Andrés was the general secretary of the *barrio* organisation, and his family was one of the first we went to visit. He and his wife Antonia were in their early thirties and they had three little girls.

Their home was in the same condition as that of their neighbours. It was made of sheets of bamboo, supported by wooden stakes. The floor was of mud and the roof was covered with plastic. Outside, on the dusty street, was a pile of red bricks, that familiar sign of hope for the future.

It was evening when we knocked on their door. Antonia politely invited us in. Andrés was slouched on a time-worn armchair, resting after his day at the textile factory. In one corner, the children were playing, sitting on a piece of fabric. Its eye-catching, bright colours, typical of those woven in the *sierra*, stood out in the Spartan surroundings.

Sitting around the table, we had briefly explained who we were and the purpose of our visit. As Antonia got up to make some coffee, she turned to Carmen:

'Priests in parishes would be better able to understand the people, if they were married. Bringing up their own families, they would be closer to the people and their problems.'

'And then, what they would have to say to us in church, would strike a chord. It would tie in with our daily experiences, and not sound like something up in the sky. But, don't get me going on this topic – I could go on all night,' Carmen added.

On a more serious note, Andrés intervened:

'You should know we have seen students, and other people, come and offer to help with this and that. Then, before we knew, they were gone. People are sceptical about offers of help.'

'On that score, Andres, you need not worry. We intend to stay around. We've come to live in the area and to try to help as long as we can be useful.'

'What do you think you can help with?'

'Well, that depends on what you think is needed. We are open to any ideas you may have.'

Antonia was quick with her suggestion:

'I would love to see a women's group here, where we can learn different manual skills and also study some things. We could meet here in our humble home in the afternoons.'

'I would be happy to help you out, Antonia. That's what I have some experience at,' Carmen said, barely concealing her excitement.

'We also need to do something for the youth. There is nothing here for them, except kick ball on the plaza,' Andrés added.

'Well that is something I would like to be involved in. I have worked quite a bit with young people. And how about doing something in the barrio with the leaders?' I asked.

'Better to go slowly. That is more complicated. Once they see some of the other work being done, they will be more open to suggestions,'

We would have more coffee and chat about our children; Kathy and Patty were the same age and would have to meet soon.

'Our home is your home too. Why not drop by on Sunday afternoon?' was Carmen's spontaneous suggestion.

Night had fallen as we made our way through the dimly-lit *barrio* and across the railway line on our way home. Street lighting, here and there, was poached from the electric poles that bordered the factories. We were relaxed and buoyed up. It was to be the beginning of a new commitment and a special friendship.

Another important figure we had to meet in the *barrio* was Amanda. She was feared by some and respected by most. Though only in her forties, her face was drawn and weather-beaten. Her pronounced chin, combined with the ever-present cigarette between her lips, and the easy ability to express her opinions forcefully, even in awkward situations, all projected an air of inner strength and wisdom.

Her life had been anything but easy. Widowed when her three children were small, she had devised ways to make ends meet, preparing lunch for workers at one of the factories, and washing clothes. She had done a good job: the two girls and one boy had finished secondary school. Immediately, they had set about supplementing the family income and relieving the burden on their mother.

Of late, she had been able to dedicate more time to her passion, being part of the struggle to improve living conditions in the *barrio*. As yet, there were no basic services. She was a leader of her own neighbourhood committee, and also part of the leaders' team that represented the central organisation.

When we spoke to her about the idea of working with children and youth, she was excited, and didn't have to think much about what to say next:

'That is such a good idea. You know, we do our best, but we never get around to doing something for the youth and the children. All our efforts are focussed on what we call the "bigger problems", like, getting water, light and sewerage. Look, I want to offer my place for your meetings and activities. This whole area here and behind those curtains, we hardly use.'

'That would be great, Amanda, but are you sure it wouldn't be too much of an intrusion in your home?'

'Not at all, it's too quiet around here anyway and I know the girls and my son will love it and want to get involved too.'

'What do you think, Amanda, is the best way to get the word out?'

'You can't beat fliers, you know.'

'Ok, we'll talk to Paulina, in the parish office, to get them printed.'

There and then, we worked on the wording for the text. She was keen to emphasise that it would be an opportunity for the children and youth to get 'Education for Life'.

'Parents always want their children to have a better preparation than they had,' she said. I could see that she was proud of the address, where the meetings would take place.

On hearing the news, my brother-in-law, Carli, was keen to work with the children. Having qualified as a primary teacher, he had gone on to study art at the university, and had experience in organising workshops on handcraft, music and dance. On Saturdays, he was to enthusiastically give of his time.

There was a bigger response than expected to the invitation. It was obvious that, what we were about to embark on, was going to mean a major intrusion on Amanda's family. Our project for the non-government organisation had been approved, and we were anxious to come to some fair arrangement.

'Amanda, things have gone faster and got bigger than we had expected,' Carmen said.

'Well, isn't that great news, just what we wanted? There is great excitement in the barrio and I'm not surprised with the response.'

'Yes, it's great to see the interest of the people, but we can't just come in and take over half your home. We need to come to some agreement.'

'You know me. I am a poor woman, but I want to do this for my *barrio*.'

'We know that, and greatly appreciate your generous offer and commitment, but Luke and I have to do the right thing. We have a small fund, and with that we were thinking of removing the bamboo sheets, putting down cement foundations and a floor, and building a wooden room.'

'Oh, Carmen, when I offered a place for the meetings, that never came into my mind.'

'We know it didn't, but it is only fair and right. We insist.'

The brave widow sobbed and they both hugged.

'God has strange ways,' she murmured to herself, as she rose to make a cup of coffee.

When in the clerical priesthood, from early on, I had learned to be mindful of the danger of creating, or deepening, an attitude of dependence when working with the poor. I had resisted the temptation to build or give handouts. The *gringo* priest, especially, was easily perceived as someone who had access to money and important contacts.

Maybe I had been a bit too careful at times. But looking back, I have no recollection of ever getting a hint that my aversion to handing out money was being held against me.

On this occasion, outside the clerical ranks, we had had a frank discussion with Amanda and felt that our agreement had left her dignity untouched.

We had begun to meet with a small group of leaders that Andrés had got together. From the outset, one could see how important an event the foundation or 'invasion' of the *barrio* had been for all of them. It had not only built a strong bond, but it was an indelible experience. I began to think of how we might recreate it.

Quite by chance, I had become interested in the use of video as a tool for popular education. I had been teaching English to a small group before they started work in the morning. They were members of a Centre of Services for Peasant Farmers, CESPAC, and were already using video, bringing technical courses to peasants. All were fervent advocates of this new tool. I could see a very different use for it. When I heard they were organising a course on video production Carmen and I availed of the opportunity.

It was there we were to meet Miguel, a Spaniard from Mallorca. He had left the clerical priesthood some years earlier, after working many years in the highlands, and had married Emilia, Emi to us. He had an arts degree from his seminary studies and had recently finished his M.A. in film production.

We quickly became friends with this tall, lanky man, whose enthusiasm was contagious. He was collaborating on the production of a film that was soon to finish and he was looking at the possibilities of video.

'Here we are Miguel, without even a video camera, and there is a programme that is crying out to be made, right now!'

'What is it? Tell me. We might be able to get the loan of a camera and I'm sure our friends in Cespac would lend us a hand to edit it.'

'Well, as you know we are working in Villa Señor de los Milagros and the memory of the "invasion" is very vivid and fresh. We have been talking to the leaders and they recall that night, and the following days, all the time. I am sure they would be delighted to re-enact the experience.'

'I am excited already,' Miguel said, as he began to jot a few ideas on a piece of paper.

The leaders were thrilled at the prospect of recording this special part of their history. There wasn't much free space in the barrio, except for the plaza. But they were adamant. It would have to be filmed near the railway line. It was from the other side of that line that the most serious challenge to the success of the whole venture had come. That whole weekend they had to withstand and fight off the efforts of the police to dislodge them. The police station was less than ten blocks away in Carmen de la Legua.

Miguel's more expert eye had calculated that the long strip of ground alongside the railway line would be adequate. For the purpose of the documentary, we needed about twenty bamboo huts to be set up.

Excitement ran high, as that Saturday afternoon drew to a close, and the time of filming came with the dusk. As if repeating a well-known routine, the 'actors' got to work. There were even a few off-duty policemen, residents in the *barrio*, who were on hand to pursue the 'invaders'.

We filmed the 'invaders' arrival, loaded down with sheets of bamboo matting and stakes. They set to work erecting their huts in haste, while their look-outs manned strategic positions. The inevitable clashes with the police were taken seriously by all participants.

There were no special effects, just black and white images, a simple recording of a momentous time in the lives of the people. But, when edited, they were never to tire of watching it. From one neighbourhood block to the next, and even out in the plaza, it held the audiences captive. They seemed to be reflecting proudly, and repeating quietly to themselves, 'We actually did all that!'

There would be no question of video replacing the proven method of awareness-raising, which many of us had been using to educate the poor. 'Formation through Action', where reflection on situations and problems from their own lives led to action and to more reflection, was the path. Nevertheless, the experience of that first little documentary, re-enacting the invasion that had led to yet another *barrio* being formed, served to convince us that video could indeed be an invaluable aid and stimulus in the process of popular education. We had witnessed its impact first hand.

The saying, 'a picture is worth a thousand words' rang true, especially when the images were from the people's own reality, and they were accompanied by the familiar sounds and voices from the *barrios*. We could see an important role in popular education for programmes that portrayed the lives, living conditions, community efforts and mobilisations of the poor.

In documentaries like the above, the poor could be shown in a totally new light – as actors and agents of their own history, breaking the political and economic marginalisation of centuries. About a year later, we were to get the opportunity to make a contribution in this area of popular education.

The poor had indeed begun their struggle for liberation, but it was about to get much more complicated than any of us could have imagined.

As the second phase of the military government rolled back on the reforms of the Velasco regime, the Peruvian economy went from bad to much worse. By 1978 inflation was over 70 per cent. There were several huge devaluations and real income for the poor fell by 50 per cent. It was a time of unprecedented mobilisation of the poor by the Left. As marches and strikes increased, curfew was regularly imposed from evening to early morning.

The atmosphere was tense and the risk, for the leaders, was constant. On the eve of a general strike, or an important march, they disregarded curfew and marched around the *barrio*, rallying their neighbours for the next day's protest marches.

Personally, it wasn't easy for me to know when, and how much, to get involved. The people understood this and were protective of the *gringo*. Nevertheless, on a few occasions, I did have the odd close shave. These, in a small way, allowed me to experience something of the risk-taking and danger which at that time were an almost routine experience for the poor.

One evening I had joined in the march through the *barrio*. It was the eve of a general strike, and we were chanting slogans like, 'Down with the dictatorship!' and 'General strike tomorrow!'

Suddenly, we were scattering in different directions, the police hot on our heels. Two women grabbed me by the arms and whisked me through a half-opened door. Breathing heavily, we watched through the chinks in the bamboo matting as the po-

lice, with their batons drawn, raced by. Two seasoned campaign-
ers, Antonia and Julia, had got me to safety.

'That was close enough,' I ventured.

'We have to keep a few steps ahead of these guys, you know,'
Julia winked at me, before turning towards the family members,
whose presence I hadn't noticed until then.

'Good night Don Julio and family, we are sorry for coming in
like this, unannounced.'

'No problem at all, you are always welcome, especially if it's
an emergency!'

During this turbulent time, just before we moved to Carmen
de la Legua, Olga and Esther, who had worked with us in Chimbote, had returned to Lima. Both girls had become close friends
and were looking for jobs, preferably related to work with the
poor.

Shortly after her return to Lima, Olga had come to visit us.
We lived on the ground floor, at the back of a block of flats. She
had come on a motor bike and had pushed it down the passage
way to our door. When I opened, there she was, her slight figure seeming an unequal match for the impressive motor cycle
at her side. After manoeuvring it through the doorway, we left it
against a wall in the sitting room, where it dwarfed my modest
machine.

'Compañera,' I said, 'they'll surely see you coming on this
one.'

'That's the general idea, my friend; one has to stand out.'

'Can you manage it alright? I mean, is it easy to drive?'

'Not a bother. The only problem I have is putting it on its
legs. It is heavy.'

She was the same girl – wide-eyed, with a contagious laugh.
After playing a while with Kathy, we had a bite to eat and a long
chat but she was asking most of the questions.

We had joined a small left-wing political party, made up of
people who had been working for some years in popular education in the *barrios*. She was interested. After she decided to
join, we met up at seminars also. Luckily, she had got a job in

a Department of Education literacy programme, and would be working in the northern sector.

One evening she visited us and I remember that she was her usual cheerful and positive self. Things were working out as she had hoped and she was relaxed. Out on the sidewalk, before she departed I had helped her ease the bike onto the street.

'That is the only part that I still have trouble with but we're getting there. Until the victory, compañero,' she had blurted out.

With that mischievous smile visible in the poorly-lit street, she revved up the engine.

'Adios compañera,' I had said, and she disappeared into the night.

On the following afternoon, we got a phone call from the Columban centre house. There was terrible news. Olga was dead.

With her companion and friend Esther on the pillion seat, she had paused at a crossing of the notoriously dangerous Pan-American Highway near Sol de Oro. My recollection is that there were no traffic lights there at that time. Then she had attempted to cross, and was hit by a car. She was killed instantly.

Esther was thrown off and, incredibly, walked away with little physical injury, only some light scratches. Her emotional wounds must have been unspeakably deep. She would however recover and continue her journey. On two occasions, in the 1980s, she was to be elected mayor of the sprawling, densely populated district of Independencia, where she had been born, reared and been a member of a parish group. This was an impressive step forward. When we first started to work in the *barrios* it was customary for an 'influential' person from the wealthy sector of the city to be chosen as mayor – it always had to be a man.

Olga's mother and sister must have found it difficult most of the time, and sometimes impossible, to keep up with, or understand, the pace and direction of her life. But they must surely have been greatly comforted, and surprised, on witnessing the size of the crowd that came to say their final farewell.

The funeral took place in her parish of Holy Cross, where I had first got to know her as a member of the catechist group. It was an honour to be asked to speak at the Mass.

Life is never simple, never just black or white. In spite of my radical opposition to the autocratic clerical institution, I felt the need for a simple Church. One that was close to the people, that didn't need power and control in order to spread the simple message of Jesus – love, solidarity and justice. We needed a Church like that as we journeyed through life, especially to celebrate the big moments such as birth, marriage – and death.

In my reflection at the Mass, I tried to pierce the dark cloud of gloom and desolation that hung over us all, in the only way I knew how – remembering her.

Olga had been snatched from our midst in her mid-twenties. But she had inspired very many people, and would continue to do so. The good she had done could not be measured by the length of time she had been amongst us.

As Carmen and I settled into our new surroundings and work in Carmen de la Legua, we were aware that Peru was passing through a crucial period in its history. The Left, though splintered, was a powerful force and was bringing the cause of the poor into the national political scene.

At that time, insecurity about the future was constantly at the back of people's minds. But life would go on. The poor struggled and raised their families. With quiet enthusiasm, we too set about balancing the raising of our young family with our commitment alongside the poor. Fortunately, none of us could have foreseen how drastically the sociopolitical situation in the country was to change for the worse in the coming years.

Though Olga's untimely passing was a heavy blow for us, once again death was tempered by a new life soon to be born. Carmen had followed her new doctor's advice and her pregnancy had been free of any serious problems. Our first son, William, was about to be born.

His birth started early in the morning, with a rush to the hospital: Carmen was already in labour. It was to be an anxious and long, drawn-out day. The doctor had come to the waiting room a few times to say they were still expecting a natural birth. But the day dragged on and now it was after visiting hours.

Out in the car park, I paced back and forth, looking up at a window on one of the top floors of the impressive Hospital del Empleado building. Carmen had been asked to walk the corridor and, from time to time, would wave to me.

Darkness had long fallen when one of the security personnel came to tell me that the doctor had come down to the ground floor and wanted to talk to me. All day, while attending his other duties, he had kept a close eye on my wife. Now, this dedicated professional, in his mid-forties, looked drained. He pulled off his glasses and wiped his wrinkled brow:

'You have a healthy baby boy. But your wife has sure made us sweat and wait!'

'She wanted to have a natural birth, so much.'

'Yes, she did; all day she persisted in her determination. I too was in agreement with her: a caesarean should not be performed unless it is necessary. But as the evening wore on, I realised that we just had to proceed.'

'What a relief.'

'And for me too,' he said.

In typical Peruvian fashion, we embraced, he, surely feeling professional satisfaction with the final outcome, and I immensely grateful to him and to the God of life.

There were nearly five years between our two children. Kathy had been at the centre of the family for all that time, and we were aware she could have feelings of being displaced. But, from the time she could make her wishes known, she was showing an independent streak.

Like she had done that morning, when we left her at the play school for the first time. The place was alive with the buzz of busy toddlers. Our baby, holding her lunch box, stood for a moment looking on. Then she turned to both of us, waved and took the teacher's hand to walk into her new world. As we watched for a while through a window, she was soon fully engaged. She had left us, just like that!

'Will she be alright? I can't believe she went in there so easily,' Carmen wondered.

'A lot of kids do cry, I know, but Kathy doesn't need to cry. You can see she is joining in already.'

'It's just that she has surprised me. I wasn't expecting that.'

We should not have been surprised. By the time she was three, she was asking to go to stay the night with her aunties. She would have packed her bag with pyjamas and a few toys and be waiting to be brought over. Her parents were always left a little perplexed – mostly surprised and happy to see she felt secure, but also perhaps a bit taken aback by her independent spirit.

She was very caring with her baby brother, and as the months went by played with him, bringing out some of her old toys and games. Of course, he got bored at times. We still have a few minutes of video, which causes her some embarrassment, and all of us, much merriment. She appears giving out to him for prematurely breaking up a jig-saw puzzle they were playing at. Her reprimand ends with a slight tap on his hand.

Willie was not yet a year old, when we travelled to Cajamarca, at that time a sixteen hour plus bus journey, into the *sierra*. We had gone at the invitation of John, an English volunteer priest who had worked with the Columbans in Lima. He had come to El Montón, for a few months, while I was there.

Ever the adventurer, while in the parish, he had taken on a night job in a bakery in the *barrio*. He came home each morning, totally white with flour.

'I want to experience what the conditions of the workers are like,' he said.

Afterwards, he had invited us to go to Cajamarca, where he was enthusiastically involved in a new project setting up libraries in the far-flung and isolated villages of the diocese. He had produced booklets full of drawings that related to the experiences of the peasants. They were to be used in adult literacy classes. He had hoped to persuade us to join him, but it was not the right moment. We were already committed.

Our visit coincided with the dry season and, as we made our way home, we were constantly surrounded by a cloud of dust, some of which got into the bus.

The morning after our arrival back in Lima, I had an English class with my friends from Cespac. Before we started, Manuel felt compelled to tell us of his ordeal the previous night.

'I am absolutely drained this morning, guys.'

'Why, what happened?'

'Well, Maria and I were awakened around 2.00 am by cries coming from Manolo's room. He has just gone two and is a healthy child. When I went to his room, he could barely breathe. For a while, we thought it would pass and Maria rubbed stuff on his chest. But he only got worse and we knew we had to get him to the hospital. Boy, were we lucky! The doctor said we had got there in the nick of time. They were able to ease his breathing after a few hours.'

'What did they say he had?'

'The doctor said it was the croup disease, a serious inflammation of the larynx and trachea. It's a bug that children pick up and some get it worse than others. I had never heard of it. But what I do want to say lads is this – if it happens to any of your children, and it's a bad dose, don't wait around. Get to the hospital as fast as you can.'

It was after eleven, that very night, when I went to have a last look-in at Willie. To my horror, I found him already turned purple and unable to cry or scream. I hadn't yet told Carmen about Manuel's saga, but my mind was already programmed.

'Love, we have to leave for the clinic now, right now. Get your coat.'

She was a staunch believer in herbal remedies, and was probably considering that route, but it must have been the urgency in my voice that told her we were in a real emergency. She had her baby in her arms in a moment and we were on our way.

About ten blocks from our house, nestled by the side of the busy airport road, was a small clinic, *San José*. It had been founded by a group of missionary sisters. If it were still open, it would be our first port of call. We were to be so lucky!

Although, at that time, it was no more than a modest primary health care centre, it proved, literally, to be our baby's lifesaver. He was quickly given an injection that helped him survive until we reached the hospital in the port of Callao.

There we kept vigil by his bedside through the night. His little frame, criss-crossed with tubes, was tense and silent. Then, as dawn broke, I was to witness something magical. A broad, relaxed smile came over his face, and I knew he was telling me, 'Dad, I'm getting better.'

I carried that smile out onto the corridor, where Carmen and her Dad were waiting. Not a word needed to be spoken. In joy and relief they hurried in to witness for themselves, while I walked the corridor, in silent gratitude for the remarkable and uncanny coincidences of that special day.

The little clinic, by the airport road, has survived the vicissitudes of life in the capital and has expanded to become a hospital. But, for me, it remains suspended in time, as that lone outpost, bravely committed to saving the lives of the poor, and where our son was given that second chance.

Willie had recovered from his brush with croup and was a few months away from his second birthday, when his brother Anthony, our third and last child, was born. His birth took place without the commotion of previous occasions. Carmen had had a good pregnancy and was able to work right up until the end.

She was very relaxed as we entered the clinic, her confidence undoubtedly boosted by the knowledge that her fond cousin, Máximo, recently graduated as a medical doctor, would be at her side too.

The small clinic was an old building, built of adobe, but without the hustle and bustle of the big hospitals. Maybe it had an affect on mother and child: our new arrival was relaxed and at ease. We named him after my brother Liam's son.

Back home in Carmen de la Legua, as the children grew up, both of us were able to continue our commitment, due in great part to the fact that we had help from family, and from Nelly and her sisters. What the latter earned was useful to help further their education. But for Carmen and me their help was simply invaluable.

15.

A Time of Conflict and Violence

AT THE END OF THE 1970s and right through the 1980s there was feverish activity by the left-wing parties. They were organising and mobilising the poor in the *sierra* and in the *barrios*. In addition, they concentrated their efforts among workers, teachers and students.

Besieged by strikes and marches, and struggling with an economy in deep crisis, the then right-wing military junta called elections to draft a new Constitution. Though competing against one another, the combined left vote was a third of the total. This was an impressive achievement.

For someone like myself, whose experience had been mainly in the much slower process of popular education, the speed of events was dizzying, and at the same time exhilarating. On the one hand, the space and time for popular education had been reduced, squeezed out by the urgency of events. However, there was no denying the fact that the marching poor were expressing their demands on a new scale, and going through a hugely important experience.

But we knew that all was not well. There were serious questions that would have to be addressed. How could a divided Left hope to represent the very different social movements in such a geographically vast and varied country, where cultures, races, and needs were all so different? Could the leaders relinquish dogmatic party positions, assume the culture, demands and grievances of these social movements, and really continue to influence them in the following years?

At the end of 1980 the United Left had been formed as an electoral front. It incorporated all the main left-leaning parties engaged in the democratic process.

This was undoubtedly a step in the right direction, and I can remember the widespread excitement and hope it had generated. Most parties on the Left subscribed to the central point made by the great Jose Carlos Mariategui, founder of the Peruvian Socialist party in 1929, namely, that the Left must create a united front, which could embrace and mobilise the majority of the exploited people in the whole country. How each party, and the united front as a whole, would interpret and try to implement this goal was to be tested for the rest of the decade.

A few years later, I had a chance to observe, from a discreet distance, the internal workings of the United Left. It was the occasion of the formation of the Federation of Young Towns, or *barrios*. The event was held one weekend, in one of the oldest *barrios* in the Northern Sector, *El Ermitaño*. Understandably, security was tight, as delegates from the *barrios* and party leaders held discussions behind closed doors. These continued long into the night.

Carmen and I, as well as other people from the *barrios*, had come along, bringing coffee and sandwiches for the participants. It was a long wait, only broken every now and then by the sight of party leaders leaving the premises. In small groups they huddled in the dim light of the lamp post and engaged in animated discussion.

What were they discussing? Were they cutting a deal, out of the sight of delegates? It certainly seemed so. Old habits were hard to break. As the decade went by, and ever afterwards, the image of the huddled leaders came to symbolise in my mind an essential malaise at the heart of the United Left.

When the event ended, the small delegation from our political party was happy. Andrés from Villa Lord of the Miracles had been designated as the new Secretary General of the Western Sector. It was very late, and we were all drained. But the occasion, and the moment, needed to be savoured.

We arrived back in the *barrio* to hold our modest celebration with Antonia and the girls. Bleary-eyed, Ronald, our irrepressible party leader, raised his glass:

'To your health, companions. It was a good night's work, don't you think?'

'Sure, companion. How it will work out, well that's for another day!' Andrés managed to say.

With that, both men, worn out but content, threw themselves on the bed behind the curtain. As we continued to chat, I could hear Ronald, humming himself to sleep, with a few verses of that haunting anthem:

> Rich mountains, beautiful lands, smiling beaches; that's my Peru.

As well as witnessing the formation of the United Left, 1980 also saw two other organisations enter the fray. Both, though very different, espoused the armed struggle.

I cannot recall my friends in the Left, or in the *barrios*, being very surprised, or indeed attaching any great importance to the news. I think the attitude was that anything was possible in the country during those years. The poverty and frustration of the poor in the *sierra* had even increased, after the failure of the agrarian reform.

It was in the poorest parts of the highlands that an offshoot of the Maoist Communist Party of Peru had been gaining followers. It was founded by Abimael Guzman, a philosophy professor in the University of Huamanga, in Ayacucho.

Better known as *Sendero Luminoso*, or Shining Path, it had preached its violent revolution among students all through the 1970s, and had quietly gained control of student councils in several universities in the sierra and in Lima.

This military-style organisation, which had no interest in any kind of democratic politics, had ironically taken its name from a maxim of Mariategui's, the man whose idea of revolution was based on the formation of a broad political front: 'Marxism-Leninism will open the shining path to the revolution.'

On the eve of the general election, in 1980, *Sendero Luminoso* declared the start of its 'armed struggle', by burning the ballot boxes in a town in the *sierra*. This act passed without attracting much attention, but soon the whole country woke up to a continually worsening nightmare.

The bourgeois state had to be taken down totally according to Guzman. He had said that 'the triumph of the revolution will cost a million lives'. The plan was to destroy state institutions, and those who represented them, and build anew. All who were seen to stand in the way would be eliminated.

Daily, the news came in of the assassination of police, members of left-wing parties, teachers, and landowners. Public buildings were destroyed. Trials were held in the public places, and unpopular local figures were executed there and then.

Due to the weak, or negligible, presence of the state, *Sendero Luminoso* was seen to provide some kind of popular justice and, in those early days, it had some support in the local peasant communities. Quickly, the organisation's influence extended across the three poorest departments of Ayacucho, Apurimac and Huancavelica.

Belaunde, who had been ousted by the military coup in 1968, had been elected President, for a second term (1980-'85), after eleven years of military rule. He was reluctant to hand over control of the conflict zone to the armed forces. However, by December 1981, he was obliged to declare a 'state of emergency'.

The army was given a free rein to deal with the insurrection and the conflict got dirtier by the day. The victims of the slaughter were the poor, utilised by, and caught between, the two forces.

Over 7,000 Defence Committees, in the *sierra*, were trained and armed by the military and would have an important part to play in the final defeat of the insurgents.

Massacres of villagers, committed by both sides, took place, with numbing frequency for the rest of the decade and beyond. Their only crime: being suspected of supporting the other side.

Alan Garcia became President (1985-90). After a promising start, showmanship and mis-management of the economy led to hyperinflation, and the internal war intensified alarmingly.

There was to be no respite for Peru, and especially not for the poor. An almost unknown figure, Alberto Fujimori, won the election in 1990. He quickly carried out a 'self-coup', with the support of the military. With the democratic institutions suspended, he proceeded to implement wide-ranging neoliberal policies – he removed price controls, sold off hundreds of state companies, greatly reduced government restrictions on capital flow and investment, and over-rode workers' hard won rights, among many others. The IMF was impressed and guaranteed loans. The economy grew. But at the centre of the regime there was a terminal cancer – corruption on an unprecedented scale.

In 2003 Peru had started to recover from the scars of the internal conflict and the soul-destroying effects of the most corrupt regime in its history – the ten years that Fujimori was President (1990-2000). The fondly-remembered interim government, headed by Valentín Paniagua, had set up a Truth and Reconciliation Commission. It reported that 69,280 people had been killed or disappeared in the 20-year conflict, about half of them by the *Sendero Luminoso* and a third by the military.

The same Commission found that the other organisation involved in the war, the Revolutionary Movement Tupac Amaru, was responsible for about 1.5 per cent of those deaths.

By 1983 *Sendero Luminoso* was active in the capital. Its members targeted electricity power stations, and large-scale blackouts became part of our lives. The kerosene lamps had to be always at the ready. Attacks on police stations were frequent and many of them were barricaded and roads closed off. Public buildings were also targeted.

Due to the work done in the previous decades by the Left, Church organisations, and NGOs, *Sendero Luminoso* followers did not easily get a foothold in the *barrios*. But we knew they were there in the shadows.

It was an eerie feeling to be working in a situation where there was no minimum trust, no basic rules which could help us predict their next move. At any moment, and for any reason, one could be seen as an obstacle to be removed.

It was not easy to talk about our feelings then. I didn't, neither did my close friends. We were all trying to cope, living close-up with terrorism.

About four blocks from Andrés and Antonia's house lived Juana with her two young boys. She kept food on the table by preparing and bringing lunches to workers at nearby factories.

Juana's out-going, trusting nature made her popular in the *barrio*. She was a regular participant in one of the women's clubs. Though she joined in protests and marches, she did not appear to have much understanding of the party-political scene. So it was a big surprise when we heard that meetings were being held in her house and that perhaps *Sendero Luminoso* was involved.

Some years later, as the conflict raged, she was arrested. When we visited her in the women's prison in Chorrillos, she held herself with dignity and was stoically serving her sentence. Undoubtedly, the recent decades of brutally-dashed hopes had deeply influenced her. This proud migrant from the Andes, like many more poor people, was receptive to the radical fire and brimstone rhetoric of *Sendero Luminoso*.

The dirty war between Sendero Luminoso and the military brought us face to face with a depravity and an inhumanity that were dumbfounding. The former cut out their victims' tongues and, after killing them, forbid the villagers to bury the corpses. The army practiced systematic torture and mass assassinations, such as that in the Andean village of Accomarca. There they rounded up the women, children and elderly men. After being kicked and abused, they were put into houses, shot and burnt to death.

One episode stands out for me as epitomising the frightening lack of respect for human life in those years. Joan was a Columban Sister who worked four days a week at the Lurigancho prison, bringing words of comfort, medicines, and news of their legal papers to the prisoners. Over 5,000 men were being held there, in the worst conditions. Only 1,000 had been sentenced. The others had been waiting for years, without ever being charged.

One morning, Joan and three of her co-workers were taken hostage. The prisoners were demanding better living conditions. Negotiations with the prison authorities went on all day, and in the evening they were given an ambulance in which to leave.

They had barely left the prison when the ambulance was ambushed by the police. It was riddled with bullets. The scene of the massacre was not far from the city centre and very quickly a television crew was at the scene.

Later, the TV station showed the footage many times, burning into our memories the sheer depth of the inhumanity of what we were watching. The police dragged the limp, dead and dying bodies from the ambulance. Over the dusty road they pulled them. They proceeded to pile them on top of one another in a heap. Some were still clearly breathing.

Sr. Joan and the eight prisoners were later declared dead. But the slight, brave nun, in her selfless service of those without any rights, would light a permanent flame of hope.

It wasn't my good fortune to have served in parishes where nuns worked. The Sisters of St. Columban, and other congregations of sisters, had come to live and work in some Columban-run parishes. I was keenly aware of their important contribution to the process of liberation of the people in the *barrios*. They too had their heated discussions over pastoral approaches. From the outside at least, they seemed to manage them most often by allowing individuals to follow their preferred line of commitment.

In spite of the fear and insecurity that was all-pervasive at that time, hundreds of lay people, accompanied by nuns and priests, carried Sr. Joan's coffin from the church in Independencia. They did so for the whole 14 kilometres, to the cemetery El Angel, on the other side of the city. Today, a tall wooden cross stands at the spot by the roadside. It bears the inscription: 'You Shall Not Kill.' It is the focal point where Christian communities gather regularly, to remember, and to highlight, human rights issues of the moment.

As the crowd accompanied Sr. Joan's remains, police had lined the route at different points. Many must have hung their heads in shame. They were poorly paid and, though a reputation for bribery was often levelled at the force, we knew scores of ordinary policemen in the *barrios* who did not fit that image. There, they brought up their young families. Some did keep to themselves, while others took an active part in community activities.

One such 'ordinary' policeman who played an active part in the community was Wendy. We got to know and become friends with him, his wife Nelly and their three boys in Carmen de la Legua. A gentle person, and kind by nature, he was from the jungle area of the country. Nelly, a vivacious woman, was from the coast.

It was late morning and we were finishing up at the market, when over the loudspeakers we heard the news:

'Did you hear that?' I blurted out to Carmen, laying down the shopping bag.

'My God, that has to be our Wendy; did you hear the last name?'

Wendy had been shot several times, at close range, and his automatic rifle stolen, while on duty outside the Bolivian Embassy. His life hung by a thread for well over a week, but miraculously he did recover and was able to do office work at the station until retirement. Never once, at the time or afterwards, had I heard a complaint, or a hint of harboured vengeance, from this ordinary 'man on the beat'.

During those years of mindless violence the whole country was gripped by fear. The upper classes coped by putting up defence systems around their homes. Their company premises were especially protected. The poor had no such defences. They suffered the most. For apart from being exposed to the violence and destruction it was a time of huge unemployment, food shortages and rising prices. Still, we picked up no sense of despondency in the *barrios*. People lived in constant fear but were managing to cope – this nightmare time too would pass.

Walking along Abancay Avenue, in the city centre, I bumped into Miguel, that confidence-exuding boss of the Columbans when I first arrived in Peru. As usual, when out and about he was dressed in full clerical garb. Standing tall and straight, he was still that imposing figure who, a quarter of a century earlier, had unrestricted access to the presidential palace.

'Let's go for a cup of coffee, we haven't met for a while,' he said as he scanned the sidewalk, teeming with people. There was no shortage of places but he brought me to Plaza San Martin, where it was quieter and more relaxed

Sitting by a window, looking out on the plaza, we began to catch up. I was keenly aware of how his world had been turned upside-down. The Church he once knew, and the country he once thought he knew, were no more. Both were going through huge upheavals.

At the height of the internal struggle among the Columbans, his approach towards pastoral work had been severely criticised. As a natural leader, and one of the first to come to work in the new mission, his frustration and disappointment must have been severe.

From my own experience as a cleric, I think it would be unlikely that Miguel would have been able to talk to any of the other priests about his deep hurt. Nevertheless, on that morning, I saw a man who, somehow, had come through it, and could still smile, something that was by no means an automatic outcome.

Miguel read a lot, on both sides of the theological and pastoral divides. I remember being surprised one Christmas, when he had come to El Montón and given me a book about the struggle of the Palestinian people. He had just finished reading it and wanted me to do the same.

On this particular morning he was to surprise me once again. I felt he was genuinely interested in how we were doing as a family. He wanted to know how Carmen and each of the children were progressing. Then he asked me about our work.

I had presumed he would not be at all interested. On that level we shared little. My answer was vague but he was insisting and not interested in differences:

'I mean is there any project you would need help with? You know, in my opinion, what you and Carmen are doing is as good as anything we are doing within the Society.'

'Well, there is actually. Some time back, we took a course in video production, and we are very enthusiastic about the possibilities it has for popular education.'

'Great, why don't you put a project together and send it in to us? I will keep an eye on it.'

Looking back now, it seems a logical thing to have done, but in the early 1980s it was almost unthinkable for me. Even though the hard line of the official Church – 'You joined, you left, be gone' – had begun to change, I was unaware of any change.

Many years later, I learned that in 1978 a letter from the Sacred Congregation of Religious went out to all organisations, with a most surprising admonition. All were told that they had an obligation, based on 'charity, equity, justice and social responsibility', to look after those who had resigned. It specifically recommended that re-training be provided. Of course, it would typically take many decades for this recommendation to be implemented in any kind of meaningful way.

Within the Columban ranks in Lima, things were not static either. Peter, who together with Tom had given shelter and support in *El Templo* to the workers, had been elected Director. But I would not have approached him for support, thinking that it could cause him problems.

In hindsight, I was holding on to an assumption that the attitude of many Columbans in Lima towards someone like me was less than sympathetic. However, because of the large number who had left the clerical priesthood in a relatively short period most Columbans had to come to grips with the exodus, and the reality of seeing friends leaving.

At the top level of the Society, the number of 'defections' in Peru had caused alarm. For some years, they decided not to send any new personnel. It was considered too risky. Meanwhile, no real effort was made to meet and dialogue with those of us on the outside, or try to come to any shared understanding of what was involved in our leaving.

It would not have been an easy journey for either side, and would have brought up the arguments for and against reform of the Church structures and policies, thorny issues like the damaging effects of obligatory celibacy and the marginalisation of women were sure to be to the forefront. And the very nature of mission would have caused much debate: preaching and converting versus getting immersed in the new culture, listening and trying to see the signs of salvation already at work among the poor.

A couple of years back, at a St. Columban's Day gathering in the centre house, I was chatting to one of the priests who had been in Lima for many decades.

'You know, Luke,' he gestured with his can of beer, 'all of you guys who have left worked for a time with the people, but then you left. We are the ones who have stayed with the people and been faithful.'

'Well, my friend, I hear what you are saying, and it is admirable on one level. But being faithful is more than that. I should say, not as simple as that.'

'I don't get it, what do you mean?'

'Guys who have left are believers and faithful too. Every one of them, that I know, believes deeply in justice, fairness, solidarity and community. Each one, in his particular work situation and community, stands on the side of the weak. He tries to be faithful to these values, as best he can, wherever he may be. Isn't that what the message of Jesus is about, and what Christians are supposed to do?'

'Sure, that is what ordinary Christians are supposed to do. But I am talking about the priest's role and responsibility, something completely different.'

We did not get to finish the conversation on that occasion. It is probably an unrealistic expectation to hope that we could do better than 'agree to disagree'. The topic cuts to the heart of the debate on Church and the need for radical reform of the whole clerical structure.

From my friend's point of view, the priest's role was defined by being a member of the clergy. He belonged to that elite clerical institution which, in spite of lip-service given to the notion that we were 'all the people of God', in practice was, and also appeared to be, of another class. All the important decisions, including who should be ordained priests, were made exclusively by that institution.

For a good number of years in Lima, married men have been ordained deacons – the last step before priesthood. They are working in their own local communities and are liked and respected. Will they ever be ordained priests? Will their communities ever have a say in deciding who is to be their priest?

Meanwhile, some dioceses in England have a sizeable number of married clergy. The latter are former Anglican clergy who have joined the Catholic Church and been ordained again. They now work in parishes, living with their wives and children – a progressive step, one might think.

Of course, it is no such thing. They left the Anglican Church for reasons such as being against the ordination of women priests and the rights of gay people. How the Church, more precisely the Pope and the Vatican curia, can justify having one law for its new arrivals and another for its own clergy, only they know.

Our growing family, the work in the barrio and the video project, all kept us busy. My visits to the Columban centre house, and priest friends in the parishes, were fewer. We did meet up on St Patrick's Day and for the celebration of the feast of St Columban. From time to time former colleagues called by to visit us.

The whole context of work in the *barrios* had changed and got more complicated over the previous five years. From the high hopes and expectations of the Velasco years, to the about-turn and clamp-down of the Morales Bermudez regime. Now there were growing signs of a dirty internal war – the road ahead was uncertain and ominous.

Those Columbans who were trying, from within the Church structures, to raise awareness among the poor of their rights, and to contribute towards the broad movement for change, were going through a soul-searching time themselves.

While still in the clerical ranks I had often participated in sessions where we Columbans bonded, reflected on issues of the moment and generally relaxed over some beers. They have left me with precious memories. At times one or other of us overpassed the prudent alcohol limit but the others were there to look after him.

I fondly remember the evening three of my best friends and I went to *Alfredo's,* one of the numerous places then for roast chicken. After the meal and a few *pisco sours*, my friends considered it unwise for me to drive my scooter. They had come in a Volkswagen which had the engine at the back and boot out front. Without hesitation they lifted the bonnet and loaded the scooter. Of course this meant that the raised bonnet blocked any vision through the windscreen. Then the driver stuck his head out the window and the occupant of the passenger seat did likewise. It was near midnight and there was little traffic. We proceeded cautiously to *Plaza Union* and a whistle sounded. My driver friend respectfully greeted the policeman:

'*Mi guardia*, forgive me but we have a bit of an emergency. My friend has been celebrating his birthday and we're taking him back to the parish.'

He got an understanding smile from the custodian of order and an onward wave. The birthday fib had touched a Peruvian's heart.

Now as a married man I joined in the reunions less frequently and had begun to notice a change. Some people were more obviously struggling with personal problems, and there was less limitation on the amount of alcohol consumed.

I had known that a priest friend was going through a rough patch. However, it was a surprise when he came to our house one morning and asked if he could stay with us for a time. He was accompanied by a middle-aged nun, a woman of many talents. She was a qualified nurse before coming to the country, and had renewed her studies in Lima and re-validated her degree.

Never the one to avoid problems, this decisive mother figure had seen the need to take on a role which a bunch of men would be less likely to give serious attention to – she was a counsellor, and a firm voice of reason, at a time she judged that health of body or spirit were in danger.

We were sitting around the table in the kitchen. My friend was, as usual, having a cup of black coffee, and pulling on a cigarette. It was he who started the conversation.

'Great to see you guys. As you know, things haven't been going too smoothly for me of late. Most of the time, I feel I'm just "pulling the devil by the tail", and I need to take some time out to clear my head. Leaving Lima is not something I can think of right now. The place, where I would feel most at ease, is with you guys, if you would have me.'

'He really admires you both. We have been talking and have come up with the idea of building a little room on the roof, if that would be alright with you,' the nun explained.

'What are good friends for but to look after one another in times like these? We will be happy to have you with us, *amigo*, for as long as you wish,' Carmen said, as she nodded in my direction.

At that time, I did not see my friend as suffering from an addiction to alcohol. If he could work through his personal problems, I thought, the alcohol issue would go away. For a short time his drinking seemed to be under control. He was enjoying his independence. I often dropped into his room around mid-morning to find him engrossed in a book. Carmen's cooking was to his liking and often, after lunch, he played with our children in the back garden. He came and went as he wished.

My friend had never been a daily drinker, but rather someone who could go on a binge for four or five days at a time. Since coming to live with us, we had not witnessed anything like that. In fact, I would share a glass of beer with him now and again and that would be all. But the problem had not gone away.

One evening he came home, obviously having had more than a few drinks. We were watching television and, unwisely, I had joined him for what I thought was a last drink. There was no more in the fridge. It was after midnight and my friend was insisting that we go out and get more.

'No way, *mi amigo*. Every place is closed. That's it for tonight.'

'Ah, come on lad, just two more bottles!'

When I flatly refused, he replied, 'I'll just have to go on my own,' and began to make his way towards the door.

I could not let him out on his own and so I found myself by his side on the street. It was dark and back streets were poorly lit. What we were doing was neither safe nor rational: the danger of being assaulted late at night was well known. I accompanied him from street to street in his desperate search. Finally, he got a sleepy response, after knocking on yet another door. After some delay the wooden shutter on the window went up, and the deal was done.

As we made our way home, I remember how that up-close experience had given me a deeper insight into the addiction. In spite of the fact that he had already consumed more than enough, he could still sniff out the beer in those dark and unfamiliar surroundings. It would take more than the support of friends like us to break the stranglehold.

Nowadays, I sometimes think of the story that another mutual friend tells. He was a Columban, several years younger than *mi amigo,* and they were good friends. Around the same time both were having problems with drink. One day they decided they would beat it by going on their holidays together and helping one another to stay dry.

The plan was going well, drinking only soft drinks. Until the second day!

'We were in a little restaurant, going to have a bite of lunch. I went to the toilet, and when I came back to the table, my friend had two big bottles of beer sitting in front of us. Do you think I objected? Not likely. That was the end of that,' and he breaks into uncontrollable laughter.

Shortly after leaving our home, *mi amigo* went into rehab and less than a year later our mutual friend did the same. Both men joined Alcoholics Anonymous, that truly inspiring worldwide organisation, which helps so many back to life after addiction. Decades later, both have remained faithful participants in AA. One remained in the clerical priesthood, working with the poor, and the other left the clerical ranks to work with the marginalised and drug addicted as a social worker.

Revisiting that precious but uncertain time, when *mi amigo* lived with us, or earlier times, when I shared sessions with my Columban friends, I can easily become nostalgic. But likewise, my throat can get blocked up. I get to thinking about the frailty of human nature. And about how some of my best friends had the courage, and the necessary support, to enable them to ride out the storms. Through the darkest night, they made it safely to a new shore.

16.

APPROACHING THE ABYSS

FOLLOWING MY CONVERSATION with Miguel, we presented a project to the Columbans and it was promptly approved. That was another life-learning moment for me. My assumptions had been proved unfounded. As the lessons of life teach us, they almost always are. I was beginning to free myself of those awkward feelings of distrust and the judgemental attitude that had taken hold of me at the height of the internal dispute.

Those men on the 'other side' were decent people, who were stubbornly holding on to a vision of Church handed down and cemented by unquestioned loyalty.

I learned to meet them, accept them as they were, enjoy the chat, and avoid the controversial topics. There were other forums for those.

It was a path I tried to follow, not always successfully, within family circles and with friends too. From time to time, in different situations, I was to find myself pushing ideas on church and society, when it was neither the time nor the place. Sometimes, I became aware of my mistake, even if a little late. On others, when the situation became embarrassing, Carmen or one of the children might give me a discreet nudge.

We now had the basic video equipment to film and edit programmes. In spite of the deteriorating social and political situation, we were excited at the possibilities this new educational aid opened up.

There was no shortage of ideas as regards documentaries that could be made. Our plan was that the project would be self-supporting; we would be able to do some work, in the form of collaboration with the popular sectors, while some organisations could afford to pay a modest fee.

One of our first assignments was to make a documentary based on interviews we recorded at a 'Congress of Relatives of the Disappeared', held in Lima. In those years, in countries like Chile and Argentina, and in Central America, cruel military dictatorships had arrested, tortured and forcefully 'disappeared' thousands of mostly young men and women. Their only crime was suspicion of being communist subversives.

One of the most brutal practices was that carried out in Argentina under General Videla. Many were thrown from aircraft into the sea during night-time flights.

But the families and relatives of the victims, all over the continent, did not allow fear to stop them calling for justice for many years. In Buenos Aires, the Mothers of *Plaza de Mayo*, with their white head scarves, and carrying photos of their loved ones, marched silently around the plaza in front of the Presidential palace. They became a powerful symbol of heroism, around the world, and of an unquenchable resolve to get justice. They continued to do this, once a week, for over three decades.

For Miguel, my friend from Mallorca, and me, the moving testimonies of the relatives seemed to belong to far-away lands. We were, as yet, unaware that a similar situation to those being recounted so vividly was festering and brewing right under our feet. The dirty war had already begun in Peru.

Over a period of about seven years, we were to produce some forty programmes. Miguel taught me a lot. Working alongside him was the best possible way to learn both theory and practice. When he had to leave us, I was confident enough to carry on.

The making of one particular programme was to be an experience that started the shattering of a stubbornly-held dream.

Backed by the United Left coalition, Alfonso Barrantes had been elected Mayor of Lima in 1984. He was its first non-party, socialist mayor. One of the problems his administration had to contend with was the urgent need to find homes for the recently arrived poor. The internal war had displaced hundreds of thousands of peasants from the *sierra*. They came to cities along the coast, some 130,000 to Lima.

The Huaycan housing project was designed and executed by the Municipality, in coordination with a group of non-party socialists and with help from some NGOs. It was planned as a self-managing urban community and was modelled on the very successful experience of Villa El Salvador, on the south side of the capital.

The location chosen was some sixteen kilometres from the city, on the left side of the central highway and the river Rimac. It was an enormous gorge, full of rocks and sand, that stretched away back into the surrounding mountains.

The plan was for 15,000 plots in the first stage. Inscriptions of future members and associations had begun. As word got out, competition among political parties, but especially among those on the Left, became intense. *Sendero Luminoso* adopted a tactic of infiltration.

The goal of the founding members was to set up a model urban community. But to achieve this they needed to have an orderly occupation of the area. The organisers were not getting cooperation from some political organisations. So, with the backing of the Municipality, they had decided to occupy the gorge in order to prevent anarchic invasions.

A management committee, comprising the founders, and Eduardo, an architect from the Municipality, had been formed by municipal resolution. Security committees controlled the occupation and a soup kitchen was set up for each sector.

While organisations within the United Left wrestled with one another for control of different sectors, it appeared that the only ones who had a clear vision of what they wanted were *Sendero Luminoso* and the oldest right-wing party, APRA. The latter wanted to win the upcoming general election, while the former's aim was to surround Lima and recruit new members.

Shortly after the occupation began, I had been asked by Eduardo, the architect, to make a documentary on the project, and had begun to accompany him in the evenings to meetings of the new communal groups. There I shot the first scenes.

The energy and excitement was contagious, but the shadow of a darkening cloud was never far away. People were aware of a threat coming from another new settlement, just 500 metres to the west. It was there that members of a radical left-wing party held sway. They had refused to join the orderly occupation and were biding their time.

One Sunday morning, about a month after the occupation had begun, I made my way up the gorge, carrying the video recording equipment on my back and a tripod in my hand. I had arranged to record some interviews with leaders and new arrivals.

As I looked up the gorge, the activity at the entrance to the settlement was noticeable. It was not the usual gathering for a day of community work. There was a definite urgency in the air. Men had arrived in big numbers and had formed a long line. Drawing closer, I could see that they were armed with clubs and sticks.

One of the leaders approached, led me through the defence line, and a little way up the gorge to a 'safe house'. There I learned of the seriousness of the situation. An attack by the people from the neighbouring settlement was imminent. Their objective was to force their way in and take control of the whole project.

It was to be a long and indeed a sad day. Leaders came and, after hurried and hushed conversations, left the bamboo hut again. I felt the growing anxiety and knew that the attackers had arrived. Many were armed with guns and sticks of dynamite. There seemed to be little doubt about the inevitability of the outcome.

As the battle raged, I was worried for my safety, but most of all I felt swallowed up by a deep, all-pervading gloom. It came from the inescapable realisation of the enormous tragedy of what was happening. This was a nonsensical battle, where the poor were fighting one another, a battle where sectarianism was the driving force in an effort to impose the correctness of a particular political doctrine.

As the evening approached, incredibly, the shouting and shots diminished and quietened altogether. The democratic leaders of Huaycan could tell me that the threat had been withstood.

There were no celebrations, just a mixture of relief and worry on tired faces. I had suspected that *Sendero Luminoso* must have played a part in the unexpected turnaround of the situation. Only later did I learn that those brave men and women who held on to the dream of a new, democratic socialism had had no alternative but to accept military support from the afore-mentioned.

That support came at a cost: *Sendero Luminoso's* presence in the settlement was strengthened. Together with the APRA, they were to control the organising committee for the First Congress of Huaycan.

That day, which I had spent as a silent and shaken witness of the extremes to which dogmatic sectarianism could lead, had served me as a stark warning of the dangers ahead. In the following months, I often talked with friends, and debated with some party members, about that seemingly endemic flaw.

But the voices of reason were all too scarce back then. Only a few years later, the collapse of the communist system, as it was then, would crack the ingrained mindset. The Left, all over Latin America, was to learn a humbling lesson: only a coalition that genuinely tried to understand, value and represent the culture and interests of all the poor would get their support.

Coming in off the street, in those momentous times, I was always thankful that children could continue to be children. Our house in Carmen de la Legua echoed with the normal sounds of little children exploring their world, the cries of anguish after falls, the shouts of joy at play. They were reassuring sounds.

The bus route passed directly outside our door. It was a narrow street and unsafe for children to play on. There was no public park nearby but, like other children in the *barrio*, they made the most of the indoors, visiting back and forth with the children of friends.

Sometimes, I have wondered about how much of the tension of those years they picked up. Looking back at old photographs, I am reassured. Kathy, the big sister, was enjoying many special moments, as she watched her brothers grow from toddlers to mischievous playmates.

Birthdays were occasions to gather together family and friends. Carmen never seemed happier than when she was in the middle of a *fiesta* or party. Not one to shrink from social commitment, she instinctively realised that 'all work and no play' would not only make me a dull boy but a burnt-out one too. Once, at her own birthday party, when proposing a toast to the birthday girl, I had said that she had 'a party in her heart'.

Next day she happily reminded me of what I had said:

'A hooley in your heart actually sounds better,' I joked.

'What is that?' she laughed.

'Oh, that's what we used to call a lively party, when I was a lad. You know, with plenty of singing and dancing'.

'I just love that; a hooley in my heart!'

As the children were growing up, we had the usual passing moments of anxiety when they got ailments, such as measles and mumps. But Willie had a more serious health problem. Ever since his brush with croup disease, he had developed breathing problems. For a number of years his ailment was manageable with medication. He was about four and a half when his health began to deteriorate alarmingly.

Our paediatrician friend was affectionately known as *El Chato*, the Short One. He was a friend of Carmen's from her college days, and I had got to know him while we were in Chimbote. There he had cured me of a serious infection, the result of letting a cut, sustained on the hard, clay surface of the football pitch, go unattended.

He told us bluntly that our son's condition was getting worse. It could not be cured in the high humidity and contamination of our surroundings. What he needed was the dry air to be found along the Central Highway.

With mixed emotions we set off one day to look around. In the very next gorge to Huaycan, we saw a sign advertising houses. Life was dictating our path. Our son's health had to be given priority. The price of the house was affordable. We sold our place in Carmen de la Legua and moved.

The weeks before we left the *barrio* went by in a whirl. It wasn't what we'd had in mind. Our close friends in Villa Senor de los Milagros and Carmen de la Legua were aware of Willie's health problems. We had a simple get-together with them in the house. Amanda expressed the general sentiment in her usual, practical way, after a long pull on her cigarette:

'We won't see as much of you, but we know you will keep in touch. It's the dry air coming from the sierra that the boy needs. God speed to you.'

An immediate concern was where to locate the video studio. Carmen's uncle, Pedro, came to the rescue. The credit union he belonged to were looking to rent a few rooms. It was in the central district of Lince and suited our needs.

Our new home was perched on a terrace, half way up the next gorge to Huaycan. There was plenty to explore and the children made friends quickly. We had come with all the medication for our son, but after a few short weeks he would not need any of it again. Incredibly, he was keeping up with his siblings and the other children as they raced and chased around.

During the year we lived there permanently, Aunt Estela came to live with us for periods. Her support meant we could leave the two older children at a nearby school in the morning and travel to work in the city. We continued to keep in touch with friends in the *barrios,* continued our political participation and forged ahead with the production of video programmes. When our son's health had greatly improved we decided to move back to Lima, a few blocks away from the video studio.

Living amidst the tension of those years, we knew of socially committed couples that had run into 'difficulties' in their relationship. Indeed, some were close friends. Raising a young family and keeping food on the table, while maintaining a commitment to the cause of the poor, was a challenging balancing act. It was no less so for Carmen and me.

It was around this time that we had our first and only crisis as a couple. We had other 'moments' too, but more akin to the ups and downs of most marriages. Our disagreement ran deep and, for both of us, was rooted in our different personal experiences: they went back to our different childhood formation and culture.

Our children were being spoiled, I felt. Too much was being done for them, and they were not learning to do things for themselves. They were learning that there would always be someone there to pick up the pieces as they went through life – a path towards disaster, I thought. And, most times, when I tried to correct some misbehaviour, I found myself being told I was wrong.

It wasn't very difficult for me to see where my thinking and reactions were coming from. I had witnessed how my Dad, as I saw it, had unwittingly spoiled my brother Liam. This had made a lasting impression on me. My experience at secondary school, where corporal punishment was the norm, must have influenced my attitude too. And so must my time in the seminary, when a lot of the emphasis was on the acquiring of habits such as self-discipline and obedience.

But being more or less conscious of the experiences that lay behind my thinking only made it more difficult to see any shades of grey, or see any reason to change. Not before time, we sought help. Lila was a psychologist and counsellor, a person herself involved in social work with sufferers from AIDS, and other marginalised people.

We met her individually at first. After my third session, I can still hear my counsellor as she gently, but firmly, invited me to let down my defences.

'I have a good picture of the influences behind your thinking on how to bring up your children. They are real, but you must remember you were sent to boarding school at an early age and were away from your family practically all the time after that. Can you seriously claim to know all about child-rearing? I don't think so. Carmen has had a very different upbringing. She can't claim to know it all either. Luke, it's not a question of who is right. Neither one of you is completely right. What we need is to get both of you really listening to each other.'

With Lila's help, we would learn to walk the path of compromise. As we did so, each of us must have had to wince from time to time. I know I did. But, I was learning to appreciate my wife's vital contribution to the formation of character in our home, to appreciate that the rearing of children involved much more than discipline. It was about giving affection, paying attention and, above all, communicating.

Soul-revealing sincerity and the ability to compromise had enabled us to put our relationship on a sound footing once again. These were qualities that, in some basic degree, were going to be needed in a very different scenario soon. An historic event, the outcome of which would be crucial for the poor and indeed the country for years to come, was at hand.

In 1989 the First Congress of the United Left was held. Alfonso Barrantes, no longer Mayor of Lima, was the charismatic leader of a shaky alliance of left-wing parties. On that coalition a vast array of organisations representing the poor had pinned their hopes. If it could be held together, the alliance was expected to get around one-third of the vote in the first round of the upcoming general elections. That would probably have been sufficient to get its candidate into the final round of the Presidential race.

All through the 1980s, the Left had played an important role in advocating for the rights of the poor, and mobilising them in far-flung corners of the country. During those years, its popularity had increased to the highest level ever.

However, the flaw that had bedevilled it from the start still hung over the alliance. By far the biggest emphasis, for each political organisation, was on its own party. The organisations of the poor, and the wider social movements, were in a weak second place. Parties utilised them, instead of working with them, respecting their cultural differences and taking on board their most urgent needs.

Some weeks before the Congress, I was asked to do a video documentary on it. The request had come from Jorge Del Prado, the General Secretary of the Communist Party, originally called the Socialist Party, which had been founded by Jose Carlos Mariategui in 1928. Both had been close friends.

The crucial event was held in the popular recreation centre of Huampani. It was located close to the river Rimac, about sixteen kilometres into the mountains from Lima. There was a large area, occupied by sports grounds, on part of which the tent for the main event was erected. Middle class families and groups normally rented the surrounding bungalows.

These however could house only a small proportion of the vast number of delegates from all over the country. The rest erected tents, which dotted every piece of available ground. It was an impressive sight, a hive of activity, excitement and nerves. The number of attendees hangs vaguely in my memory at around 3,000.

The place was familiar from more than twenty years earlier. With my Columban friends, I used to come there on our 'day off' to play six-a-side soccer with the workers at their lunch break. We played in the mid-day tropical sun, oblivious to the need for protection for our *gringo* skin. Some of us were to carry the hidden hurt of those happy hours. Just last year, I listened philosophically, my thoughts wandering back, as my doctor told me that the spots of skin cancer on my face had to be removed.

The circumstances of my return to our former playground were dramatically different now. The whole atmosphere was tense. Security, organised by the parties, was at its tightest. I still have the pass which we had to show at every check-point.

The offensive of *Sendero Luminoso* had dramatically increased over the previous years and large sections of the population were in the grip of fear, and near to panic. The actual carrying out of the Congress, in itself, was a statement about courage and hope.

Just about a kilometre away, the self-managing urban community of Huaycan, once the depositary of so much hope, was still heavily infiltrated by *Sendero Luminoso*. There was a real possibility that they might try to impede, or disrupt, the event.

As a show of strength and determination, a large column of delegates of the United Left marched from Vitarte right past the settlement. At the head was Javier Diez Canseco, one of the most charismatic leaders. Slight, and carrying a noticeable limp from childhood polio, he was bravely making a statement.

As the Congress opened, word spread that Barrantes, the acknowledged leader of the alliance, was not going to attend. He was not a member of any party and, up to that point, it had seemed to give him a freedom to act as a moderating and consensus-building voice. At public rallies, this lawyer by profession had the ability to connect with followers, speaking in a simple language that touched and inspired ordinary people. The importance of his active presence in the event could hardly be overstated.

That weekend I watched the event unfold into a hardening of positions. Like so many others, I felt a growing anger and frustration at our absent leader's decision not to attend. We had to contemplate the unthinkable.

Just like we had witnessed some years earlier, at the formation of the Federation of Young Towns or *Barrios*, once again the same destructive habits were on show. Groups of leaders were huddled together outside the arena, bargaining and taking decisions, removed from the main body of delegates.

I can still see Jorge Del Prado, then in his seventy-ninth year, his voice weakened by age and emotion, appealing to the delegates and party leaders to put the hopes of the millions of poor before personal and party ambitions.

For some sixty years he, who was at heart an artist, had dedicated his life to helping to build a new society in Peru, one where socialism and democracy went hand in hand. Over the long years of commitment, he had suffered persecution and imprisonment. Through it all, his fairness and human decency was acknowledged, not just on the Left but across the political divide.

Now, he stood tall and frail, a lonely figure, fighting a losing battle. He had faced many challenges, but at that crucial juncture the tide against him was to prove too strong.

On a human level, Del Prado desperately needed support but, more importantly, the outcome at stake was nothing less than the destiny of the country for a full two decades to come. Had Barrantes been there, and taken up the cause of compromise and unity, the result would most likely not have been different.

For the key element was missing. We lacked a collective leadership with the vision and courage to put the interests of the millions before those of their individual parties. Helpless and emotionally battered, like so many others, I was left to take in the worst of outcomes – a split.

17.

AFTERSHOCK AND UPROOTING

IT WAS NOT EASY TO ADMIT to myself that the split in the United Left had affected me more than I wished to acknowledge. I had stubbornly held on to a romantic notion of the coalition. Now, I had watched it crumble and something deep inside me had shattered too. It was not difficult to see that the consequences would follow the 'enlightened' leadership of the Left, and be suffered by the poor, for years to come.

Rattled also by the ever-present and growing violence in the city, the idea of taking a break, and of moving, had begun to circle in my mind. Carmen and I discussed our options for continuing to work in Peru. We could see that trying to run an NGO like we had would be a very shaky prospect into the future. I could not imagine myself in the country doing work that had nothing to do with the poor. My soul companion could appreciate that. Our thoughts turned to Ireland.

IN SEARCH OF A JOB I TRAVELLED to my native land. It was autumn 1989 and the country was coming out of a recession once more. The government had been trying to get the fiscal deficit in order, imposing cut-backs. Thousands of young people had to emigrate each year. Young families were struggling. I could empathise with people as I walked the streets of Dublin.

At that time, the capital city had a population of just over half a million (today it has more than doubled). Coming from the bustling metropolis of Lima, it seemed to me that here everyone could, and most likely did, know everyone else.

211

My goal was to get a job in community development or education. The prevailing system placed high priority on degrees obtained within the country. The idea of re-validating my sociology degree was unrealistic. I had a young family to look after.

In reply to advertisements in the papers I had applied for hundreds of jobs, but not a single invitation for an interview came my way. It was at the home of a friend from secondary school that I was advised to contact another friend from that time, and that contact did get me employment. Fundraising for a foundation attached to a hospital was not something I had remotely thought of. But I was greatly relieved to have a contract to start work in mid-January.

During my life as a cleric I had witnessed, from that detached position, the joys and sorrows of people. Every family had its good and bad times, the poor always getting more than their fair share of the latter.

Now I was part of a normal family. We shared the joyful times and supported one another through the pain and darkness. A few days after getting the job, heart-breaking news was to come from Lima. My brother in law, Carli, had been killed in an accident. He was only thirty-three. His daughters, Desiree and Dafne, were the same age as our own children and were very close.

         ❧   ❧   ❧

I HAD ARRIVED BACK IN LIMA in time for the funeral. Amidst all the gloom and sadness, Carmen was managing to comfort others: 'My brother is at peace and resting,' she said repeatedly to family and friends. Not so her father. He was to carry that scar forever, like a permanent look of shell-shock.

He and I were to go several times to the cliff from which his only son had fallen to his death. There we dwelt for long, silent moments. In silence too we walked away and, over a cup of coffee in his favourite little haunt, he would say: 'Thanks Lucas, I feel a little better now.'

There was less than two months to go before our departure. We all had to go through a soul-wrenching process of uprooting, each in a very personal way. I was aware that it would have the biggest consequences for Carmen. She would miss her language, the predictable weather, her family and friends and much more. But, typically, she was putting all that behind her and we, her family, came first. She was telling me she was confident we were doing the right thing:

'The children will get to experience the land where you were born, get to know your roots. That's important,' she would say.

However, there was something else that weighed on her mind, and from which I think she took a lot of the motivation she needed to go forward. We talked little about it, but I was aware that she had become increasingly worried for my safety. As the internal war raged, working behind a camera, in the *barrios*, had become a riskier occupation.

The children were to suffer their own sense of loss, of being torn away. Kathy, going on sixteen, went to an all-girls school run by nuns. She had her close group of friends and volleyball had become a passion in her life.

The rain-free climate of the Peruvian coast meant that this sport could be played outdoors at any time. In the *barrios,* quiet streets and plazas served to set up playing courts. The sport had become popular due especially to the success of the women's national team which had achieved spectacular success on the international stage.

Its finest hour was at the 1988 Olympic Games in Seoul. Several girls from the *barrios* were on the Peruvian team. In the final of the competition, facing the Soviet Union, they had gone two sets up and were winning 12-6 in the third – they needed just three points to win. The Soviet coach called time out. He was seen on television reading the riot act to his charges. Unbelievably, they went on to beat Peru by a whisker.

On a typically overcast winter's day we had gone to the national stadium to welcome home our heroes. They were a genuine source of joy and a ray of hope for a country badly in need of an uplift.

For a number of years Kathy had taken to the sport but more seriously of late. She had been called to be part of a group of players that trained with the hope of some day representing their country. That was hard work. But playing for her school was very different. The spectators, a mixture of students, teachers and parents, crowded around the outdoor court and got passionately involved.

In her last year at the school, Kathy was team captain and they won the competition organised by the association of schools run by religious organisations in the capital. Leaving now was going to hurt.

Our two sons had the good fortune to go to a mixed school that had an alternative vision of education. It had been recently set up by Juan and his sister Chopi, both single, in their mid-30s and totally dedicated to their calling. The large home of their parents had become the school premises.

Juan, the robust director with an infectious smile, was a man of many talents and boundless energy. For him education was a persistent process of helping students to learn to think for themselves and develop their individual gifts. So from an early age, group projects, art and drama were all an important part of the curriculum. The two boys were proud of their little school and had made friends they would dearly miss.

The school year ended just before Christmas, which meant that our children were able to finish their year's study. They had begun to stay overnight in friends' houses more than usual. Surely, I thought, they were assimilating, in their own way, the magnitude of the event ahead, engraving memories to carry away.

In those turbulent days for Peru, some were taking decisions of a different kind. I recall a visit to the video studio by a youth I had known in one of the *barrios*. Once before he had come and shown me a small video camera he had acquired. This time he had come to say he was going to El Monte, an expression used to indicate one was going to the jungle to join the guerrilla movement. No questions were asked or explanations given. Respectfully, deliberately, we hugged and he went slowly down the stairs. I was left to reflect on his courageous commitment and on his farewell gesture. Along the way, in spite of our different paths, I must have meant something special to him, maybe someone he could trust.

One of the things we had to do, before leaving, was to find a home for the video equipment, and the many tapes of programmes. We left them to an organisation which was run by women and worked with women's groups.

Those last weeks were awkward ones for me. Faced with political and economic chaos in the country, leaving was not an option for our friends in the *barrios* or those of the middle-class. Though it was not something I looked forward to, we had to do our leave-taking. The decision had been made and our focus now was more and more on the mundane matters for the journey.

Carmen was ensuring that each of our children brought as many of their 'special things' as possible. Then, there was the delicate matter of our cocker spaniel. 'Oh, it will have to come with us,' was the almost unanimous voice. I was out-voted four to one.

So I started the *tramites* or red tape necessary to ensure it could travel. After a number of weeks and trips to the vet, the Ministry of Agriculture and the airport, I had an impressive bunch of papers. They showed that our pet had all the vaccinations and health checks necessary. Staff at the airline desk in the airport had assured me, on a number of occasions, that all was in order. A special cage for our doggie would be at hand on the day of our journey and put where the luggage was stored on the plane.

The morning had come, and we were all at the airport, with our bags and pieces. I carried our canine in a wicker basket, which closed around its body, leaving its head sticking out. When we got to the check-in desk, there was no special cage available. After some frantic phone calls, we were told there would not be any.

Our plan was unravelling fast, but the unwavering advice of the friends who had come to see us off was clear: 'Have dog, must travel.'

Columban Sister Eileen was in no doubt: 'It's the airline's fault. This dog means so much to the children. You must take it with you.'

Carrying our pet, I had got through the check-points, joined the boarding queue, gone up the steps and into the plane. A stewardess had expressed not a little surprise, but we were allowed to take our seats. Tony and I were four rows in front of Carmen and Willie, who had their pet on the floor between them. They were the most attached to it. Kathy sat just ahead of them.

Commotion among the staff grew as the time for take-off approached. The captain was brought to inspect the situation. Visibly annoyed, he vowed the problem would be rectified at our next stop. For a brief time after the plane took to the sky, we could relax.

Then, all of a sudden, pandemonium broke out behind me. It was a mixture of screams and barks. The passengers behind us were frantically trying to raise themselves out of their seats, as our four-footed friend scrambled its way along the floor beneath them, making a bee-line for Tony and me.

Amid the nervous laughter of disconcerted passengers, order was gradually restored. With help from staff we tried to make the basket a more secure holding-place. During the brief stop-over in Quito, Ecuador, our pleas for proper transport of our pet were unsuccessful. We returned to our seats on the plane, and it travelled with us to our next stop in mainland Europe.

By the time we arrived at the European airport the staff there already knew about our problem. They took our dog, put it in a cage and took it to its proper travelling quarters on the plane. Beforehand they warned us that Ireland had one of the strictest control regimes for the entry of animals to the country. But we had all the necessary papers, didn't we?

In Dublin, we had gone through customs, and were in the arrivals' area, when loud barking soared above the usual din. Across the hall, surrounded by men in white coats, our furry friend had spotted us.

It looked emaciated after the long journey, and its minders weren't the least impressed with the certificates I produced. Instead, they had grim news. The best I could hope for was that it would go into quarantine for six months, costs to be met by yours truly. It was simply not a feasible option.

To avoid having to take a decision there and then, a kind airport employee who had listened to our predicament offered to keep our pet in her office until the morning. Then we would get a phone call and a decision would have to be taken.

Next day, I was told there were only two possibilities: either the dog was returned on the same airline to Peru, or it would be put down. I quickly chose the less hurtful option and later had to break the news to Carmen and the children. Their beloved pet was to find a home with Wendy, our fondly-remembered policeman, and his family in Lima.

Alas, it was never to chase around the fields of Maynooth, our home to be. A precious link to our lives in the land of the Incas would not be at our side, to brighten the trying days of transition. But life never stands still. Some months after our arrival, our oldest son got a cocker spaniel from a dog shelter. Today, over two decades later, Willie and his girlfriend Grainne are both dog lovers and they dote over two pets.

18.

CHALLENGES OF AN IMMIGRANT FAMILY

IT WAS MID-WINTER WHEN we arrived in Ireland, having left summer behind us in Lima. This timing was not something we had chosen, or had control over. The change of weather was particularly bewildering for Carmen.

There were those days of near gale-force winds and pelting rain. Then the hurrying clouds could suddenly allow the sun to break through, and create moving shadows on the ground around her. She was to have moments of near panic too, like when an unruly gust of wind got under her umbrella, turning it inside out.

The cold she could manage, putting on several layers of clothing. To this day, the rest of her family are amused to see how, after coming in off the street, she goes through the ritual of removing a number of the outer ones.

We had made some provision to shield ourselves against cold. A few weeks before leaving Lima, I was talking to Uncle Manuel about our need to get some trousers made of heavier material. His eyes sparkled because he knew the very man who could deliver. So, one evening we had all set out to meet Don Remigio.

He plied his trade near the marketplace, in a little attic above a shop. The experienced tailor, with his measuring tape draped around his neck, his glasses hanging on the point of his nose, did what he had done on so many occasions before. We were measured, and notes of measurements and materials were written in his notebook. It did catch my attention that, a number of times before we departed, Uncle Manuel had cautioned the good man: 'Don Remigio, on your life you better do a top job for my family, or I will be after you.' We had picked up the goods on the evening of our departure and only examined them on arrival in Ireland.

I had got a suit made for work and it fitted perfectly; not so the other garments. Not just the colours had gone awry, but critically the measurements too. The worst case was probably Tony's trousers – the legs were wide as a barn door and barely covered his knees. After finishing the suit, our trusted tailor must have done the rest with a bottle of *pisco* handy. We haven't ever had the courage to let Uncle Manuel know of the misadventure.

Carmen never quite managed to judge the weather, or knew how to prepare for going out on any particular day. No discredit to her, I suppose, seeing that the weather experts make sure to include a bit of everything in their forecasts, down to the 'odd clap of thunder'! My own bit of advice wasn't of much use to her either: 'The clouds seem to be fairly high in the sky today. It might not rain.'

A problem we were faced with on arrival was accommodation. Peadar and Toni kindly took us into their home for a few weeks; we had become friends when they worked in Peru. After getting the new job I had put a deposit on a house under construction in Maynooth, a town some thirty kilometres west of Dublin. Now we were told it was not going to be ready for another four months. But Paddy, the approachable, easy-going foreman from Connemara in County Galway, came to our rescue and lent us a house he had in the neighbouring town of Leixlip.

Kathy was the only one of the children who went to school during those months. She had no time to lose, if she were to do the Leaving Certificate just two years later.

The popularly called 'Leaving Cert' was the final examination at the end of secondary school. Huge importance was placed on it, many would say far too much. It was largely an academic, memory-cramming exercise that determined each student's possibilities of getting into a university to study for a particular career. Success depended on the number of points accumulated over the different subjects. The system is still in vogue today, but crucially there are also many courses available that allow the non-academic-minded students to go on to third level education.

A problem that had no immediate solution but was a formidable barrier to be faced by Carmen and the children was their lack of English. We had arrived in Ireland totally unprepared in that regard. Why had I not done much more to ensure all were prepared for this important part of the challenge? The accusatory finger of the judge followed me around in those first years. But, with time, seeing my wife and children gradually take down that obstacle, I began to realise that I shouldn't be too hard on myself.

When the children were small I had made a few attempts to teach them English. But at that time I did not know that one parent could speak in a 'foreign' tongue all the time and the children would get accustomed to it and learn. Rather, I felt I was just confusing them and always said to myself, 'maybe later.'

Of course, there was a more fundamental problem: we were by no means a 'normal' middle-class family. Our commitment with the poor meant we were out a lot and when at home people frequently called in. This had been the way up to our departure, something which had not even been considered until about six months beforehand.

In Ireland now we spoke Spanish at home, it was our comfort zone. The two boys were to take their own route to come to grips with English. With their friends, whether in the house or sitting on a wall in the estate, they were listeners, concentrating on absorbing as much as possible from the chatter around them. It was nearly a year before they felt confident enough to join in – and by then they were sporting a credible North Kildare accent.

Meanwhile, Kathy was involved in a challenge of her own, the outcome of which would mean more parting. She had started her preparation for the Leaving Cert. Because of her weak English, it was going to be an uphill struggle to the end.

When I looked at her school textbooks, I noticed that the pages were covered with her handwriting. Her method was to pencil in the Spanish equivalent of the many words she didn't understand. She said it helped her fix their meaning in her memory.

Her heart was set on becoming a primary school teacher. In order to be able to work in Ireland, she needed to pass the Irish language examination. For a few months she had studied it, until she realised it was a step too far, given the pressure of the other subjects, and the sheer lack of time.

It was then that she turned her thoughts to getting into a teachers' training college in England. One of her teachers told her about Liverpool Hope University where entry required getting honours in at least three subjects.

I vividly recall that one of the subjects she aimed to get honours in was Biology, with its myriad formulae. It seemed like an insurmountable obstacle to her teacher. Some months before the exams were to start, Carmen and I were called to a meeting with him. He advised us to persuade our daughter to take the pass level course. He told us that while her efforts were admirable, she was unlikely to achieve her goal.

We did talk to her, but she continued on her path. She burned the midnight oil and got the cherished result. I travelled over to Liverpool with her, leaving behind a mother and brothers, who pondered over another uprooting, which had come all too soon.

For the first year, Kathy was to live on campus. We had barely left her few belongings in a corner of the room when there was knocking on the door. A group of curious, also newly onboard young girls, began to introduce themselves. In that endearing way that young people can make light of drama and protocol, they protectively surrounded my daughter, and proceeded to guide her to the small community room. Some sat on the available chairs and others squatted on the floor.

I stood at the door taking in that scene, until I caught my daughter's eye. Then with nothing more than a little wave to each other, I was on my way, quite overwhelmed with mixed emotions.

That parting image of the contagious and optimistic companionship of youth, which my daughter had been so spontaneously invited to share, would stay anchored in my memory. It would serve to comfort both Carmen and me. However, there was no avoiding the reality: our daughter had well and truly flown the nest, and we had to learn to 'let go'.

'You remember that morning, when we left her at the play-school. She was only two and a bit. There was no crying, she just took the teacher's hand and went into the room to join the other kids,' I recalled.

'Yes, she was always confident and sociable. But, this is such a change for her and it's so far away,' Carmen reflected.

'It seems to be a long way but it's not anymore. It's only seventy odd miles across the Irish Sea.'

'But that's a long way for us. A daughter needs to be able to talk to her mother. There will be days she will a bit down, and she'll be far away.'

'But you both like to write and you can keep in touch that way.'

'I need to see where she is. Do you think we can make it over?'

'Sure, we'll get there, don't worry', I said reassuringly.

At that time, third level education in the UK was free. We had to pay for her accommodation and she needed some pocket money. Carmen had tried, to no avail, to get into a training course in the hope of getting work. But she was determined to provide some vital supplementary income, and had come up with a plan of her own.

Maynooth University was expanding, and each year there were students looking for accommodation with families. Hastily, we had converted the garage into a bedroom, and the adjacent utility room into a kitchen. We took in four students, two in the newly prepared bedroom, one in the dining room, which we hardly ever used, and one in Kathy's room upstairs.

It did indeed mean a certain loss of privacy in our home, but it also had its positive side. Word got out about my Mayo ties. Parents usually wanted to check out where their offspring, especially those starting their first year, were going to be living. Nearly all the students we accommodated in the following years came from the county of the green and red. Most stayed with us for their four years at college, always feeling free to join us in the sitting room. They were to remain long-time friends.

As the children struggled with their own process of adaptation I was trying to come to grips with my job. As a promotion officer for the foundation I was expected to seek out, encourage and support individual people and groups to organise fundraising events. I had been assigned an area that covered five counties in the midlands. The only way to learn how to do the job was by going out and trying. Though many families around the country had one of their own treated at the hospital, we were not allowed access to their names or contact details. Of course, they would have been the people most likely to be responsive to a plea for support.

So, on a wet and windy morning in early January, I began my apprenticeship by the banks of the Shannon in Athlone. It was to be the first day of many dedicated to 'cold calling'. My first call was to the Garda station, where I was hopeful of getting the sympathetic attention of a member of the force.

'Noel is your man, he knows everyone around the place. He will be back in an hour or so.'

After meeting the soft-spoken Garda, I left with the names of contact persons for local sports and community organisations, among others, though no precise home addresses or telephone numbers. On that first day, and for months to come, my efforts to actually meet people face to face were very 'hit and miss'. What a difference with today and the instant-contact mobile phone. Then the pay-phone, often out of order, was still the 'old reliable'.

So, in those first months I was only able to meet a few people on any day. Times were hard, and while I was always received graciously, I often felt I was the bearer of an uncomfortable request. Nevertheless, some hopeful responses were coming my way: 'Certainly, if there is something being organised for the hospital in the town, I will give a hand.'

After a number of months I had begun to find some rhythm in the job and, from the midlands, it was possible to get home each evening. But all that was about to change drastically. The boss had managed to involve a dairy company in the sponsorship of a national fundraising day for our charity.

The opportunity would only be successful in the measure that we could promote it and motivate people to participate. In the absence of a team, which could effectively do justice to the project, for the following three months I found myself travelling frantically against the clock, covering long distances and staying in B&Bs four nights a week.

One typical pressurised journey is etched in my memory. I had finished a meeting in Tralee, County Kerry, after six in the evening, and had started out for Kilbeggan in County West-meath. There, I was to meet some people who worked in one of the plants of the dairy company that sponsored the upcoming fundraising day.

It was a particularly wet and windy night at the end of February, and time was not on my side. I did not yet know the roads, and was straining to keep my eyes fixed on the way ahead. My view was not helped by the lashing rain and the swishing back and forth of the windscreen wipers. Soon I got a searing head-ache, which lasted all the way to my destination.

As on that night, and many others to come, I was to reflect dolefully, with a strong dose of self-blame, on the job I had taken on. The big fundraising day came and went. My original area around the midlands was increased by more than double. Nights away from home became part of my life, and so did attending functions, often until the small hours of the morning.

But gradually my job did develop an attractive aspect, one that made the downside of it more bearable. I was enjoying meeting people and making friends, once more getting to know my country and its people. After a few years, I had to do much less cold calling. In each town, I now had a few friends whom I could call on the phone beforehand.

A habit I got into, from the start, was to serve me well. In a way, it was a continuation of one I had enjoyed in Lima – playing soccer and later jogging. Now, conditions had radically changed. The challenge of the Irish weather, and the small time space available, were two big obstacles. But I had extra motivation: to be able to cope with the pressures of a demanding job, and to try to meet my responsibility as bread-winner.

Whenever I left home, my running gear was always in the boot of the car. Three times a week I went out for jog. In win-ter, especially, the most difficult test was putting one foot on the bedroom floor. But, once out on the road, just after six in the morning, whether it was dark or bright, wet or dry, a special time began. The roads were quiet, the adrenaline began to flow, and I knew that the positive feeling would accompany me all day. So, the roads around many places like Ballina, Galway City, Birr and Cavan Town became familiar and friendly.

Both of our boys were now in secondary school. Carmen, never one to easily accept being housebound, was eager to explore and learn in her adopted homeland. First, she got a diploma in Women's Studies from Maynooth University, and then joined a women's group in a deprived area near Dublin. True to character, my wife quickly felt at home there. She made wonderful friendships that were to stand the test of time. With a group of those friends, she took a creative writing course led by Anne, their inspirational motivator.

Back in secondary school, she had first begun to write poetry, and only sporadically after that, until our children were growing up. Then the dormant muse had inspired her to put pen to paper once more. Before we departed from Peru, she had a book of her poems published. Now she was motivated to write once again.

None of the above took her eye off the family's welfare. To supplement our income she took on tedious tasks, with a persistence and patience that belied the poet within. Into the small hours of the morning, she could sit at the kitchen table making up raffle baskets, or sorting raffle tickets, for the Foundation I worked for.

Secondary school for the two boys was to be a very different experience to that of their sister. The academically orientated regime, where memorising information was almost the total emphasis, seemed to just turn them off. In Lima, they had a very different experience of school from Kathy's. In Juan's visionary project, education had been principally about motivating students to begin to think for themselves, ask questions and work in groups.

When the two boys began to show worrying signs of disaffection with school, I began to take notice. I felt it was something more than not liking school. We had several conversations.

'Your mother and I can see that you guys are not exactly jumping up and down to go to school or do your homework. Having to leave Peru and your friends, trying to make new friends and get into things here, it all must be hard to get used to.'

'No Dad, it's not about getting used to the change. That is going alright. It's about the classes, they are just downright boring. We're supposed to sit there and listen all the time and keep quiet. The teachers are just concerned about discipline and controlling us.'

'But surely there are some teachers whose classes you like.'

'There are a few who try to be friendly. We can see that, but their way of teaching is the same. It bores the hell out of us and we can't get interested.'

'That's a pity,' I would say. 'You know the most important part of a teacher's job is to get the students interested in the subject: to take the time to motivate them so that they feel they are part of the learning too, and can participate asking questions and expressing their ideas.'

'Your idea of teaching, Dad, is very different. That is not the way it is in the school. Teachers come into class, and are not in the least interested in whether the students are tuned in or bored, and anyway they don't see it as their problem. They give out their lesson, and you take it or leave it.'

'That's the way it is here. In Juan's school there was discipline too, but the difference was that we were made to feel part of everything,' the other boy would add.

Neither of them was to find the self-motivation to exert themselves within the system, much less accept it, or feel comfortable with it. They did enough to get by.

Willie had got a second-hand guitar and, after a few initial lessons, was teaching himself to play. A few of his friends, all in their own way anti-system too, and proudly wearing their shoulder-length hair, were also interested in heavy metal music. They formed a band.

Ever anxious to keep in touch, Carmen and I went to their gigs. The music wasn't to our liking, but the teenagers were energised and making a statement. They were breaking loose, without any precise notion of where to. These were the early days of the Irish economic boom or Celtic Tiger. The traditional values and moral constraints of our society were to be questioned, loosened and replaced as never before.

Globalisation, or deregulated capitalism, let loose to follow its ruthless path of profit and greed, brought with it an insatiable, soul-destroying consumerism in Ireland. Personal and community values suffered from the race by individuals to accumulate more and more material things. These were to be the empty expression of newly-found self-worth.

Our country's leaders, time and again, assured us that we were enjoying the best of times. 'Let's ride on' was their message. In collusion with the mega-builders, and giving a nod and a wink to the gambling banks, they shouted down the dissenting voices.

The rising tide was going to lift all boats, we were told. For a time the country could show some impressive figures regarding low unemployment and the growth in the standard of living of the working and middle classes. But, side by side with this 'progress' there were large areas in the big cities deprived of the benefits of the Celtic Tiger. Violent crime and drugs increased alarmingly.

As the boom took off, jobs became more plentiful. It became popular for secondary school students, especially in their final years, to work a few evenings a week. The money earned was spent on their social outings. Sometimes it meant saving for a rock concert, but most often the money was spent on a night out with friends in the pub.

It was to be a particularly worrying time for us parents, as significant numbers of teenagers took to binge drinking. A typical Friday or Saturday evening could start off with several cans of beer in one of the youngsters' homes, then on to the pub, where they could consume five or six pints of beer and several shots of hard liquor. After that it was a few hours in a club or disco to have more drinks. Females as well as males were involved. To add to the madness, drugs, especially cocaine, were coming in.

After the pubs and clubs closed, in the early hours of the morning, the youth spilled out onto the streets of cities and towns around the country, many of them literally out of their minds. Vicious fighting and screaming often followed.

I had witnessed first-hand the tumult on the street after a disco. The shouting and arguing had quickly turned nasty. As I waited uneasily in the car for my sons to appear, I clung to the consoling thought that I knew their friends.

But, many a time I asked myself if that would be enough to see our sons through. We talked about facing up to peer pressure, and taking more control of their drinking. About drinking more slowly, as people did on the continent. Could they not take shandies and avoid shots?

They listened and smiled. Then one of them would say:

'It's not that easy Dad. Each of us buys the round when it's his turn. It's all pints, and now and again shots.'

'But, surely, one can change to a shandy no matter whose turn it is to buy the round?'

'Not really. No one drinks shandies. But don't worry, we don't let our sessions get out of control.'

I would have to trust them and the formative upbringing, such as it was that we had given them down the years. It hadn't been very structured, more trying to teach the basic human and Christian values by example.

We weren't a regular church-going family. However, we did go to the main Christian celebrations, like Christmas and Easter. We used to go to a parish, where two Columban friends, from our time in Lima, then worked. This was a deprived area on the north side of Dublin.

Sometimes, we had a relaxed session at home, sitting around the kitchen table, before lunch on Sundays. We might pick a topic from the newspaper, or more often it was about letting each one say whatever was on his or her mind. It was what my resigned Columban friend, Joe, calls a 'go around'.

Problems in secondary school, like boredom and bullying, came up in the early years. Later issues such as friendship, peer pressure, binge drinking and violence came to the fore. At the end we would ask ourselves what Jesus thought of what we were discussing.

Our two sons had, for the most part, the same friends. We had got to know them from their visits to our home. They were a tight and loyal group who looked out for one another, and their friendship has endured and grown down the years. Most are married now. Some have emigrated and still keep in touch.

There was a morning some years ago, and an image from it that I hold dear. Willie had recently got a mortgage approved and had moved into his new house here in Kinnegad. Still involved with his band, he had plans to sub-divide the garage, in order to make a place for music sessions. He had let the word go out, among his friends, that he needed help to build a dividing wall and do some other modifications.

It was a Saturday morning and I had gone along to see if I could be of any help. There was no shortage of volunteers, ready and willing at the appointed hour, among them just one brickie.

Work had proceeded apace all morning, and by midday the wall was half built. I hadn't been of much use, except to provide cups of tea and coffee. The whole operation had come to a full stop and I went to have a look. Our brickie had run out of steam. He was stretched out on the floor of the garage, fast asleep, with a bag of cement for a pillow. Around the place, his companions, with an understanding smile on their faces, were winding up for the day.

'What happened, is he alright?' I enquired.

'He's just out for the count. He worked behind a bar until 2.30 this morning.'

The place was tidied up quietly, so as not to wake the sleeping companion. I have held on to that picture of young, loyal friendship. It was to reassure me in these giddy times.

An experience that served the whole family to take stock of our individual journeys happened in 1994. At the first opportunity, we travelled to Liverpool. Kathy was in her second year in college.

All returned reassured, but Carmen was especially relieved. She had sat on the bed, in the semi-detached house, where her daughter lodged with her three classmates. They were companions and friends and had casually dropped in and out of the room to join in the conversation. Indeed, their friendship has lasted down the years.

As Carmen soaked up the atmosphere in Kathy's room, the two boys and I had cut the over-grown grass in the back garden. Then, on that balmy afternoon in late summer, we all sat outside, some on chairs and most of us on the newly-mown grass. The girls were chatting freely with Carmen and the boys. Over to one side, I was in a reflective mood. I thought once again of the precious gift of friendship, and the natural ability of young people to bond. About how they could face, and make light of, challenges, about their natural enthusiasm and ability to enjoy life.

During our short stay, Kathy insisted we visit the Beatles Museum. She seemed to know it would be an important experience for her brothers. Like her, Carmen and I were pleasantly surprised to see how they soaked up the atmosphere, reading the story and listening to the music. We had to urge them to move along and reluctantly finish the tour. In the following months it was obvious that the visit had indeed helped to open up a whole new world of music for them.

Another place we visited, at the boys' insistence, was Anfield, the grounds of Liverpool FC. They were both soccer fans. I had tried to get them interested in Gaelic football and they had played it for a time, but never really got into it. I sometimes lament how work had kept me away from home, and I was not around on those wintery evenings to give some necessary encouragement.

At work, my life was about to get much more complicated. There were about twenty staff, all female, working in the offices of the Foundation. They worked in administration and did back-up for people like me who travelled around the country meeting voluntary supporters.

Their workload was heavy, but I never heard any complaints about that side of their work. Rather, it was their low wages, well below the going rate, that was the source of their discontent. They, like the rest of us, had mortgages and other bills to pay.

On a number of occasions, I had approached our boss, and pleaded with him, to no avail, to rectify the situation.

'I run a tight organisation,' he told me. 'Things are going well. Keep doing your job. You are doing well but this matter has nothing to do with you. It's none of your business.'

The idea of setting up a trade union began to occupy my thoughts. There could be no justification, I told myself, for such unfairness and lack of transparency. The fact that this was a charitable foundation could in no way justify that staff should be paid a pittance.

In my mind, I was clear about what had to be done, but its implementation was to cause me much emotional turmoil. I had given the job my best effort, and been successful. In that sense, I felt that I didn't owe anything.

On the other hand, I recalled how my boss had given me the job, and how loyalty was something fundamental for him. We had known one another from secondary school. I couldn't escape the fact that my action would cause him hurt. From his point of view, he had 'built' the foundation from scratch, and it was considered to be very successful. He had assembled a board that had some of the most familiar names in the country.

It was a most uncomfortable crossroads. I was torn between loyalty and avoiding hurting a friend on the one hand, and doing what I believed was right on the other.

The majority of the staff joined the trade union. We had a few meetings outside the offices, when our boss made the surprise announcement that he was taking early retirement. Immediately, a new chief executive was appointed. It was common knowledge among the staff that he happened to be the nephew of the then chairman of the hospital board, a person who had no previous experience in the field of fundraising.

On several occasions, I was called to his office, at first on my own, and later, at my insistence, accompanied by a union member. His purpose was to try to get us to disband the trade union.

The efforts did not succeed, and we were getting ready to go on the picket line, when an agreement, satisfactory to our members, was reached. After work we celebrated that proud moment, hitherto almost unthinkable, with a little get-together. For the rest of my time at the Foundation, whenever I stepped into the offices, I got the sense of a warm atmosphere. I could hear the busy banter of companions at work, the fruits of recovered dignity.

19.

PERSONAL CRISIS AND NEW HORIZONS

IN THE YEARS AFTER THE SUCCESSFUL outcome of our trade union efforts, my relationship with the boss was civil but strained. I was aware that the setting up of the union had not endeared me to the powers that be in the Foundation. My retirement at sixty-five was nigh. Because my personal pension was almost non-existent, I felt it necessary to continue to work.

Naively, I was hopeful that I would be given the opportunity to do so. A colleague several years my senior had been given a new contract after retirement and was still working for the Foundation. But when my time came I was given no such opportunity.

I was in a new and awkward situation. For most of my adult life I had been part of struggles to get better living conditions and secure rights for others. Now I was about to fight for myself and didn't feel comfortable about it.

Over a period of many months, at two different instances of the Labour Court, the trade union fought my case. But it was to be all to no avail. The Foundation could not be obliged to take me back.

Carmen and Kathy had accompanied me for the last session of negotiations. The result was a foregone conclusion, and as we made our way to the coffee shop on the premise, I was counting the cost of a futile enterprise.

'It was so hard to sit through all that. It was a mistake to try to continue working there but I felt I was being treated very unjustly and found it so hard to let go.'

'You had to do it for yourself. They can't afford to have prying eyes around,' my daughter said.

'You can let go now. It's been a painful journey for us all. That whole business needs serious reform,' Carmen consoled me.

It had been nearly a year of personal tension for me. My family had not been immune from it either. The long months had taken their toll. I was feeling tired. Carmen insisted I go to my local doctor for a general check-up.

I had mentioned to him, not expecting any great reaction, that now and again I had been getting a stab of pain in my lower stomach. It used to last for less than half a minute and then go away.

'I am not going to take any chances with that. I'm sending you for a colonoscopy,' the doctor had said, taking me by surprise.

Before leaving the hospital, on the day of the procedure, Carmen accompanied me to the consultant's office. We were subdued and speechless when he told us that I had colon cancer. Then in a matter-of-fact manner he enquired about which hospital we preferred to have the operation in.

Stunned, for a few whirling moments, I soon realised there was no going back. The struggle of the previous months fell into perspective. It just faded from my consciousness and lost all importance.

During the slow-moving time before my operation, I began to read about cancer, its causes and treatment. It was a powerful enemy, but there was hope. Much depended on the type of cancer and how early it had been detected. I became interested in alternative, herbal treatments for the disease. Perhaps they could complement the standard chemotherapy.

People seem to react differently when stricken by cancer. Some prefer that their struggle be kept within their close family. My own reaction took me by surprise. I felt the need to draw on the spiritual energy and prayers of my extended family and friends. Contacting them, bringing them into my corner, and having their positive energy coming my way, gave me great comfort.

The night before the operation, I was in the hospital and had taken the prescribed number of litres of liquid, when I developed a total stomach blockage. All night I walked my room in distress, longing to be in the operation theatre and drift into that anaesthetic sleep.

It was a few days after the operation before the full weight of what had taken place hit me. The incisions, tubes and drains, I could accept as part of the whole procedure. But a visit by the colostomy nurse made me face a new level of reality.

The experienced, patient woman explained my prospect simply: 'You should know that it is quite possible that you will have to live with this bag for the rest of your life. So, you just have to get used to it.'

By the time she had left the room, I was deflated. My self-confidence had suffered a severe blow. I wasn't worrying about whether I would survive the cancer. Somewhere, deep down, I had buried that challenge for another day. No, I was distraught at the sudden realisation that quite possibly I might never run or cycle again. How would I manage without that rush of adrenaline a couple of times a week?

As I recovered and took my first steps along the hospital corridor, I slowly began to see things more realistically. I drew inspiration from the way some friends made light of the same limitation. There was Kathleen, always cheerful and ready for a laugh, who joined our walking challenges to raise funds for the Foundation. She always finished her walk well up the field. Then, there was my friend's Dad. He had the same operation at eighty and lived to the age of ninety-nine. It probably did no harm that he regularly walked to the town for a pint of the black stuff.

In the days prior to leaving the hospital, the team of young doctors were anxious to impress on us the importance of my undergoing chemotherapy. However, Carmen and I were gradually moving towards an alternative remedy.

On the morning that I left the hospital, I met the surgeon in his office. He was widely respected in his profession and I had two questions for him.

'Professor, your team are telling me that I must have chemotherapy but I am more inclined to use alternative medicine. What is your opinion about chemo?'

'Well, there are two schools of thought on the matter. One of them believes that it should be used in all cases, the other does not recommend it in all situations. Basically, it's your decision.'

'Thank you. I have one more question. Now that you have successfully removed the malignant tumour, what changes in my lifestyle would you recommend me to make, so as to keep the cancer from returning?'

A faint, whimsical smile crossed the good surgeon's lips. There was a pronounced pause as I awaited his considered reply:

'You take care now and be sure to make an appointment to see me in about three months' time.'

His message was clear. He had done his job and my lifestyle was not his specialty or responsibility. The non-response to my question had not really surprised me. It was no secret that the majority of medical practitioners, at all levels, had little preparation for, or interest in, advising patients about healthy diet, how to overcome tension or avoid harmful chemicals.

Because I was faced with a life-threatening ailment, I had avidly read about the causes for the alarming increase of cancer, especially in the western world. Causes such as the widespread use of processed foods, and poor diet in general; the use of dangerous chemicals in prescription drugs and personal care products; and the tension that was all too prevalent in the competition-based societies of our day. I was learning fast about the importance of taking responsibility for my own health.

In the past, like most people I'm afraid, I had handed over the responsibility for my health to my doctor. Though an infrequent visitor, I always expected to leave with a prescription to cure whatever symptom was bothering me at a particular time. Indeed, if I didn't get one, I almost felt cheated. Neither he nor I ever talked about my primary responsibility, that of looking after my own health and preventing ailments.

Our son, Willie, knew we were looking for quality, natural health supplements. He believed he had found them. We were aware of the gravity of our decision, of not going down the conventional route of chemotherapy. But we had a plan that consisted of not relying solely on these natural supplements. I was going to follow a healthy diet and learn to relax at yoga.

My recovery was rapid and life was more precious now. Walking regularly in the countryside, I was observing nature with a new-found wonder and eagerness. As I had sometimes heard people recovering from cancer say, I too was grateful. The whole experience has brought a new balance and harmony to my life. Six months on, I was able to have the colostomy reversal operation and the bag removed. I had got a second chance and the storm had passed.

I was to discover that the two worries I had harboured in the lead-up to my retirement were largely without foundation. Would I ever get work again? How would I continue to provide for my family?

Getting work was not the impossible task I had imagined. At different times I was approached by two foundations that worked for different causes, and was employed by them for a few years. Both were small, tension-free and friendly places to work.

My responsibility as breadwinner was also something in my own head. Life had moved on and the children were grown-ups now. After graduating, Kathy worked for a year in England. Afterwards she returned to Ireland and was teaching here.

She had not come back alone. While at college she had met Dale through their mutual involvement in volleyball. Carmen had been the first to get the nod to meet the six foot four Welsh man. She could tell me: 'I think he'll be good for Kathy. He is very patient with her. It's serious between them and it seems he'll be moving to Ireland soon after she does.'

We had picked up our son-in-law-to-be at the airport and apart from some difficulty understanding each other's accent, we had got on well. Kathy told me later:

'I was really nervous and had given out to him. He had a few drinks on the plane to calm his nerves, and I was afraid that you would get the smell of beer off him, and it being your first encounter.'

'Not at all, you needn't have worried,' I replied. 'He's a tall lad, far too tall for me to get a whiff of anything.'

Two years before my brush with cancer Kathy and Dale had got married. The two boys were men now. Both had finished their university studies, had their first jobs and were in relationships.

Right up to the time of my illness, absorbed and pressurised by the circumstances of work, I had not fully appreciated that the boys had indeed moved on. They were making their own way in life and I no longer needed to see myself as their 'minder' or 'provider'.

As I became more aware of the above reality I felt a great relief. I had my State pension. In the mindless years of the Celtic Tiger it wasn't considered much, but it was and is one of the better expressions of caring social legislation in our country. Our basic needs into the future would be looked after, and the matter of work now took on a freedom of choice that was life-giving.

For a while I was the one resting on my oars, ready for every opportunity to meet family and friends for a cup of coffee and a chat. But there was also space and ease of mind now to give attention to some of our deepest interests. One of the closest to our hearts had to do with the leaders and friends in *barrios* of Lima. All our family had managed to go to Peru together months before my retirement. Carmen and I had organised a couple of gatherings with the people. Over a weekend of moving reencounter and remembrance each person had an opportunity to make a contribution to the dialogue.

These brave people were still recovering from the nightmare of the dirty internal war which they wanted to forget. But what we had done together was still a bright light on which they could build their future – the rest was a woeful mistake never to be repeated.

There were two generations present at those remarkable reencounters. Parents who had young families over three decades earlier were now in their sixties and seventies, their children of long ago had their own families now. Both generations had been active in their *barrios*, the elders in adult groups and their children in youth ones. Our children had come to the last session and soaked up the atmosphere.

It was at that last gathering that the idea of recording the oral history of those leaders and friends surfaced; it would be an important legacy for the next generation. On our return to Ireland we prepared a project and presented it to the Columbans.

Missionary organisations could access funding from the Irish government's programme for aid to under-developed countries. After our request was approved Carmen and I, over a number of years, recorded meetings and interviews. The video recordings are ready for editing, if only I could finish this memoir!

In those years of new-found energy after illness, I became involved in another project. A dozen or so of us resigned Columbans used to meet for a meal before Christmas each year. We shared a special bond, one that reached back to our time with the Columbans but also went beyond that.

After leaving the clerical priesthood, making our way on different paths, whether we realised it or not we were part of a worldwide social phenomenon – one that was to question the clerical institution, and the wider Church, in a manner probably not seen since the Reformation. It is estimated that between 80,000 to 100,000 priests have left the clerical institution since the 1960s.

Thrown on the waste pile by the clerical powers, and without any retraining for the vast majority of us, we each ploughed our furrow in the real world. Most of us had shared our lives with female partners. Some were in same sex relationships. Many were raising young children. Without the status or the platform, we were bringing the simple message of Jesus to those around us by example.

In stark and total contrast to the official Church's characterisation of us, as traitors to the cause, a current Columban states that we are much more likely to be seen, in the course of time, as pioneers.

As we each made our way through life, there was an internal process going on. We were at different stages of disentanglement and discovery. This ensured there was always a wide variety of opinions and shades thereof at our reunions. But there was a tolerance and an understanding in the room which encouraged us to say what we felt.

It was at one of those get-togethers that Jimmy had challenged us to go beyond reminiscing. The idea of reconnecting with all the resigned Columbans around the world began to take shape. Joe, the proud Sligo man from, as he always reminds us, the 'foot of the Ox Mountains', was our natural leader. Ever anxious for the welfare of the scattered brothers, he led the efforts to locate them. We pooled our information but it came up short. However, some individual Columbans were able to help. Many long-distance phone calls and emails were needed to complete the full picture of the diaspora, and have an up-to-date contact list.

Then we took a step in hope. We sent a simple questionnaire to each person, asking him to tell us, in a few pages, about his life after resigning and give us any reflections he might have.

We were aware that there was a possibility that people might be reluctant to reply. Some might feel they had made their own way up to that point, and might not be keen on any re-connection. The traumatic experience we had all gone through had affected us in different ways. In the official Church's eyes, we had done the worst possible thing a priest could do, namely, leave the clerical institution. It was a bigger offence than assaulting and abusing children. Those men were to be cared for and protected, their crimes covered up.

However, the response far exceeded our expectations. Just short of 200 Columbans had resigned. Of these nearly forty were already deceased. We received some 135 replies from countries around the world. Clearly, our initiative had struck a chord with our dispersed brothers. They welcomed the opportunity to recall their journeys and reconnect. Two aspects of their stories stood out.

One was the great variety of jobs people took on initially in order to make ends meet. They worked on the building-sites, in security, in pubs, door-to-door selling – whatever they could get. Gradually, most found employment in organisations working with people on the margins. Those who had done better financially were known for their generosity and social awareness. The banished brothers had held on to basic human and Christian values, and were quietly doing their bit to make the world a better place.

The other striking point was that, in spite of their disenchantment with the wider clerical institution, most still held dear their bond of friendship with individual Columbans. The majority also had a positive relationship with the leadership of the Society. But for some it had been a conflictive one.

We had put the contributions from all resigned Columbans into a book for private circulation. A second edition was circulated to all current Columbans. Only a few of the latter contacted us about it afterwards. We got no acknowledgement or comment of any kind from the Society leadership. What feelings and thoughts had our collective stories stirred up for them?

In the following years, we have had numerous private conversations with individual Columbans, and many official meetings with the leaders of the Society. For the first time some of us were to understand the deep pain and sense of loss that our leaving had caused to our friends within the organisation, pain and loss that had not been expressed for years.

We, resigned Columbans, had set up a committee and were holding frequent meetings. Top of our agenda was the rebuilding of the relationship with the Society and the support of our brothers in difficulties of one kind or another. We engaged in formal dialogue with the Columban leadership. It was to be a long five-year process and often a frustrating experience for those of us directly involved. My friend Brian tells me that his computer now holds close to 13,000 emails, testimony to the many and varied exchanges.

The frustration arose around the very different understanding each side had regarding the nature of the support to be given to resigned Columbans who needed it. On our side it was seen as vital that whatever 'help' given be acknowledged as a *right*: it could not be seen as charity, a hand-out that could hurt the dignity of the recipient.

Coming at the problem from our experience of life in the world, we believed that resigned Columbans had a basic civic right to have had provision made for pension contributions for their years of service, the average was fourteen years. This had not been done. Now, surely, that grave omission should be corrected by giving the support some needed as a right.

Personally, it took me a long time to come to grips with the fact that the leadership was not for accepting our arguments. We were nearing the end of the first decade of the twenty-first century but the leaders would not move on this point. In fact, as they saw it, they could not move. They were subjects of another legal code, canon law. One of the canons, which today echoes of a world long gone, states bluntly:

'Whoever lawfully leaves a religious institute, or is lawfully dismissed from one, cannot claim anything from the institute for any work done in it.' Not even contributions to a pension.

In spite of this internal regulation, devoid of humanitarian and Christian spirit, most religious organisations seem to have offered some support to resigned members in more recent times. But there were of course cases of the worst kind of treatment, like that meted out to Elena.

I first met her in the early 1990s. Her easy, relaxed and enthusiastic manner belied the journey she had made. For thirty-three years she had served on the missions as a nun, a member of a religious congregation. During her last two years in the congregation she had been in hospital, suffering from depression and mental anguish. Then she was told by her superiors that they could no longer afford to pay her medical fees.

She had returned to Ireland where, as a social welfare recipient, she got a place to live and medical treatment. Living in a poor area of the city, she began to organise workshops for women. There she began to walk towards personal freedom, shaking off the shackles that had bound her mind and spirit. She broke loose from endless feelings of guilt and began to think for herself. Having come out the other side, she discovered that her vocation was more alive than ever. Vocation, she would say, is not a question of the garb one wears. It is in the heart.

As I, and others on our committee, began to accept the reality that the representatives of the Society could not acknowledge that resigned Columbans had a right to anything, there was less tension in our meetings with them. Today, as has always been the case with the Society, support is available to those who need it and ask.

As regards re-building the relationship between the two sides, the efforts have been noticeably successful. There is new warmth and understanding manifest in encounters at all levels these days.

At the recent funeral Mass, after the untimely death of a re-signed Columban, the Director of the Irish region dwelt at length on the contribution the deceased had made to the missionary ef-fort of the Society in the Phippine Islands. Then he spoke of his dedication to his family, as an exemplary husband and father, and of his commitment at work. It was a simple, honest gesture and something refreshingly new.

Another gesture was to touch all resigned Columbans in Ire-land. Again, it was a simple thing to do but had been a long time coming. We received an official thanks for our years of service to the Society and to the countries we had worked in.

In this time of retirement, with its welcome surprises and opening of new avenues, there is one dimension whose demands are especially rewarding. We have four grandchildren. They sur-round us in a world of wonder and surprise.

A year prior to my illness, Liam was born. He lit our hearts with special joy, and for six years he was to hold pride of place as our only grandchild. For four of those he and his parents, Tony and Linda, lived in the independent unit at our house. While they worked, Grandma Carmen looked after him most of the time.

By the time he was ready for school, I was 'the Dada', some kind of ancient one. Even today, every now and again, he will suddenly ask:

'How old are you again?

'Wow, that's really ancient, Dada,' he will tease me.

He loves nothing better than accounts of how we lived 'long ago'. For him, they have a ring of real adventure – going to school in our bare feet in summertime, doing our chores on the farm, footing turf in the bog, fishing our Sundays away.

Liam is now eleven years old and he and I have been having chats for a number of years. Sometimes I brought him to school or picked him up afterwards. One of us might suggest we go for a little something at the local hotel. There, I have been a privileged confidante, as my grandson has related his escapades with the local GAA team, or told me about the things that have been bothering him.

I heard of his distress at the way a black boy was being treated in his class:

'They all make fun of him, all the time.'

'Why do they do that?'

'They just pick on him because he's black.'

'That's so wrong. Do you know what it's called?' I ask.

'Yes, that's racism. I know.'

'What does the teacher do about it?'

'I don't think she knows. They do it in the school yard when she isn't looking.'

'What do you think you could do?'

'Well, I walk to school with him.'

'That's very good. But maybe somebody should tell the teacher.'

'I don't want to be a tell-tale.'

'You know, sometimes we have to do what is right, even though it isn't easy to do.'

One morning I had left Liam in the school yard. He had lined up with his classmates as normal, their school bags on the ground beside them. Having noticed nothing unusual in his demeanour, I had left the vicinity of the school and was walking down the village, when I heard screaming. It was my grandson, struggling with his school bag, as he attempted to catch up to me.

'Dada, I can't go to school today. Don't make me go!' he blurted out between sobs. I put my arm around him:

'Relax, that's not a problem. Let's go and have something and talk about it.'

By the time he was sitting down, sipping a cup of hot chocolate, he was ready to talk.

'I hate school now. The teacher has it in for me. She punishes me for anything.'

'Like what?' I asked.

'Well, it's about talking most of the time. Sometimes it's about not paying attention. She says I don't focus in class.'

'And you do a good bit of both, I imagine.'

'Yes, but she always picks on me, Dada. That isn't fair.'

'What kind of punishment do you get?'

'She makes me stand at my desk for half an hour at least. Everyone is looking at me.'

'Well, I am sure it seems like an awful long time but it's hardly half an hour. But, you know you are quite a talker and you do daydream. I sometimes have to call your name a few times to get your attention, especially when you are watching television.'

'Yes, but that's different.'

'I used to daydream a lot when I was young.'

'Did you, Dada?'

'You remember how I told you that I went to a boarding school. Well, in those times we got slapped with a cane for not keeping quiet in class. I used to find the classes very boring, and I think when one is bored one easily daydreams.'

'Yes, that's it, I daydream too when I'm bored.'

'The problem everyone has is how to get interested in school subjects, and then how to keep that interest going. It is called getting motivated.'

'But, how do you do that when it's so boring?'

'Well, let's take an example. When you want to be able to score with your left foot in Gaelic football, what do you have to do?'

'I know, practice kicking with the left. But, I like to play Gaelic.'

'A very good point. Now, as we grow up, we have to learn to do many things that are not as pleasing to us as playing football, like getting up for school on time, dressing, making the bed, getting school things together.'

'Boring, boring ...' he laughs.

'Ok, but just because we don't like some things, it doesn't mean we don't have to do them. Actually, we can learn to do them, and even get to like them.'

'How is that, Dada?'

'Well, if we do these things many times, repeat and repeat them, they become easy to do. Then we have habits. That's the trick.'

'Dada, I think I would like to go back to school now. Soon they will be on a break. Could you come with me and you might have a word with the teacher?'

As we walked back to the school, relaxed and silent, I was profoundly grateful for having been at my grandson's side for those precious couple of hours. Thankful too for those less burdened days of retirement that allowed me to share a special relationship.

Spending time with the two younger grandchildren, each day I seem to grasp a little more how vitally important those first few years are for character formation. Jack is four and Eva six months older. The former has an independent character; he is as we say 'his own man'. Sometimes when he looks at me I can hear him say:

'Yes, big fella, what's your problem? I am a baby boy and I am free, not like you, with all your rules and dos and donts.'

Then, wearing his mischievous smile, he turns away to continue in his toy fantasy world.

Jack and Eva are frequent playmates. They can spend hours together with only the odd spat. The slightly younger cousin, a sturdy, strong-willed lad, as many a kid before him, is not always enamoured of the idea of having to share toys. His petite, ladylike companion is a talker who can make her feelings known.

The impasse can start with both cousins pulling on the same toy. Then I hear Eva's plea for reason:

'Jack it's my turn now. You have to share. Jack you are not listening!'

She confronts her playmate who presses the toy closer to his chest.

'Enough is enough, Jack,' she mutters resignedly as she makes her way for outside help.

Little Grace is our latest grandchild, just three months old. She brings back the magic of those early weeks and months of a baby's life, which can somehow fade from a man's memory. Women seem to immerse themselves in it continually and with ease, spontaneously drawn to a pram whether on the street or out shopping. Babies are so dependent and helpless, but they have their winning, gratuitous smile. Grandchildren can capture our attention and affection, melt away worries and lighten our step.

In these more carefree autumn years of life there are two other passions that energise my days. One has to do with keeping abreast of developments in Peru, the land of my awakening, and the country to which I am bound by many ties and days of great hope and bitter disappointment too. Daily I use the internet to skip through a few newspapers and keep up to date on its onward march.

These are days of hope and expectation for Peru. After two decades of a cruel internal war (1980-2000), with the last of those decades witnessing the most corrupt regime in the country's history, it has had a decade of democratic governments. A transition government set up a Truth and Reconciliation Commission to help people come to grips with the horrors of the nightmare. The corrupt and Machiavellian pair, former President Fujimori and his accomplice Montesinos, are serving lengthy jail sentences. So too are top military and hundreds of *Sendero Luminoso* members.

During the decade of democracy the Peruvian economy has grown spectacularly, mainly based on the export of minerals. Two successive governments have followed neoliberal policies, and the promised 'trickle down' to the poor has been almost negligible. Today, Peru has its first ever democratically elected centre-left government. It has come to power promising 'Growth with Social Inclusion'. Its programme for government talks about 'Rights for the Poor', no more 'buying' of sympathy and votes with handouts. After a year in power Humala's government has some achievements to show.

It has raised the minimum wage twice in its first year. Starting in the poorest areas of the country, it has begun to roll out three programmes: a pension at sixty-five, crèche facilities for children up to three years of age, and scholarships for students – all acknowledged by the State as rights. These days of hope have been a long time coming. As a part of a progressive section of the Church and later as part of the Left, Carmen and I made our contribution. We were part of a process, which, with all its advances and setbacks, made today possible. With muted pride we can say, 'We are part of this day too.'

The other interest that has taken hold of me lately is the radical reform of the Church. For many years I had come to accept that my generation would not see any real reform in our lifetime. My personal experience of clericalism seemed to have convinced me of that.

I had gone through the seven years of training and domestication in the seminary, and come out accepting I was one of an elite caste, above, and separated from, the mere faithful. Gradually I had grown more uncomfortable with that mantle. It is my impression that it hung awkwardly too on the vast majority of the simple, unpretentious men I have known in the Columban Society, and on so many other priests too. Today I see clericalism, structured and empowered as it is has been over the centuries, as an unjustifiable division of the People of God.

In Peru, I had the good fortune to join a nucleus of people committed to the vision set out in the Second Vatican Council. As the evidence of the betrayal of its own Council, by the Vatican elite, became more and more evident, like so many people around the world my hopes were dashed too.

After all, the historic gathering had sat for three years, and some 3,000 people, mainly bishops, had attended. Its resolutions were passed by huge majorities.

Among the disappointed were many priests working in parishes around the world. They had hoped for a new spring. For decades they have borne the frustration silently. Those who spoke out were 'silenced' or harassed by the Vatican.

During the long night of counter-reform by Rome, the ability of the hierarchical, obedience-based structure to keep the rank and file clergy in line has always impressed me. Those men in parishes, in direct contact with the people, have largely remained quiet. Privately, they will speak of their frustration. Now most of them are older and over-stretched with work. It is understandable that they may be daunted by the thought of getting involved in a grass-roots reform movement; their energy for such a mission may be low.

Nevertheless, some stirring events give hope. The international movement of Roman Catholic Women Priests (RCWP), though small in number, is a breath of fresh air. They boldly state: 'The voice of the Catholic people – the *sensus fidelium* – has spoken. We women are no longer asking for permission to be priests. Instead, we have taken back our rightful God-given place ministering to Catholics as inclusive and welcoming priests.'

In Austria, an organisation of clergy, called Priests' Initiative, has declared that it has had enough of the Vatican's 'delaying tactics', and is advocating pushing ahead with policies that openly defy current practices, such as allowing lay people to lead religious services and give sermons, allowing priests to be married, and allowing women to be ordained priests and take positions in the hierarchy.

Here in Ireland, an Association of Catholic Priests has been formed. The founders are known for their clear position on the need for serious reform in the Church. Interested, but sceptical, I watched on as some of them were 'silenced' by Rome.

Then, in a positive and radical move, this new clerical organisation turned towards the people. It commissioned a survey on the opinion of Catholics in Ireland. The results only confirmed the reality, known for the last couple of decades: over three-quarters of people are in favour of radical reform of Church governance, and practices such as compulsory celibacy, the marginalisation of women and discrimination against gay people.

But these reform-minded clerics, who now number close to a thousand, were to go much farther down the road of pitching their tent among the people. They organised a meeting open to lay people with the theme, 'Towards an Assembly of the Irish Catholic Church'. It was a heart-warming, hope-giving event.

Over a thousand people attended from all over the country. As I walked around the venue in the morning, it was hard to distinguish lay people from clerics. During the event people identified themselves before speaking. It was evident that the great majority were lay people.

It was no surprise to meet several Columbans there. They, like the other clerics, were comfortable among the people. There was expectation and silence in the air as people rose to speak. Many voices warned of a difficult struggle ahead. But above all, there was energy and enthusiasm for action. Were we witnessing the beginning of a new dawn?

A movement has been formed at the base. The primacy of the individual conscience, over out-dated dictates from the top, has been loudly asserted. Who knows what effects the pressure and shaking will have on the whole edifice?

Kevin is a priest working on the Atlantic coast of my native county. Thirty years ago he entered the seminary, buoyed up by the vision of a Church in the image of the Second Vatican Council. In the words of the poet Matthew Arnold, he describes his life as, 'Wandering between two worlds, one dead, the other powerless to be born.'

Many years ago in Peru we saw how marginalised people could become the agents of their own destiny. How analysis could lead to ever broader action.

Along that path, the making of history is possible. We, the ordinary people, can make a difference.

A new world can be born.

EPILOGUE

I AM ALWAYS CONSCIOUS THAT the time I spent in Peru was the most life-changing part of my life. There, in that captivating land, among its brave and hospitable people, I had received and given and grown as a person. But, our arrival in Ireland in early January 1990 was to be the beginning of a process that was to change and mould each of our lives, especially those of my wife and children.

Like the tens of thousands of emigrants that came to Ireland in the nineties, my family bravely faced, and gradually integrated into a new reality – of language, culture, study, work and friends. I watched them walk that extra mile, overcome obstacles and, each passing day, fit in a little more into their new homeland. But nestled deep in their thoughts and feelings was that faraway land of so many precious memories.

Carmen and the children nurtured their bond with the land of their birth. There was no danger it would be allowed to weaken. We continued to speak Spanish at home. The possibility of meeting the odd visitor with the latest news from Peru was special.

Our children always harbour the desire to visit the land of their childhood. They plan, save and go when they can. For several years they have been organising fundraising activities for crèches that provide pre-school facilities in some of the poorest *barrios*. I know they join with Carmen and me in saying to so many people in Peru: 'Thanks dear friends, a thousand thanks for joining us on our inter-connected journey – of receiving and giving.'